# BUSINESS ENGLISH

商务英语(本科)系列教材

# 商务英语笔译 （第2版）

陈永生 于 璠 主 编
叶一粟 李静玉 副主编

## BUSINESS ENGLISH TRANSLATING

U0361968

清华大学出版社
北京

# 内 容 简 介

本书系统介绍了商务词汇、商号与商务名片、商标与品牌、商务广告、商品说明书、商务礼仪及祝词、商务信函、商务合同与协议、国际商务信用证、备忘录、商务报告、上市公司年报、企业介绍、宣传资料等知识,并通过强化实践实训提高学生的应用能力与技能。

本书既可作为本科国际贸易、工商管理、金融保险等专业的首选教材,也可用于商务从业者的在职岗位培训,并为广大中小微商贸企业和大学生就业创业提供有益的学习指导。

**图书在版编目(CIP)数据**

商务英语笔译/陈永生,于璠主编. -- 2 版.

北京:清华大学出版社,2024.8. --(商务英语

(本科)系列教材). -- ISBN 978-7-302-66811-4

Ⅰ. F7

中国国家版本馆 CIP 数据核字第 2024J9T317 号

**责任编辑:**贺 岩
**封面设计:**李伯骥
**责任校对:**王荣静
**责任印制:**沈 露

**出版发行:**清华大学出版社

网　　址:https://www.tup.com.cn,https://www.wqxuetang.com

地　　址:北京清华大学学研大厦 A 座　　　　邮　　编:100084

社 总 机:010-83470000　　　　　　　　　邮　　购:010-62786544

投稿与读者服务:010-62776969,c-service@tup.tsinghua.edu.cn

质量反馈:010-62772015,zhiliang@tup.tsinghua.edu.cn

**印 装 者:**三河市人民印务有限公司

**经　　销:**全国新华书店

**开　　本:**185mm×260mm　　　　**印　　张:**16.75　　　　**字　　数:**396 千字

**版　　次:**2014 年 8 月第 1 版　　2024 年 8 月第 2 版　　**印　　次:**2024 年 8 月第 1 次印刷

**定　　价:**49.00 元

产品编号:092953-01

# 编审委员会

# 序 言

随着我国改革开放和社会主义市场经济的快速推进,中国经济已经连续40多年保持着持续高速增长的态势,并进入了一个最为活跃的经济发展时期。近年来国家"一带一路、互联互通"经济建设的快速推进和全球国际贸易的迅猛发展,不仅有力地促进了我国经济产业的国际化发展,也使中国市场的国际化特征更加凸显。

外向型经济依靠外语工具支撑,国际贸易、商务活动的顺利开展需要大批商务英语人才作保证。商务英语涉及国际贸易、商务往来、通关报检、运输仓储、会展旅游等各领域,并在国际交往、商务活动、文化交流、解决就业、促进经济发展、丰富社会生活、构建和谐社会、弘扬中华文化等方面发挥着越来越大的作用,因而成为我国服务经济发展的重要支撑,在我国外向型经济发展中占有举足轻重的位置。

当前面对世界经济的迅猛发展和国际市场激烈竞争的压力,我国企业要生存就必须走出国门,中国经济要发展就必须参与国际竞争。为此急需大量既懂专业知识,又掌握外语工具的新型商务英语人才。加强商务英语的推广普及,加速商务英语专业知识技能型应用人才的培养,已成为我国经济转型发展亟待解决的问题。

需求促进专业建设,市场驱动人才培养。针对我国高校商务英语教材陈旧、知识老化而急需更新的问题,为了配合"北京市国际化大都市"的建设,为了适应国家经济发展、满足社会商务英语人才市场需求,为了扶助"中、小、微"企业发展,也为了解决学生就业问题,在北京联合大学、燕山大学、北京交通大学、山西大学、北方工业大学、郑州大学等全国10多所高校的支持下,我们组织多年从事商务英语教学和实践活动的国内知名专家教授及业界精英,共同精心编撰了本套教材,旨在提高我国商务英语专业大学生和从业者的专业技术素质,更好地服务于我国外向型经济。

本套教材作为普通高等院校商务英语专业的特色教材,融入了商务英语最新教学理念,强化"听、说、读、写、译"理论与实践的紧密结合,注重岗位技能应用方法、应用能力的培养训练,并为中国教育部考试中心与英国剑桥大学考试委员会联合组织的全国商务英语资格证书（Business English Certificate，BEC）考试打好基础。

　　本套教材根据高等院校"商务英语"专业教学大纲和课程设置编写，包括《商务英语阅读》《商务英语写作》等5本教材。教材的出版对商务英语从业人员的教育培训，对帮助学生尽快熟悉商务英语操作规程与业务服务，毕业后顺利走上社会具有特殊意义。

　　本套教材既可作为普通高等教育院校"商务英语"专业教学的首选教材，也可作为商务、贸易、工商企业在职员工的培训教材。

牟惟仲

2024 年 1 月

# 第2版前言

外语既是敲门砖,也是对外交流的主要工具。商务英语是开展国际化经济活动的基础,也是提升涉外企业核心竞争力的关键。商务英语在国际贸易、商务活动、商务谈判、商务会议、市场营销、会展旅游、涉外文化交流合作中发挥着非常重要的作用,并在我国服务经济中占有极其重要的位置,因而越来越受到我国教育与企业界的高度重视。

商务英语笔译是商务英语专业非常重要的课程,也是涉外企业从业者必须掌握的基本知识技能。当前,全球经济一体化进程加快,国际商贸市场竞争激烈,对从业者专业技术素质的要求越来越高,社会经济发展和国家产业变革急需大量具有理论知识与实际操作技能的复合型商务英语专门人才。保障我国外向型产业经济活动的顺利运转,加强现代商务英语从业者应用技能培训,强化专业综合业务素质培养,既是加快我国与国际经济接轨的战略选择,也是本书出版的目的和意义所在。

本书自出版以来,因写作质量高,深受全国各高校广大师生的欢迎。此次第2版修订,作者审慎地对原教材进行了案例更新、补充新知识,以使其更贴近现代国际经济活动,更符合社会发展,更好地为我国国际贸易和商务英语教学实践服务。

本书作为高等教育商务英语专业的特色教材,严格按照教育部关于商务英语本科"培养具有扎实的英语基础、宽阔的国际化视野、合理的国际商务知识与技能,掌握经济、管理和法学等相关学科的基本知识和理论,具备较高人文素养和跨文化交际与沟通能力的复合型人才"的教育教学要求,根据教育教学改革与国际商贸业务接轨的实际需要,设计教材的体例和内容,使其更贴近现代经济发展实际,更符合社会用人需要,从而更好地为国家经济建设服务。

全书共16个单元,以学习者实用笔译能力培养为主线,根据国际经济发展新形势,依照涉外商贸活动和职业岗位技能要求,结合商务英语笔译的特点和翻译原则,系统介绍:商务词汇、商号与商务名片、商标与品牌、商务广告、商品说明书、商务礼仪及祝词、商务信函、商务合同与协议、国际商务信用证、备忘录、商务报告、上市公司年报、企业介绍、宣传资料等知识，并通过强化实践实训提高学生的应用能力与技能。

由于本书融入了商务英语笔译最新的实践教学理念，力求严谨、注重与时俱进，具有知识系统、案例丰富、突出实用和通用性等特点，因此既可作为本科国际贸易、工商管理、金融保险等专业的首选教材，也可用于商务从业者的在职岗位培训，并为广大中小微商贸企业和大学生就业创业提供有益的学习指导。

本书由李大军筹划并具体组织，陈永生和于璠为主编，陈永生统改稿，叶一粟、李静玉为副主编，由杨昆教授审定。编者编写分工：牟惟仲（序言），于璠（第 1 单元、第 3 单元、第 8 单元），叶一粟（第 2 单元、第 4 单元、第 6 单元），陈永生（第 5 单元、第 7 单元、第 9 单元、第 10 单元、第 14 单元），张凤霞（第 11 单元、第 13 单元），李静玉（第 12 单元、第 15 单元、第 16 单元）；李晓新（制作教学课件）。

本书再版过程中，我们参阅了大量商务英语笔译的最新书刊、网站资料，并得到有关专家和商贸界精英的具体指导，在此一并致谢。为配合教学，本书提供电子课件，读者可以扫描书后二维码免费下载使用。因作者水平有限，书中难免存在疏漏和不足，恳请专家和读者批评指正。

编　者

2024 年 2 月

# 目 录

**1 Unit 1 Introduction to Business English Translating**

**12 Unit 2 Business Terms and Expressions**

Section 1 Theme Lead-in ·············································· 12
Section 2 Translation Warming-up ······························ 13
Section 3 Topic Features and Translation Principles ······ 14
Section 4 Translating Strategies, Samples and Training ··· 17
Section 5 Extensive Expression ·································· 24

**28 Unit 3 Company Names and Business Cards**

Section 1 Theme Lead-in ·············································· 28
Section 2 Translation Warming-up ······························ 29
Section 3 Topic Features and Translation Principles ······ 30
Section 4 Translating Strategies, Samples and Training ··· 37
Section 5 Extensive Expression ·································· 43

**46 Unit 4 Brands and Trademarks**

Section 1 Theme Lead-in ·············································· 46
Section 2 Translation Warming-up ······························ 48
Section 3 Topic Features and Translation Principles ······ 48
Section 4 Translating Strategies, Samples and Training ··· 50
Section 5 Extensive Expression ·································· 57

**60 Unit 5 Business Advertisement**

Section 1 Theme Lead-in ·············································· 60

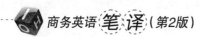

商务英语 笔 译（第2版）

Section 2  Translation Warming-up ·············· 61
Section 3  Topic Features and Translation Principles ··············· 62
Section 4  Translating Strategies, Samples and Training ··············· 66
Section 5  Extensive Expression ··············· 73

## 75  Unit 6  Commodity Specifications

Section 1  Theme Lead-in ··············· 75
Section 2  Translation Warming-up ··············· 76
Section 3  Topic Features and Translation Principles ··············· 77
Section 4  Translating Strategies, Samples and Training ··············· 80
Section 5  Extensive Expression ··············· 89

## 91  Unit 7  Ceremonial Address

Section 1  Theme Lead-in ··············· 91
Section 2  Translation Warming-up ··············· 92
Section 3  Topic Features and Translation Principles ··············· 93
Section 4  Translating Strategies, Samples and Training ··············· 94
Section 5  Extensive Expression ··············· 104

## 106  Unit 8  Business Correspondence（Ⅰ）

Section 1  Theme Lead-in ··············· 106
Section 2  Translation Warming-up ··············· 107
Section 3  Topic Features and Translation Principles ··············· 108
Section 4  Translating Strategies, Samples and Training ··············· 111
Section 5  Extensive Expression ··············· 120

## 124  Unit 9  Business Correspondence（Ⅱ）

Section 1  Theme Lead-in ··············· 124
Section 2  Translation Warming-up ··············· 125
Section 3  Topic Features and Translation Principles ··············· 126
Section 4  Translating Strategies, Samples and Training ··············· 129
Section 5  Extensive Expression ··············· 142

## 145  Unit 10  Business Contracts and Agreements

Section 1  Theme Lead-in ··············· 145
Section 2  Translation Warming-up ··············· 146

Section 3    Topic Features and Translation Principles ·························· 147
Section 4    Translating Strategies, Samples and Training ····················· 150
Section 5    Extensive Expression ············································· 160

## 163  Unit 11    International Business Credit

Section 1    Theme Lead-in ····················································· 163
Section 2    Translation Warming-up ············································ 164
Section 3    Topic Features and Translation Principles ·························· 165
Section 4    Translating Strategies, Samples and Training ····················· 169
Section 5    Extensive Expression ·············································· 176

## 179  Unit 12    The Memorandum

Section 1    Theme Lead-in ····················································· 179
Section 2    Translation Warming-up ············································ 180
Section 3    Topic Features and Translation Principles ·························· 181
Section 4    Translating Strategies, Samples and Training ····················· 184
Section 5    Extensive Expression ·············································· 192

## 195  Unit 13    Business Reports

Section 1    Theme Lead-in ····················································· 195
Section 2    Translation Warming-up ············································ 196
Section 3    Topic Features and Translation Principles ·························· 197
Section 4    Translating Strategies, Samples and Training ····················· 199
Section 5    Extensive Expression ·············································· 207

## 210  Unit 14    The Annual Report of Listed Companies

Section 1    Theme Lead-in ····················································· 210
Section 2    Translation Warming-up ············································ 211
Section 3    Topic Features and Translation Principles ·························· 212
Section 4    Translating Strategies, Samples and Training ····················· 216
Section 5    Extensive Expression ·············································· 222

## 225  Unit 15    Company Profile and Publicity Materials

Section 1    Theme Lead-in ····················································· 225
Section 2    Translation Warming-up ············································ 226
Section 3    Topic Features and Translation Principles ·························· 227

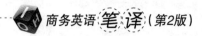

Section 4    Translating Strategies, Samples and Training ················· 231
Section 5    Extensive Expression ················· 239

**241 Unit 16    Tourist Publicity Materials**

Section 1    Theme Lead-in ················· 241
Section 2    Translation Warming-up ················· 243
Section 3    Topic Features and Translation Principles ················· 243
Section 4    Translating Strategies, Samples and Training ················· 246
Section 5    Extensive Expression ················· 251

**255 参考文献**

# Unit *1*

# Introduction to Business English Translating

### Unit Objectives

In this unit you should

➢ familiarize yourself with the types, characteristics and criteria of business English translating.

➢ learn how to practice, develop and master business English translating skills.

➢ enable yourself to acquire the method of business English translating quality assessment.

➢ understand and comply with the code of conduct for public service translators.

　　商务英语笔译在对外商务交流中起着不可或缺的桥梁和纽带作用。随着我国社会经济的发展，以对外贸易为中心的涉外商务活动已经深入社会的各个层面，国际性商务活动日趋频繁，社会对商务英语笔译人才需求也越来越旺盛。

　　为了适应形势，近些年来，我国高等院校也加大了商务英语专业建设的力度。据统计，在全国 700 余所本科院校中，设立商务英语专业的有 500 所以上，相关专业课中也大多包含了商务英语笔译课程。

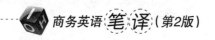

## 一、翻译及商务英语翻译的界定

### 1. 翻译的界定

中国自商周时期开始就有了跨语言翻译（interlingua translation）。中国的翻译理论和实践在世界上具有显著的地位。《礼记》已有关于翻译的记载；《周礼》中的"象胥"，就是四方译官的总称；《礼记·王制》提到"五方之民，言语不通"，为了"达其志，通其欲"，各方都有专人，而"北方曰译"。后来，佛经译者在"译"字前加"翻"，成为"翻译"一词，一直流传到今天。由于中国早期历史所处的环境，中华文化的近邻在很长时间内都没有自己的文字，所以直到佛教传入前，翻译并不广泛存在。

我们在这里所谈论的翻译实际上就是跨语言翻译，"是把一种语言文字（文化）的意义用另一种语言文字表达出来。"从现代符号学的观点说，翻译的实质就是以两种不同的语言符号来表达同一个思想、意思。因此，翻译的中心任务就是再现（reproduce）原文的思想。

《大英百科全书》（*Encyclopedia Britannica*）将翻译定义为"the action or process of content transformation from a language or a set of linguistic symbols to another language or a set of linguistic symbols"。约翰·卡特福德（John Catford）将其定义为"to use an equivalent textual material to replace another kind of language text material"。

以上两种定义，尽管陈述形式不一样，但都是从翻译作为一种行为这一角度来界定，而且其核心内容是一致的。首先，翻译是一种行为或者过程。其次，翻译涉及两种语言（或两套语言符号）。再次，翻译的结果是一种语言被另一种语言所取代。最后，翻译是一种语言的内容而非形式被另外一种语言所替代，或者是一种语言的文本材料被等值的另一种语言的文本材料所替换。

从功能和目的两个方面讲，"翻译是思想交流的桥梁（使不懂原语的人，能通过译文懂得体现在原文信息中的作者的思想、意图、观点和所表达的思想感情）和接力（使原文信息能传播得更远，能传播到更多的人那里）。"《韦氏新大学词典》（*Webster's New University Dictionary*）对"翻译"的定义为"to turn into one's own language or another language"；《牛津高阶英汉词典》（*Oxford Advanced Learner's English-Chinese Dictionary*）对"翻译"的定义为"to give the meaning of（something said or written）in another language"。

翻译是运用一种语言把另一种语言所表达的思想、内容，准确而完整地重新表达出来的语言活动。范仲英对"翻译"的定义为"is an intercommunicative process of cross-linguistic, cross-cultural information and sentiments"，是一种跨语言、跨文化的信息与情感的交流过程。翻译通过把一种语言（原语）表达的信息用另一种语言（译语）再现出来的方式，帮助译语使用者了解原作者意欲传达的信息内容，并获得与原语使用者大致相同的感受，以达到帮助不同语言的人相互沟通、理解的目的。

当代美国翻译理论家奈达（E. A. Nida）认为："所谓翻译，是指从语义到文体在译语中用最切近而又最自然的对等语再现原语的信息。"中国著名翻译家孙致礼认为："翻译是把一种语言表达的意义用另一种语言传达出来，以达到沟通思想感情、传播文化知识、促进社会文明，特别是促进译语文化兴旺昌盛的目的。"

结合各个学者的观点，本书作者认为，翻译就是在准确通顺的基础上，把一种语言信息转变成另一种语言信息的行为，是两个语言社会之间的交际过程和交际工具。

### 2. 商务英语的界定

商务英语是英语的一种社会功能变体（anamorphous of social function），是专门用途英语（English for specific purposes，ESP）中的一个分支，是英语在商务场合中的应用，是一种包含了各种商务活动内容、适合商业需要的标准英文。

英国商务英语专家尼克·布里格尔（Nick Brieger）在1997年提出了"商务英语范畴"（category of business English）理论，即"商务英语应包括语言知识（language knowledge）、交际技能（communication skills）、专业知识（professional content）、管理技能（management skills）和文化背景（cultural awareness）等核心内容"。

商务英语实质上就是商务活动（business activities）与英语语言（English language）的综合（integration），并具有以下功能：

（1）信息功能（informative function），即为商务活动参与者提供信息交际功能；

（2）交流功能（intercommunicative function），即帮助商务活动参与者进行交际和沟通；

（3）祈使和呼唤功能（imperative/vocative function），即促使商务活动参与者作出相应的反应。

在当今这个经济不断发展的世界上，国际商务活动日益频繁。这些商务活动包括技术引进、对外贸易、招商引资、对外劳务承包与合同、国际金融、涉外保险、国际旅游、海外投资、国际运输等，在涉及这些活动中所使用的英语统称为商务英语。

商务英语源于普通英语，并以普通英语为基础。因此，商务英语完全具有普通英语的语言学特征；同时，商务英语又是商务知识和英语的综合，具有独特性，属于功能性语言（functional language）的范畴。随着国际商务的空前繁荣，人们对于商务英语越来越关注，不仅关注商务英语教学，关注对商务英语语言的研究，还关注对商务英语的翻译。

## 二、商务英语的语言特点

作为英语的一个功能性变体，商务英语在语言使用方面有专业性（professionalism）、规范性（standardization）、简明性（conciseness）、具体性（concreteness）和礼貌（courtesy）等特点，主要表现在以下几个方面。

### 1. 语言形式、词汇及内容与专业密切相关

商务英语的语言形式、词汇以及内容等方面与专业密切相关。商务英语所承载的是商务理论和商务实践等方面信息，没有承载商务理论和商务实践等方面信息的英语不能称为商务英语。

### 2. 用词明白易懂、正式规范

商务英语的用词明白易懂、正式规范、简短达意、语言平实。在用词的明白易懂方面，尽量多用较为常用的词语，如表示"赞同"多用"approval"而不用"approbation"；表示"改善"多用"improve"而不用"ameliorate"，以保证所用词语具有国际通用性，能为普通大众所理解，又不过于口语化。也就是说，商务英语所使用的语言不能过于非正式。

商务文书因为具有规范性、约束力等公文性质，因此会使用一些正式的、冷僻的单词，如表示"之前"多用"prior to""previous to"，而不用"before"；表示"期满"多用"expiry"，而不用"end"；表示"证明"多用"certify"，而不用"prove"；表示"寻求"多用"solicit"，而不用"seek"；

等等。在动词的使用方面，多用非常正式的单个动词，而不使用小巧的日常生活中常用的动词，或"动词+介词副词"，或"动词+名词+介词"等动词短语，如表达"约会"时，多用"appoint"，而不用"make an appointment of"；表达"继续"时用"continue"，而不用"keep on"或者"go on"；表达"附加"时用"supplement"，而不用"add to"；等等。

在介词和连词的使用方面，由于现代英语中的介词和连词非常通俗简短，将这些介词和连词置于商务英语中，会与商务英语中所使用的比较正式和规范的名词和动词等不相协调，因此商务英语中往往采用复合的介词短语来替代简单的介词和连词，如用"in the nature of""along the lines of"替代"like"；用"for the purpose of"替代"for"；用"in the case of"替代"if"；用"in the event that"替代"if"；用"on the grounds that"替代"since""because"；用"with reference to""with regard to"替代"about"；等等。商务英语很少使用俚语或者粗俗用词。

### 3. 句意简明扼要，句子结构较为复杂

商务英语句子结构通常较为复杂，句式规范，文体正式，尤其在招标文件和投标文件以及合同中更是如此，如下面"公司年报"的部分内容。

The offer price of this global offering was HK $9.00 per H share, and the Company offered 355,700,000 H shares for the global offering, of which, 35,570,000 H shares were offered in the Hong Kong public offering and the remaining 320,130,000 H shares were offered in the international offering. 35,570,000 state-owned legal person shares were transferred to NSSF Council due to the reduction of shareholding state-owned shares by the Company's relevant state-owned corporate shareholders, and were converted into overseas listed Foreign shares (H shares). A total of 391,270,000 H shares were listed on the main board of the Hong Kong Stock Exchange on 18 June 2021.

**译文：**

本次 H 股发行价格为每股 9.00 元港币，本次全球公开发售 355,700,000 股 H 股（其中，香港公开发售 35,570,000 股 H 股，其余 320,130,000 股 H 股为国际发售），以及公司相关国有法人股东未进行国有股减持而划拨给全国社会保障基金理事会并转为境外上市外资股（H 股）35,570,000 股 H 股，合计 391,270,000 股 H 股，于 2021 年 6 月 18 日在香港证券交易所主板挂牌交易。

### 4. 陈述事物具体、明确

商务英语在陈述事物时往往具体、明确，绝不能含糊其辞、不着边际，应力戒笼统、抽象。例如，表达"确定某天发电传"，要用清晰明了的句子"We confirm our telex of July 2nd, 2021"，而不用含糊、笼统的句子"We wish to confirm our telex dispatched yesterday"。

### 5. 礼貌用语非常重要

在国际商务英语应用文，特别是国际商务信函中，礼貌是其中非常重要的语言特点之一。这是由国际商务交往的特点决定的。一封彬彬有礼的书信能使你在读者的心目中树立起一种正直、热情、有良好文化素养和职业道德的形象，使收信人愿意同你合作，愿意竭诚为你服务。

**案例**

商 业 信 函

Dear Sirs,

We have learned from Smith Company of Birmingham that you manufacture a range of high-fashion leathers handbags in a variety.

We operate a quality retail business and although our sales volume is not large, we obtain high prices for our quality goods. Would you please send us a copy of your handbag catalogue with details of your prices and payment terms? We would find it most helpful if you could also supply samples of the various leather from which the handbags are made.

Yours faithfully,<br>×××

**译文：**

敬启者：

从伯明翰史密斯公司获悉贵公司制作了一系列款式新颖的皮革手提包。

本公司经营高档零售业务,虽然销量不多,但货品属优质高档。现恳请惠寄货品目录、价格表和付款方式细则。此外,如蒙提供各类皮革样本,不胜感激。

×××谨上

## 三、商务英语的翻译过程

在语言翻译过程中,必须经过"语言符号"(linguistic symbols)转化为"思想"(idea)、"思想"转化为另一"语言符号"这两个主要程序。第一个程序就是理解(comprehension),第二个程序就是表达(expression)。任何翻译都必须经过理解与表达这两个主要程序,即透彻理解原文的意思,然后用译文语言确切地把它再表达出来。

翻译的过程就是理解和表达的过程,或者说,翻译的过程由理解和表达两个阶段组成。要做到理解正确和充分,译者必须能够从以下角度对原作进行深入细致的分析：句法分析法(syntactic analysis)、语义分析法(semantic analysis)、语体分析法(stylistic analysis)、语用分析法(pragmatic analysis)、语篇分析法(discourse analysis)和文化分析法(cultural analysis)。

## 四、翻译的方法和技巧

翻译的目的就是将原作的内容或者信息非常充分地传达给读者。翻译既可以在同一文化内进行,也可以在不同的文化之间进行。

在同一文化或语言内进行的翻译叫作文化内翻译(intracultural translation)或者语言内翻译(intralingual translation),在不同的文化或语言之间进行的翻译叫作跨文化翻译(intercultural translation)或者跨语言翻译(interlingual translation)。将中国的古代典籍翻译成现代汉语属于文化内翻译或者语言内翻译;将英文翻译成中文或将中文翻译成英文就属于跨文化翻译或跨语言翻译,所以商务英语的汉英互译属于跨文化和跨语言的翻译。

### 1. 翻译的方法

在不同语言之间进行翻译转换,往往可以采取两种方法:

(1)直译法(literal translation)

直译就是指译文不但表达原文的内容,而且还保留原文表达的形式,比如保留原文所使用的比喻、原文的形象、原文的民族特色等。

(2)意译法(free translation)

意译就是指不拘泥于原文的表达形式、形象、民族特色等,而只是将原文的意义传达出来的翻译。直译和意译相互补充、相得益彰。请看下面两个句子的翻译:

 **例句 1**

Smashing a mirror is no way to make an ugly person beautiful, nor is it a way to make social problems evaporate.

直译:砸镜子不能使丑八怪变漂亮,也不能使社会问题烟消云散。

意译:砸镜子并不能解决实际问题。

**分析**:在这里,直译形象生动,并且能够很好地为读者所理解,而意译则过于笼统,将原文中生动形象的东西丢掉了。因此,将这里的原文翻译成汉语就需要进行直译而不要进行意译。

 **例句 2**

It seems to me what is sauce for the goose is sauce for the gander.

直译:我觉得煮母鹅用什么酱油,煮公鹅也用什么酱油。

意译:我认为要求别人怎样,自己也应该怎样。

**分析**:这里的直译让人对译文所传达的意思摸不着头脑,在这种情况下就不宜直译。这里的意译则可以成为阐释性的意译,阐释性的意译把原文中所传达的意思充分地表达出来了。

从以上的例子中可以看出,我们既不能说直译的翻译方法比意译的翻译方法更好,也不能说意译的翻译方法比直译的翻译方法更好。两种翻译方法各有所长、各有所短、互为补充。陆殿扬先生在谈到直译与意译的关系时说,在实际的翻译当中,"能直译就尽量直译,不能直译就采用意译"。我们完全可以在翻译过程中按照陆先生的观点去处理翻译中直译与意译的关系问题。

### 2. 基本的翻译技巧

一般而言,最基本的翻译技巧有以下几种:

(1)选词用字(diction);

(2)增益(amplification);

(3)省略(omission);

(4)重复(repetition);

(5)转换(conversion);

（6）词序调整（restructuring）；

（7）正说反译，反说正译（negation）；

（8）长句拆译（division）等。

**3. 本书中涉及的翻译技巧**

本书中涉及的翻译技巧包括以下几个方面：

（1）词义的选择、引申与褒贬色彩（diction of word，amplification and the appraisal）；

（2）英汉句式对比——形合与意合、静态与动态、有灵主语与无灵主语、主动与被动、重复与替代（hypotaxis and parataxis，static and dynamic，animate subject and inanimate subject，active and passive，repetition and substitution）；

（3）音译、意译、半音半意（transliteration，free translation，the combination of transliteration and free translation）；

（4）直译法、意译法、创译法、增补法、浓缩法、零译法（literal translation，free translation，creative translation，supplementary translation，concentrated translation and no translation）；

（5）习语与俚语（idioms and slangs）；

（6）比较句式（the comparative sentences）；

（7）词类转换（conversion of parts of speech）；

（8）否定句式（the negative sentences）；

（9）被动句式（the passive sentences）；

（10）常用修辞格——明喻、暗喻、借喻、提喻、通感、拟人、夸张、排比、委婉、讽喻、反语、双关（simile，metaphor，metonymy，synecdoche，synaesthesia，personification，hyperbole，parallelism，euphemism，allegory，irony and pun）；

（11）拆译与合译（division and combination）；

（12）主语的翻译（the translation of subject）；

（13）数词的翻译（the translation of the numeral）；

（14）语序的调整——顺译与逆译（translation in order and inverse translation）；

（15）增词与减词（the word amplification and the word ellipsis）。

## 五、翻译的通用标准和商务英语的翻译标准

翻译是将一种相对陌生的表达方式转换成相对熟悉的表达方式的过程。其中，"翻"是指对交谈的语言转换，"译"是指对单向陈述的语言转换。这是一种轮流的、交替的语言或信息转换。

翻译的任务是把原作品中对现实世界形成的逻辑映像、艺术映像和思想感情等完好无损地从一种语言移注到另一种语言中去。这个过程从逻辑上可以分为两个阶段：首先，必须从源语言中获得译码含义，然后把信息重新编码成目标语言。

所有的这两步都要求对语言语义学的知识以及对语言使用者文化的了解。除了要保留原有的意思外，一个好的翻译，对于目标语言的使用者来说，应该要像母语使用者说或写得流畅，并要符合译入语的习惯。

因此，翻译不是简单的文字对等，不能把"四喜丸子"翻译成"four glad meatballs"（四个

高兴的肉团），而应译为"four meatballs"；不能把"红烧狮子头"翻译成"stewed lion head"（烧红了的狮子头），而应译为"stewed pork ball in brown sauce"；不能把"麻婆豆腐"翻译成"bean curd made by a pockmarked woman"（满脸雀斑的女人制作的豆腐），而应译为"spicy bean curd with shredded pork meat"；不能把"童子鸡"翻译成"chicken without sexual life"（还没有性生活的鸡），而应译为"spring chicken"。

### 1. 翻译的通用标准

翻译标准是翻译活动必须遵循的准绳，是衡量译文质量的尺度，也是翻译工作者应该努力的方向。翻译标准是翻译理论的核心问题，历来众说纷纭，却都莫衷一是。古今中外从事翻译理论研究的工作者对翻译的标准各抒己见。

在唐代，玄奘在佛经翻译的过程中提出了不同于前人的"直译兼意译"的翻译标准，他强调译文"既须求真，又须喻俗"，就是译文既要忠实地反应原文的意思，又要通顺易懂。

清代的翻译大家严复在《天演论》中的"译例言"讲道："译事三难：信、达、雅。求其信已大难矣，顾信矣不达，虽译犹不译也，则达尚焉。""信"指"The translation should give a complete transcript of the ideas of the original work."（译文完整地再现原文的风格），意义不背原文，即译文要准确，不歪曲，不遗漏，也不要随意增减意思；"达"指"The translation should have all the ease of the original composition."（译文应像原文一样流畅自然），不拘泥于原文形式，译文通顺明白；"雅"则指"The style and manner of writing should be of the same character with that of the original."（译文的风格、语调应与原文性质相同），译文时选用的词语要得体，追求文章本身的简明优雅。

此标准一经提出，即为翻译界所承认和推崇，在相当长的一段时期内，对我国的翻译工作起到了积极的推动作用。鲁迅在《题未定草》中提出："凡是翻译，必须兼顾两面，一则当然力求其易解，一则保存原作的丰姿。"傅雷在《高老头重译本序》中提出"神似"说，"以效果而论，翻译应当像临画一样，所求的不在形似而在神似。"钱钟书在《林纾的翻译》一文中提出"化境"说，"把作品从一国文字转变成另一国文字，既不能因语文习惯而露出生硬牵强的痕迹，又能完全保存原有的风味。"

英国翻译理论家泰特勒（Alexander F. Tytler）在他的《翻译之原理》（*Essay on the Principles of Translation*）一文中，提出了翻译的三要素：译文应与原文的思想完全相符、译文应与原文的风格和体裁相同、译文应与原文一样通顺自然。美国翻译理论家奈达在《翻译的科学探索》一书中认为"所谓翻译，是指在译语中用最贴切而又最自然的对等语再现原语的信息，首先是意义，其次是文格。"国外的一些翻译家还提出了"三似"的翻译标准：形似、意似、神似。所谓"形似"就是强调译文要保持原文的形式美；"意似"是要保持原文的内容美；"神似"是要保持原文的神韵美。

我国现代的翻译家们对翻译标准的阐释更为通俗。张培基提出"忠实、通顺"；阎庆甲提出"深刻理解原文，确切表达译文"；庄绎传认为，"如果一篇译文在内容上是忠实的，在语言上是通顺的，在风格上是得体的，那的确就是一篇很好的译文了。"

综合上述，作为语际交流过程中沟通不同语言的桥梁，翻译的一般标准是"忠实和通顺"；最高标准是"功能对等"，也就是严复所说的"信、达、雅"。

### 2. 商务英语的翻译标准

商务英语问题的涵盖面非常广，包括各种招商简介、商务广告、进出口业务文献、电子商务文献、外贸英语应用文、备忘录、会议记录、商务合同和协议书等。对于招商简介和商务广告的翻译,"信"固然重要,"达"则更加重要,因为对于这两种类型的文体的翻译要以"达到最佳推介效果"为原则。(王永泰,2002)

"达"在这里的意思不仅是译文要"通顺明白",还意味着译文要符合译入语的文化习俗以及译入语受众的可接受性,这才是完整意义上的通达。对于进出口业务文献、电子商务文献、外贸英语应用文、备忘录、会议记录、商务合同和协议书的翻译,译文既要忠实于原文,做到"信",又要明白晓畅,做到"达"。因此,对于商务英语文体的翻译,"信、达、雅"的翻译标准可以依照不同文体而对这三个要素各有侧重。

从功能和目的来讲,"翻译是思想交流的桥梁和接力。"(范仲英,1994)说它是桥梁,是指通过翻译,使不懂原语的人通过译文了解作者在原文中的思想、意图、观点和情感;说它是接力,是指通过翻译,使原文信息能够传播得更远,受众更多。

商务英语的译者除了要精通中英两种语言,熟悉东西两种文化,掌握基本翻译技巧,具备商务专业知识之外,还要了解商务各个领域的语言特点和表达方法。在严复提出的"信、达、雅"翻译标准的基础上,2002 年刘法公先生提出了"忠实(faithfulness)、精确(exactness)、统一(consistency)"的商务英语翻译标准。这三个原则成为商务英语翻译比较合理的标准。

(1)忠实

"忠实"是指译文能将原文的语言信息正确地传达给读者,不苛求语法和句子结构与原文一致。"忠实"要求信息内涵上的对等,即信息要等值。比如"经济技术开发区"要译为"economic and technological development area"才忠实于原意,而不能译为"economic technology development area",因为此处的"经济"和"技术"是并列关系。

(2)精确

"精确"是指译者将原文语言内容转换到译文语言的过程中选词准确,做到概念表达确切,物与名所指正确,数码与单位精确。比如"食品冲调方法"中的"热开水"要译为"boiling water",而不能译为"hot water",因为"hot water"不能精确地表明水"热"到哪种程度。在翻译度量与数量时,译者一定要核实原文。比如"美元"就不能简单译为"dollar",而应译为"US Dollar",因为港元、加元、澳元也用"dollar"作为货币单位。

(3)统一

"统一"是指在翻译过程中译名、概念、术语等应始终保持统一,不允许将同一概念或术语随便变换译名。比如"世界贸易组织"只能翻译为"world trade organization",不能译为"international trade organization"。要达到"统一"的标准,就需要译者在翻译的过程中对于经典术语、概念和名称使用最权威、最恰当的译法。对于一些新词的翻译,可以参考权威的杂志和报纸,如 *China Daily*,还可以参阅国际商贸英语文献和专门商贸英语词典的译法,如《汉英对外经贸词典》《汉英英汉实用外经贸词典》《汉英中国商品品名词典》,力争做到"统一"。

商务英语翻译同普通英语翻译或者文学翻译有着很大的区别。对于普通英语的翻译或者文学翻译,译者只要精通源语语言、译语语言以及源语文化、译语文化,再加上具备娴熟的翻译技巧,就可以进行翻译了。因为普通英语中以及文学中的场景和故事等都来源于人们熟悉的日常生活,而且原文中的用词等一般不涉及专业化的知识。

商务英语翻译比起普通英语或者文学翻译要复杂得多。译者除了要精通两种语言及其

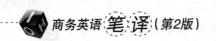

文化,以及熟悉翻译技巧之外,还必须熟悉商务方面的知识,了解商务各个领域的语言特点和表达法,才可能进行翻译。下面,以一段译文来说明商务英语中"忠实、精确、统一"的翻译标准。

 **案例**

In the contract, the buyer and the seller must arrange payment. The buyer will want possession before paying, and the seller will want payment before making delivery. Since each party often has an incomplete knowledge of the other, there is a certain caution to their dealings. At this point, the letter of credit can be extremely useful. The buyer requests his bank to issue a letter of credit in favor of the seller. Assuming that the credit risk is acceptable to the bank, it issue its letter of credit.

**译文：**

在合同中,买卖双方必须确定支付问题。买方希望在付款前拿到货物,而卖方希望在发货前拿到货款。由于双方常常不完全了解对方,就需要在交易时非常谨慎。基于这一点,信用证就十分有用了。买方要求银行开出支持卖方的信用证明,这样,就由开信用证的银行来承担信用风险。

**分析**：这里的汉语译文可谓从"忠实、精确、统一"这三个方面很好地再现了原文信息。其忠实性主要体现在：第一,汉语译文在语言风格上同原文一样平实。第二,汉语译文几乎都是以直译的方法再现了原文信息,尽管使用了增词法(如第一句中增加的"问题"),但丝毫没有增加任何额外信息。原文第三行中的"there is"(这里有)在汉语译文中被省略掉了,但实际上,汉语译文中已经包含了原文信息,如果将其翻译出来反而显得啰唆。

为了使译文充分再现原文信息而进行的增词翻译、减词翻译、引申、词类转换等都是忠实于原文信息的具体表现。汉语译文在这里的精确性表现在,译文是地道的汉语商务语言。译文的统一表现在专业术语的前后统一,比如原文中的 letter of credit 在译文中无一例外地被翻译成"信用证",让读者对所指内容非常明白。

## 六、商务英语翻译与跨文化交际

罗进德指出,"文化意识(cultural consciousness)就是译者认识到翻译是跨越语言文字、跨越文化的信息交流,而文化的差异跟语言文字的差异一样,可能成为交流的障碍,在进行语言文字转换的同时,还要注意克服文化差异造成的障碍,以保证信息交流的顺利实现;为此,译者不仅要精通译出和译入语言,还要了解和研究诸多语言背后的文化,并且要在正确翻译观的指导下知道在每一具体情况下如何处理文化差异、文化障碍。"

语言是文化环境的产物,又是文化的载体。每一种语言都有各自的文化特色,英语和汉语产生于不同的文化背景,所体现的文化也不尽相同。因此,处理文化差异也是英汉两种语言在信息转换时译者应首先考虑的问题。

例如,把"相声"翻译成"comic dialogue"比翻译成"cross talk"更容易让外国人明白。我们不能只是翻译"相声"的形式,还要翻译其内涵。把"以外贸为龙头"翻译成"with foreign trade as the flagship"比直接翻译为"with foreign trade as the dragon head"更能让外国人看懂,因为"以……为龙头"这个说法是源自中国人"耍龙灯"的习俗,外国人未必知道。

此外,也不能机械地对待一切类似的翻译问题,比如汉语的"鱼米之乡"(land of fish and rice),在英语里有一个类似的说法"land of milk and honey",但由于"land of fish and rice"外国人也能理解,不会造成跨文化交流的障碍,所以我们可以采用这一译文。再有,"摸着石头过河"用来形容中国的改革开放是没有先例的,应译为"Since there is no previous experience to fall back on, we have to 'wade across the stream by feeling the way', as we say in Chinese.",而不能按字面翻译为"crossing the river by feeling the stones",会让读者摸不着头脑,造成理解上的障碍。

## 七、商务英语笔译对译者的要求

翻译是一门实践性很强的学科。商务英语作为一门特殊用途英语,具有自身的词汇特征和运用的特殊性。因此,在商务英语笔译的过程中,译者除了熟悉英汉两种语言及翻译技巧外,还必须通晓商务专业知识,了解国际贸易惯例和习俗。一般来说,译者在翻译之前必须具备以下条件:

### 1. 译者要有良好的汉语功底

在英汉翻译过程中,对于比较正规的汉语文体,译者理解上的偏差会影响译文的准确性。因此,译者在平时要强化汉语功底,学习掌握地道的汉语表达,翻译才会得心应手。

### 2. 译者要加强英语语言能力的培养

译者不仅要掌握语法,保证翻译的准确和流畅,还要注重词汇的积累,学习正确的英语表达方式,译者的翻译水平才能不断提高。

### 3. 译者要熟悉翻译技巧

翻译技巧可以帮助译者解决翻译中一些棘手的问题,但是译者不能生搬硬套翻译技巧,而要在翻译中灵活运用、触类旁通。

### 4. 译者要具备广泛和专业的知识

译者只有具备了丰富的百科知识,对商务专业非常了解,才能准确理解原文的意思,表达译文的内容。

此外,要想成为优秀的笔译人才,译者还须具备勤于苦练、勤于思考的学习精神,并善于总结前人和自己的翻译经验,培养严谨、细致、求实的工作作风。

# Unit 2

# Business Terms and Expressions

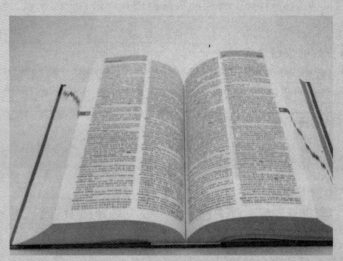

Unit Objectives

In this unit you should

➢ familiarize yourself with characteristics of business English vocabulary.

➢ enable yourself to acquire the technical terms, business formulas and abbreviations in this unit.

➢ have a good command of the translating skills of the choices of words and word meanings, the extension of word meanings and the semantic judgments.

## ❓ Section 1   Theme Lead-in

**Read the following passage to gain a better understanding of this unit.**

Business English（BE）, which involves finance, trade, insurance, accounting, marketing, advertising, securities, etc. belongs to one category of English for Specific Purposes（ESP）. It differs from English for General Purposes（EGP）and therefore has got its own distinctive features.

One notable feature is the use of vocabulary.

Firstly, BE employs a large number of technical words, which come from general words but have carried with them different meanings in business fields. For instance, words like document, honor, offer, inquiry, credit, bill, policy, and discount all bear specific meanings in BE.

Secondly, formal words are frequently used in BE. Though conciseness is stressed in modern BE, formal words are frequently employed. For example, formal words inform, initiate, terminate, utilize, purchase and assist often replace small words tell, begin, end, use, buy and help. Sometimes ancient words like hereinafter, hereby, therein, thereof, whereon, whereby appear in BE to show uniqueness and formalness.

Thirdly, lexical repetition can often be seen in BE to stress preciseness and formalness. For example, such terms as losses and damages, terms and conditions, methods and procedures, controversies and difference, by and between, on and after, etc. often appear in BE. It is through lexical repetition that formalness is stressed.

Fourthly, a shortened form of a word or a phrase, known as an abbreviation, is often found in Business English. An abbreviation is usually written in capital letters and used in trade terms, cables and facsimile, business correspondence and advertisement. The characteristic of an abbreviation is that it is vivid and easily written, spoken, and remembered.

Lastly, English formulas and jargons, which are developed through international business encounters, are also an important feature of BE. Although some of these expressions have lost their freshness, they are brief and to the point. There are quite a few such expressions in BE as "we hereby confirm" "enclosed please find" "please be informed that" "with a view to" "in line with", and so on.

All in all, vocabulary plays a significant role in BE. Just as the British linguist Jeremy Harmer once said, "If language structure makes up the skeleton of language, then it is vocabulary that provides the vital organs and the flesh. An ability to manipulate grammatical structure does not have any potential for expressing meaning unless words are used."

## Section 2   Translation Warming-up

### A: Translate the following sentences for business into Chinese.

1. If your price is reasonable, we plan to order the leather shoes.

2. This is our latest catalogue and pricelist, and you will find our price is competitive.

3. It will be appreciated if you inform us of the details of the prices and sizes.

4. Enclosed please find our latest catalogue and pricelist.

5. Upon receipt of your inquiry, we will immediately send you the samples and offer you most favorable prices.

6. A great number of textile articles are exportable by us.

7. We are interested in the import and export of bicycles.

8. We will be grateful if you reply us in time.

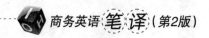

9. We are glad to have received your letter of July 10.

10. We have established good relationship with all the major dealers in England.

11. Our business has slackened a lot in the past few months. We hope you can use your advertising to drum it up.

12. Since the joint conciliation doesn't work, we have to submit the case for arbitration.

13. Claim, if any, must be put forward within 30 days after the arrival of the goods at the destination.

14. Enclosed is our confirmation of order in duplicate, of which please return us one copy duly signed for our records.

15. We appreciate the efforts you put in pushing the sales of our products and would like to renew the sale agency agreement for another 5 years.

**B：Translate the following sentences for business into English.**

1. 本报盘7日内有效。

2. 本报盘以收到你方订单时，货未出售为有效。

3. 兹报实盘，以我方时间5月4日星期一下午5时以前答复为有效。

4. 此盘五日内不接受，就会撤销。

5. 我方向你方报盘，以先售为条件。

6. 我方向你方报盘，此报盘如有变化恕不另行通知。

7. 我们相信我们所报的价格会得到你方认可。

8. 我们确信贵方将接受我们所提供的价格。此报盘至回传真为止都有效。

9. 此系特惠报盘，我方通常折扣不适用此盘。

10. 为了开展双方的业务，我们很高兴向你方报盘，以我方最后确认为有效。

11. 我们将从投产之日起五年内付清全部款项。

12. 包装不仅直接关系到产品的销售，也会影响产品的信誉。

13. 现寄我方目录，提供我方各项产品的详细情况。

14. 投标之前，我们必须搞清招标条件的细节。

15. 我想我们应该定一下合同的期限。

## Section 3　Topic Features and Translation Principles

### 一、商务英语词汇

商务英语作为普通英语的一种变体，所涉及的专业范围很广，包括经贸、金融、保险、广告、法律、股票、证券、旅游、人才管理等。商务英语在词汇使用上的最大特点就是它包含了大量的专业词汇、缩略语、套语、行话、外来语、古体词和新词，正是这些缤纷的词汇赋予了商务英语独有的特色。

### 二、商务英语词汇的翻译原则

#### 1. 专业词汇的翻译

英语的词汇可以分为普通词汇（general words）、半专业词汇（semi-technical words）和专业词汇(technical words)。商务英语属于特殊用途英语(ESP),许多普通词汇在商务英语中都具有其特定含义。例如,instrument、balance、policy、honor、literature、article 在普通英语(EGP)里意思分别是"仪器""平衡""政策""荣誉""文学""文章"的意思,但是在商务英语中它们的意思却分别是"契约""余额""保险单""承兑""宣传资料""条款"的意思,相差甚远。

商务英语词汇含义具有固定性和约定俗成等特点,所以当我们面对这些专业词汇时,一定不要想当然地按照普通英语词汇的意思去翻译,要从它们所处的语境和搭配入手,准确把握词义,要多查多看,不能随便按照字面意思去翻译。例如,在商务英语中,red tape 是"繁文缛节"的意思,不能想当然地翻译成"红带子"。它的来历可以追溯到很久以前,当时繁复的英国官方文件都是用红带子系成一扎一扎的,red tape 的比喻就此而来。又如,soybean futures 不是"大豆的未来",而是"大豆期货"的意思;special package 不是"特别包裹",而是"优惠套餐"的意思;blue chip 不是"蓝色芯片",而是"蓝筹股,绩优股"的意思。

**2. 缩略语的翻译**

缩略语是商务英语词汇的重要组成部分,是人们在长期语言使用过程中演变的结果。许多商务英语专业术语都以约定俗成的缩略语形式出现,为业内人士所熟知并广泛应用。因此,缩略语的翻译也是商务英语学习者必须掌握的技能之一。缩略语主要有以下几类形式:

第一类是首字母缩略语,它是缩略语中最多的一类,应该特别引起学习者的注意。例如,IPO(initial public offering)首次公开发行股票,CIF(cost,insurance and freight)成本、保险加运费,REP(request for a proposal)招标书,VAT(value-added tax)增值税,ROI(return on investment)投资收益率,I O U(I owe you)欠条,L/C(letter of credit)信用证,I/P(insurance policy)保险单。

第二类是剪裁缩略语,它是从一个词的前边、后边或中间剪掉几个字母缩略而成的。例如,com.(commission)佣金,dep.(deposit)定金,disc.(discount)折扣,inv.(invoice)发票,int.(interest)利息,invt.(inventory)库存,cont.(contract)合同,FRT(freight)货物,D/Y(delivery)交货,drt.(draft)汇票,dbt.(debit)借方。

第三类是拼缀缩略语,也就是说把两个或两个以上的词通过省略字母的方式合成一个新词。例如,forex(foreign exchange)外汇,hi-tech(high technology)高技术,advertics(advertising statistics)广告统计,workfare(work welfare)工作福利制,motel(motor hotel)汽车旅馆,Medicare(medical care)美国联邦医疗保险,newscast(news broadcast)新闻广播。

**3. 古体词的翻译**

商务英语中还经常使用一些已经不太流行的古体词,古体词的使用给人一种庄重、严谨、优雅的感觉。古体词常由 here、there、where 为词根,加上一个或几个介词构成合成副词。例如,herein(于此,此中),hereof(于此,关于这点),hereby(特此、据此),thereinafter(以下,此后),thereby(由此,因而),therein(在那一点上,在其中),thereof(其中,关于……),whereby(以……方式,凭借……),wherein(在那方面,在那儿),等等。

尽管古体词的词义和用法相对比较固定,但是有时翻译起来也有一定难度,这就需要学习者多看一些例句,多做一些翻译实践,切实抓住古体词的使用和翻译特点,这样才能做到胸有成竹、运用自如。请看下面的例句。

 **例句**

例1. We hereby revoke the agreement of the 1st May, 2022.

我们特此宣告 2022 年 5 月 1 日的协议无效。

例2. This contract shall come into force from the date of execution hereof by the buyer and the builder.

本合同自买方和建造方签署之日起生效。

例3. All expenses and risks thereinafter shall be borne by your side.

此后所发生的一切风险和费用由你方承担。

例4. We must hold you responsible for all consequences arising therefrom.

由此引发的一切后果必须由你方负责。

例5. Thereafter they never changed their package design.

此后他们再也没有改变产品的包装设计。

例6. He devised a plan whereby he might evade taxes.

他想出了一个可以逃税的办法。

### 4. 商务套语的使用

在长期的国际商务交流中，人们逐渐形成了一系列简洁实用的商务英语套语。例如，Kindly let us know…（烦请告知……），Kindly send us…（烦请寄给我们……），This is to certify that…（兹证明……），Enclosed please find…（随函附寄……），Enclosed is…（现附寄……），On behalf of…，I would like to invite you to…（我谨代表……邀请您……）等。这些套语的形式和意义相对固定，只要学习者多加注意，经常总结就不会出现翻译上的错误。

 **例句**

例1. Enclosed please find our latest illustrated catalog and price list.

兹附上我们最新的图示目录及价格单。

例2. Allow us to thank you for the kindness extended to us.

对贵方之盛情，不胜感谢。

例3. We have duly received your valued favor of the 25th August.

我们如期收到了 8 月 25 日的贵函。

例4. It would give us a great pleasure to render you a similar service should an opportunity occur.

我方如有机会同样效劳贵方，将不胜欣慰。

例5. We should be grateful if you would change the invoice and let us have a corrected copy.

如蒙贵方重换发票并寄给我们更改后的副本，我方将不胜感激。

### 5. 新词的使用

语言在不断变化，随着社会的发展，几乎每天都有新词出现。对这些新词的认知、记忆和翻译是商务英语学习者必做的功课。请看下面这些新词：

double dip(经济二次探底)      BRICS（金砖五国）

anti-dumping（反倾销）      downsize（公司裁员）

gelivable（给力）      cybercash（电子货币）

electronic broker(网上经纪人)      cyber-marketing（网络化营销）

online publishing（网络出版）      virtual store(虚拟商店)

open-collar workers（敞领工人,特指那些在家中完成工作的从业者）

quaternary industry（第四产业,指信息产业）

yettie（自创或经营高科技公司的 20 多岁的年轻人）

##  Section 4   Translating Strategies, Samples and Training

###  Translating Strategies

#### 一、词与词义的选择

无论是普通英语还是商务英语,一词多义、一词多类的现象十分普遍。一词多义是指同一个词在同一个词类中,又往往有几种不同的含义。一词多类是指一个词属于几种不同词类,由于词类不同,意义也有所差异。因此,译者在翻译时,一定要根据文章的题材、语境、词类、词语搭配等来确定词义。在词义难以确定时,一定要多查词典,多向专家请教,切不可想当然。例如,英语中的名词 security 就有多种含义,它既有安全、保安措施、保安人员、保安部门等意思,也有保险金、证券、抵押品等意思。请看下面的几个例句,特别注意 security 一词的几种不同含义:

#### 📝 例句

例 1. We are now under a great deal of pressure to tighten our airport security.

我们目前承受着加强机场保安措施的巨大压力。

例 2. Mary got a big loan from Bank of America,but she had to put up her house as security.

玛丽从美国银行得到一大笔贷款,但她必须以自己的房子作为抵押品。

例 3. There has been heavy trading in government securities.

政府发行的有价证券交易十分活跃。

例 4. I'll have to inform security about what is happening here.

我不得不将这里发生的事情向保安部报告。

例 5. These laid-off workers were mainly on social security.

这些下岗工人主要靠领取社会保险金生活。

又如,英语中的 like 虽然是个普通词,但是它兼有多种词类。它既是名词、动词、形容词,也可以充当副词、介词和连词。所以译者翻译时就要根据不同的主题和词类确定其含义。请看下面的几个例句,注意 like 一词的词类和译法:

例句

例 1. These government officials have like attitudes in foreign trade policies. 这些政府官员在对外贸易政策上的观点大致相同。（形容词：相似的，同样的）

例 2. I'd like you to conduct a market research and then quote your best prices.
我想请你进行一次市场调查，然后开出你方最优惠的报价。（动词：希望，想要）

例 3. As far as the project is concerned，twenty million US dollars will be nothing like enough.
就这个项目而言，两千万美元根本不够。（介词：像）

例 4. Mr. Smith acts like he is the CEO.
史密斯先生的举动就像他自己是总裁一样。（连词：像，如同）

例 5. Like attracts like.
物以类聚，人以群分。（名词：同样的人或物）

以上所谈到的主要是在英译汉时的词义选择问题，实际上，在汉译英时经常会出现词的选择问题，而且，词的选择比词义选择更难。例如，商务英语中保险费、保险单、保险条款、保险事故、保险范围应该分别翻译成 insurance premium、insurance policy、insurance clause、insurance risk、insurance coverage，而不能想当然地译成 insurance expense、insurance bill、insurance term、insurance accident、insurance scope。

由此可见，词和词义的选择十分重要，它是商务英语学习者和翻译者的一门基本功，切不可小视。

## 二、词义的引申

在英译汉时，有时会遇到某些词在词典上找不到合适的词义，如果非要生硬翻译，句子就会不通顺，甚至会造成歧义。在这种情况下，我们就可以尝试将词义加以引申。所谓词义引申是指从原词的内在含义出发，结合语境和译入语的表达习惯，在译文中对某些词语作一定的语义调整，以达到句意和句式的完美呈现。常见的词义引申有以下几种形式：

### 1. 词义抽象化引申

在翻译时，我们常常会遇到必须将一些较为具体化的词进行抽象化翻译的情形，这就是词义抽象化的翻译方法，请看以下几个例句：

 例句

例 1. Having only one person to take charge of sales promotion has caused a real bottleneck.
只有一个人负责促销影响了整个销售工作的进展。

分析：本句中的 bottleneck 原意为"瓶颈"，由于瓶颈具有使缓慢和阻滞的效果，所以在这里被抽象地引申为"影响"。

例 2. A personnel deficit has existed for years in the advertising department of our company.
人员欠缺情况在我们公司的广告部已存在很多年了。

分析：该句中的 deficit 一般都作财务上的"赤字""贸易差额"。但在现代英语中，往往又从这些释意中引申出"不足"或"欠缺"之意。说"人员赤字"是无论如何也讲不通的。

例 3. As far as the head goes, at least he has done credit to the on-going economic system.

就智力而言,他起码为现行的经济体制增了光。

**分析**:此句中的 head 是"头,脑袋"的意思,在此句中引申翻译成"智力"。

例 4. The EEC's Common Agricultural policy is a dinosaur which is adding £13.50 a week to the food bill of the average British family.

欧共体的农业共同政策已不合时宜,它使英国家庭平均每周在食品开销上多支出 13.50 英镑。

**分析**:此句中的 dinosaur 是"恐龙"的意思,"恐龙"是一种早已绝迹的远古复杂的动物。在现代英语里,dinosaur 常被引申为"要被废弃的落后的庞然大物"。在该句中是指不合时宜的政策。

### 2. 词义具体化引申

在翻译时,我们也经常会遇到必须将一些较为抽象的词翻译得比较具体的情形,这就是词义具体化引申的翻译技巧。请看下面的几个例句:

 **例句**

例 1. The first step might be to bring about an efficacious UN presence in the area.

第一步也许应该在该地区设立联合国有效的办事机构。

**分析**:句中的 presence 如果生硬翻译成"出席、到场、存在"等意,读起来会显得很不自然,翻译腔十足,所以还是引申翻译为"办事机构",使译文更顺畅自然。

例 2. As the politburo gave the go-ahead signal to Brezhnev, Nixon and Kissinger were meeting in the President's Kremlin apartment, prepared to accept a setback on sale.

当政治局向勃列日涅夫开绿灯时,尼克松和基辛格正在克里姆林宫的总统下榻处开会,准备承受马上就会到来的挫折。

**分析**:此句中的 go-ahead signal 没有直译成"向前的信号",而是根据上下文引申翻译为"开绿灯",这样的翻译也许更符合汉语的习惯。

例 3. The tsunami was the despair of the Tokyo Electric Power Co.

这次海啸使东京电力公司陷入绝境。

**分析**:此句中 despair 的本意是"失望、绝望",意思比较抽象,这里用来表示"令人绝望的事情",因此根据上下文翻译成"陷入绝境",更符合汉语的习惯。

### 3. 专有名词普通化引申

在英语漫长的历史发展进程中,沉积了大量的专有名词。专有名词原本是指称那些独一无二的人物、事件、地点等,但是在长期的使用过程中,专有名词所表达的意思逐渐泛化,独特的本义转化为普通意义。《圣经》和古希腊、古罗马神话是西方文化的源泉,所以,英语中很多这类词语都来自《圣经》和古希腊、古罗马神话,当然也有一些词语来自诗歌、小说、戏剧等。例如,Judas kiss 字面意思是"犹大之吻",引申意为"出卖朋友,阴险的背叛";the Trojan Horse 直译是"特洛伊木马",引申翻译为"奸细";the Heel of Achilles 直译是"阿基里斯的脚踵",引申翻译为"弱点";poor as Job 字面意思是"穷得像约伯",引申翻译为"一贫如洗"。

由此可见，对于专有名词的翻译，一定要追根寻源，查清楚、搞明白，否则就会出现错误，贻笑大方。在这点上，最经典的例子莫过当年赵景深先生把"the Milky Way"（银河）误译为"牛奶路"。当然，后来也有人说他是故意这样翻译的。不管怎样 the Milky Way 应该翻译成"银河"已经成为常识。所以，专有名词的翻译的确需要引起学习者的注意。

### 三、词义的褒贬

翻译时，词的褒贬也是译者值得注意的问题。在英语中，有些单词本身就是褒义词，有些单词生来就是贬义词，还有些单词本身并没有褒贬之意，属于中性词，但是作者却赋予了它们褒贬之意。因此，在翻译过程中我们必须准确把握原文作者的意思，要以原文为基准，把握好原作者的褒贬倾向。

**1. 褒义词与贬义词**

英语中有些词本身就带有褒贬之意，翻译时译者一定要把这种意思准确地表达出来。请看下面的几个例句：

 **例句**

例 1. The speech of the president has been exposed as pure propaganda.

事实表明，总统的讲话纯属宣传。（propaganda 宣传。常带有贬义）

例 2. The management felt continual pressure to cut the workforce.

资方长期处在需要裁员的压力之下。（continual 持续不断的。贬义）

例 3. The firm is renowned for its excellent technical support.

这家公司以其优良的技术支持著称。（renowned 有名望的，著名的。褒义）

例 4. The after-sale service of their company is praiseworthy.

他们公司的售后服务是值得称颂的。（praiseworthy 值得称颂的。褒义）

例 5. He didn't accept the job offer because it was a notoriously inefficient company.

他没有接受那份工作，因为那是一家人人都知道的效率极低的公司。（notoriously 臭名昭著地、声名狼藉地。贬义）

**2. 褒贬兼可的词**

英语中有些词既可以用于褒义，也可以用于贬义，这要看上下文和笔者的意思来确定。请看下面的例句：

 **例句**

例 1. The government should spend more money on really important things, not on prestige development like new airports.

政府应该把钱花在真正紧要的事业上，而不是花在像建新机场这类炫耀门面的事情上。（prestige，讲究排场的，摆阔气的。贬义）

例 2. It was his responsibility for foreign affairs that gained him international prestige.

正是他在外交中的尽职尽责为他赢得了国际声望。（prestige 威望，声望。褒义）

例 3. He needs to be a bit of a politician to succeed in this company.

他要想在这家公司获得成功,就需要耍点政治手腕。(politician 政客。贬义)

例 4. From him I learn that a good politician is marked to a great extent by his sense of timing.

从他那儿我懂得一名好的政治家在很大程度上在于其善于审时度势。(politician 政治家。褒义)

**3. 中性词**

英语中还有些词是中性的,没有明显的褒或贬的含义,但在一定的上下文中可能就具有褒贬的意味,所以翻译时要注意掌握褒贬分寸。请看下面的例句:

 **例句**

例 1. They persisted in their wrong course.

他们执迷不悟。(persist 坚持,持续。按贬义翻译)

例 2. They urged the organization to persist with its efforts to push the sales of their products.

他们敦促该组织坚持努力推动他们产品的销售。(persist 坚持,持续。按褒义翻译)

例 3. He was a man of integrity, but unfortunately he had a certain reputation.

他是一个正直诚实的人,但不幸有某种坏名声。(reputation,名誉,名声。按贬义翻译)

例 4. The company has acquired a reputation for their quality goods.

这家公司的产品质量优良尽人皆知。(reputation 名声,名誉。按褒义翻译)

例 5. Those who forget the past are condemned to relive it.

凡是忘掉过去的人注定要重蹈覆辙。(relive 再经历,再经受。按贬义翻译)

例 6. They relived the days when they worked together in the United Nations.

他们重温了在联合国一起工作过的日子。(relive 重温。按褒义翻译)

**Translating Samples**

**一、各类汇票的翻译**

1. 即期汇票 sight draft

2. 远期汇票 time draft

3. 长期汇票 long bill

4. 短期汇票 short bill

5. 逾期汇票 overdue bill

6. 本票 promissory note

7. 跟单汇票 documentary draft

8. 商业汇票 commercial draft

9. 银行汇票 banker's draft

10. 国外汇票 foreign bill

11. 国内汇票 inland bill

12. 空头汇票 accommodation bill

13. 原始汇票 original bill

14. 普通汇票 clean draft

15. 银行承兑汇票 banker's acceptance bill

16. 商业承兑汇票 commercial acceptance draft

17. 凭即期汇票付款 available by drafts at sight

18. 付款交单 documents against payment (D/P)

19. 承兑交单 documents against acceptance (D/A)

20. 开立 30 天的期票 draft to be drawn at 30 days sight

## 二、商务英语套语的翻译

1. It was a pleasure to receive your letter of 21st June.

很高兴收到你 6 月 21 日来信。

2. In reply to your letter of March 20, we have pleasure to enclose our order 2155.

兹复你方 3 月 20 日来函，我们高兴地附上我方第 2155 号订单。

3. We take pleasure in informing you…

我们谨愉快地通知您……

4. Please send us a copy of your catalogue and current price list for laptops.

请寄给我们一份笔记本电脑产品目录及价目单。

5. I shall appreciate your answers to these questions.

对于上述问题，请予以答复为盼。

6. We look forward very much to the pleasure of receiving an order from your company.

我们期待有幸收到贵公司的订单。

7. Through the courtesy of Mr. Black, we are given to know that you are one of the leading exporters of electronic products in China.

承蒙布莱克先生介绍，我们获悉贵方是中国最主要的电子产品出口商之一。

8. Enclosed please find our latest catalog and price list.

随附我们最新的目录和价目表。

9. We are enclosing the following copies of shipping documents.

随附下列船运单据。

10. Please notify us when the goods are shipped.

一旦货物运出，请尽快通知我方。

11. Being specialized in the export of…we express our desire to trade with you in this line.

我们专门出口……愿与贵方展开这方面的业务。

12. In terms of payment, we could only accept confirmed irrevocable L/C.

就付款条件而言，我方只接受保兑的、不可撤销的信用证。

13. Please insure us the goods detailed below.

请替我方投保下列各项货物。

14. If your order is large enough we are ready to reduce our prices by 8%.

如果你们的订单足够大，我们可以给你降价 8%。

15. Please note that this quotation is subject to acceptance within a month.

请注意本报价一个月内接受有效。

16. We would be very pleased to act as your exclusive agent if your terms and conditions are right.

如果贵方条件合适，我们非常乐意做你们的独家代理。

17. It should be made clear to you that we normally take every possible precaution to ensure that our goods arrive at the ports of destination in prime condition.

必须指出,我们通常会采取一切措施确保我们的货物完好无损地到达目的地。

18. In line with the purchase contract dated May 25, 2021, the goods we ordered should have been delivered by the end of July at the latest.

根据 2021 年 5 月 25 日所签订的购物合同,货物最迟应该在 7 月底交付。

19. I'd like to have your lowest quotations, CIF London.

我想请你们报 CIF 伦敦的最低价。

20. Your immediate reply would be highly appreciated.

盼望贵方早日答复。

21. Please confirm that you can supply…by the required date.

请确认你方能按期供应……。

22. I have pleasure in accepting your offer on…

兹接受贵方……的报盘。

23. We would ask you to let us have a quotation for…

我们想请贵公司寄一份……的报价单。

24. I must write to say how much we appreciate the promptness with which you have settled the dispute.

我写此信是要感谢您如此迅速地解决了此争议。

25. We hope this will be a good start for a long and profitable business relations.

我们希望这是长期互利商业关系的一个良好的开端。

### Translating Training

**A: Translate the following sentences into English, paying attention to the technical terms or business formulas.**

1. 诚然,信息产业的关键是保持技术的前沿地位,但如果技术革新速度太快,商家就难以收回成本。

2. 在整个出口额中,发达国家占 40%,发展中国家占 60%。

3. 运输和通信技术的进步降低了货物运输、劳务运输和生产要素运输以及知识和技术传播的成本。

4. 互联网的零售能力在于其能够在商人和客户之间创造一种更深层次的关系,这种关系赋予客户很大的权力,并且完全改变了现代营销模式。

5. 信息时代,创新成了公司在充满竞争的社会中生存和进步的永恒真理。

6. 改革开放以来,上海走出了一条具有中国特色、体现时代特征、符合上海特点的发展新路。

7. 虽然诸如现金和支票处理这样的传统业务依然正常进行,但是今天的出纳员面对的是一个自动化环境,在这个自动化环境中,进入远程数据库使得所能获得的信息成指数倍增长。

8. 我们更希望应用多年累积的国内外房地产操作经验,推动本地房地产市场的发展及人才培训;带领各方迈向国际化,以达到更有效的投资管理领域。

9. 合并和兼并浪潮背后的最主要因素，与全球化过程背后的因素是一致的：交通、通信成本下降，贸易额降低，投资壁垒减少，市场扩大。

10. 很多服务型企业，由于其质量没有达到消费者的期待值以及其产品不为消费者所熟知，所以在开放的商场中遭受失败。

**B. Translate the following sentences into Chinese, paying attention to the technical terms or business formulas.**

1. The trade surplus was down 19 percent from January as a government spending spree aimed at cranking up the economy fuelled demand for imports.

2. Of course, though consumers may tell pollsters they will pay a premium, getting them to do so at the shop may be trickier.

3. The Dow's bold advance this week, which included a 280-point surge Wednesday, wiped out more than 40 percent of the average's losses over the last two months.

4. First-quarter figures, which showed an alarming jump in labour costs and annual growth in domestic demand of 8%, suggest that inflation is likely to pick up.

5. If you are opening your own business, you will lose the security of a paycheck and the company benefits you take for granted.

6. Amazon.com, based in Seattle, opened its virtual doors in July 1995 with the mission of using the Internet to offer products that would educate, inform, and inspire people at a customer-friendly, easy-to-navigate Website that would offer the broadest possible selection.

7. A working environment that gets the best from people is more than just a place to work.

8. It is obvious that the strength of a country's economy is directly bound up with the efficiency of its agriculture and industry, and that this in turn rests upon the efforts of scientists and technologists of all kinds.

9. Economics involves the study of topics like wealth and poverty, money and banks, incomes, taxes, prosperity and depression, big business and labour unions, and hundreds of other matters that intimately affect the way we live.

10. A loaf of bread is the end result of a long series of operations that begins with planting and harvesting grain and proceeds through milling, baking, and shipping to the point at which the housewife can pick the loaf off the grocer's shelf.

## Section 5 Extensive Expression

### 一、商务英语常见缩略语

| | | |
|---|---|---|
| 1. agt.（agent） | | 代理 |
| 2. appt.（appointment） | | 预约，约会 |
| 3. B/P（bill payable） | | 应付票据 |
| 4. bal.（balance） | | 余额 |
| 5. c.a.d.（cost against document） | | 凭单付现 |

| | |
|---|---|
| 6. c.c.(carbon copy) | 副本 |
| 7. CFR(cost and freight) | 成本加运费 |
| 8. OZ(ounce) | 盎司 |
| 9. c.i.a.(cash in advance) | 预付款 |
| 10. C/O(care of) | 烦转交 |
| 11. contr.(contact) | 合同 |
| 12. cy.(currency) | 货币 |
| 13. dbt.(debit) | 借方 |
| 14. dep.(deposit) | 定金 |
| 15. disct.(discount) | 折扣 |
| 16. prox.(proximo) | 下月的 |
| 17. Div.(dividend) | 红利 |
| 18. drt.(draft) | 汇票 |
| 19. dupl.(duplication) | 副本 |
| 20. Expo(exposition) | 博览会 |
| 21. f.i.t.(free of income tax) | 免所得税 |
| 22. FRT(freight) | 货物 |
| 23. FYI(for your information) | 仅供参考 |
| 24. GWT(gross weight) | 毛重 |
| 25. insp.(inspection) | 检验 |
| 26. inv.(invoice) | 发票 |
| 27. j/a(joint account) | 共有账户 |
| 28. mtg.(mortgage) | 抵押贷款 |
| 29. NAV(net asset value) | 净资产值 |
| 30. c&f(cost and freight) | 成本加运费价格 |
| 31. FPA(free from particular average) | 平安险 |
| 32. S/C(sales confirmation) | 销售确认书 |
| 33. SME(small and medium enterprises) | 中小型企业 |
| 34. SOEs(state-owned enterprises) | 国企 |
| 35. T.T.(telegraphic transfer) | 电汇 |
| 36. v.v.(vice versa) | 反之亦然 |
| 37. VAT(value-added tax) | 增值税 |
| 38. WPA(with particular average) | 水渍险 |
| 39. FOB(free on board) | 离岸价 |
| 40. AAR(against all risks) | 一切险 |
| 41. ARM(adjustable rate mortgage) | 可调利率按揭 |
| 42. CIF(cost,insurance and freight) | 成本加运费和保险费 |
| 43. ICB(international competitive bidding) | 国际竞争性招标 |
| 44. MFN(the most favored nation) | 最惠国待遇 |

45. NP（notary public）          公证处

46. L/G（letter of guarantee）      保证书

47. L/A（letter of authority）       授权书

48. CPA（certified public accountant）  注册会计师

49. TQM（total quality management）    全面质量管理

50. I/P（insurance policy）         保险单

51. CPI（consumer price index）     消费者价格指数

52. F/P（fire policy）            火灾保险

53. GNP（gross national product）    国民生产总值

54. L/U（letter of undertaking）     承诺书

55. MBO（management by objectives）   目标管理

## 二、商务英语常用词汇

1. 财务简报              briefing on finance

2. 财务预算              financial forecast

3. 财务状况              financial situation

4. 次货                  shoddy goods

5. 大路货              fair average quality

6. 付款方式              mode of payment

7. 公众形象              public image

8. 股本                  share capital

9. 股票经纪人            stock jobber

10. 股票转让             stock transfer

11. 关税                customs duty

12. 互惠协议            reciprocal agreement

13. 检验报告            the survey report

14. 降低成本            cut cost

15. 交货期              time of delivery

16. 阶段性审核          phase review

17. 客户订单            customer order

18. 库存管理           inventory management

19. 离职通知书         resignation notice

20. 利润限度           margin of profit

21. 利润预测           profit forecast

22. 列入议程           place on the agenda

23. 潜在需求           potential demand

24. 投标                submission to tender

25. 人才流失           loss of talent

26. 商标侵权           trademark infringement

| | | |
|---|---|---|
| 27. 商业信用 | commercial credit |
| 28. 损失清单 | a statement of loss |
| 29. 索赔清单 | claim statement |
| 30. 索赔书 | claim letter |
| 31. 公开招标 | open bidding |
| 32. 违约 | breach of contract |
| 33. 销售确认书 | sales confirmation |
| 34. 销售业绩 | sales performance |
| 35. 印花税 | stamp duty |
| 36. 优惠价 | favorable price |
| 37. 资产负债表 | balance sheet |
| 38. 贸易壁垒 | trade barriers |
| 39. 总值 | total value |
| 40. 进口许可证 | import license |
| 41. 机构投资者 | institutional investor |
| 42. 期货交易所 | futures exchange |
| 43. 横向收购 | horizontal acquisition |
| 44. 企业兼并 | enterprise merger |
| 45. 数量折扣 | quantity discount |
| 46. 技术转让 | technology transfer |
| 47. 上市公司 | public listed company |
| 48. 索赔 | claim for compensation |
| 49. 最惠国待遇 | the most favored nation |
| 50. 授权书 | letter of authority |
| 51. 财务报表 | financial statement |
| 52. 独家代理 | exclusive agent |
| 53. 预付款 | cash in advance |
| 54. 质量不符 | non-conformity of quality |
| 55. 提出动议 | make/put forward a motion |
| 56. 提出索赔 | make/register/file a claim |
| 57. 重量检验证书 | inspection certificate of weight |
| 58. 品质检验证书 | inspection certificate of quality |
| 59. 企业利润总额 | gross profits of enterprises |
| 60. 企业亏损 | loss incurred in an enterprise |

# Unit *3*

# Company Names and Business Cards

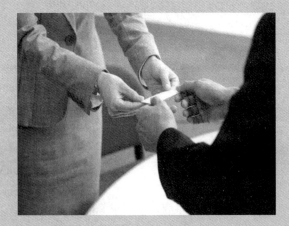

Unit Objectives

In this unit you should

➤ familiarize yourself with the format of business cards and formation of company names.

➤ enable yourself to acquire the translating characters of company names and business cards.

➤ have a good command of the translating skills of hypotaxis and parataxis, animate subject and inanimate subject, static and dynamic, repeatation and substitution.

## ? Section 1   Theme Lead–in

**Read the following passage to gain a better understanding of this unit.**

Although company names and business cards are not the decisive factors in the success of a company or an enterprise, they can be one of the most effective ways to help these businesses publicize themselves and promote the sales of their products.

A company's name is just like a person's name. It serves as the symbol of the company and it is an intangible asset to it. A considerable significance for a good company name lies in the fact that it is conducive to the promoting of its products and the enhancing of its fame and competitiveness. The charm of a good company name is so immense that it can lead the company to prominence whereas the negative effect of a bad company name might be strong enough to bankrupt it. This may seem far-fetched and exaggerative, but it is true.

Translation of company names is a comprehensive and creative process which covers linguistics, translation theory, aesthetics, intercultural communication, marketing, advertising and consumer psychology. It serves as a medium of communication and plays a significant role in modern business world and transaction. A good translation of a company name is so powerful that it can assist multinationals in penetrating international market.

A business card is an effective tool in business communication. A good card can open up a good opportunity. It is a necessity for modern businessmen to identify themselves and get acquainted with each other in a short period of time. A well-designed business card is a good advertisement because many prospective customers make assumptions and first impressions of a business or an enterprise from their business cards. Cards can really help these organizations establish their credibility, advertise their products and enhance their brand images.

The information that must go with a business card includes the name, titles, contact ways of a person as well as the name, logo and address of a company. Not only should the arrangement of these elements be aesthetically appealing, but they should also be functionally presenting and displaying. In a word, business cards should be beautiful and dignified, showing individuality.

To sum up, with the globalization of economic development, more and more foreign companies are expanding into the Chinese market and the translation of their company names, brand names and business cards becomes virtually inevitable. As a business English learner, to acquire the translation skills of them is a must and there cannot be enough emphasis laid on it.

## Section 2　Translation Warming-up

**A: Please match the Chinese translation in column B with the English expressions in column A.**

| | |
|---|---|
| 1. Kao | A. 迎宾牌香烟 |
| 2. Safeguard | B. 得利斯食品 |
| 3. Skinice | C. 金盾 |
| 4. Mickey | D. 舒肤佳 |
| 5. Welcome | E. 米奇 |
| 6. Delicious | F. 高姿 |
| 7. Nice | G. 肤美灵 |
| 8. Cadillac | H. 花王 |
| 9. Cogi | I. 纳爱斯 |

10. KinDon                    J. 卡迪拉克

B：Translate the following company names into English.

1. 沃尔玛百货公司              2. 好事达公司

3. 通用汽车公司                4. 英国石油公司

5. 美国邮政服务公司            6. GMS 能源公司

7. 苏格兰皇家银行              8. 珀金-埃尔默公司

9. 波音商用飞机集团            10. 印度储备银行

# Section 3  Topic Features and Translation Principles

## 一、商号的翻译

商号就是我们常说的公司或企业名称。虽然公司、企业的成功不完全取决于名字的好坏，但名字无疑是影响其发展的一个重要因素。所以，对于外国公司、企业而言，如何起一个响亮的中文名是很关键的；同理，对于国内商家来讲，起一个漂亮的洋名也非常重要，因为它是企业、公司开拓国际市场的有力工具。下面我们就探讨一下商号翻译的几个问题。

### （一）商号的翻译原则

在商号翻译时，第一点要注意的就是译名的准确性，译名要尽可能地表达出原商号的发音和词义。例如，American Home Products（美国家庭用品公司），如果此商号翻译成"美国家庭产品公司"就会让人迷惑，不知道它到底是经营什么的。又如，JP Morgan Chase & Co.（摩根大通银行），如果翻译成"摩根大通公司"也不能很好地体现该公司的主营业务。

商号翻译需要注意的第二点是译名要通俗易懂、优雅大方、具有美感。公司名称应尽量避免使用生僻字。译名力求简洁生动，发音朗朗上口，使人过目不忘。例如，Goldman Sachs Group（高盛集团公司），该公司译名采取音译的方法，并且"高盛"二字通俗易懂、寓意深刻，如果直译为"金人集团"，就显得俗气很多。又如，Mercedes-Benz AG.（奔驰汽车公司），Benz 音译为"奔驰"，既简洁又响亮，令人联想到驱车驰骋的速度与激情，与该公司的经营项目极其吻合，可谓翻译得神形兼备。

商号翻译需要注意的第三点是译者要有文化意识，要注意译出语和译入语国家的文化差异，在翻译时适时做出调整。例如，上海蝙蝠电器有限公司，如果翻译成 Shanghai Bat Electric Appliances Co.，Ltd. 就有问题了。蝙蝠在汉语中谐音为"福"，有吉祥之意，但在西方 bat（蝙蝠）则与眼瞎、吸血鬼等不好的事情联系在一起。蝙蝠在西方人的眼中是一种让人恶心的动物，代表凶恶和丑陋，所以英译时不宜直接翻译成 Bat，可以使用汉语拼音或者换个其他词。以上例子说明，在商号翻译时，文化因素不可忽视。

### （二）商号的翻译方法

将英文商号翻译成中文主要有以下几种方法：

### 1. 音译法（transliteration）

音译法顾名思义就是根据原公司、企业名称的英文发音找到与之语音相近的汉字进行翻译的方法,其优点是简单易行、译文具有异国情调。这种方法一般用来翻译以人名、地名、缩略语等构成的公司名称。翻译时要根据公司的特点,译语力求通俗易懂、优雅大方、富有美感,切忌使用晦涩难懂的字眼。

 **样例**

例 1. Walt Disney Company 华特·迪士尼公司(美国)

例 2. Adidas AG.阿迪达斯公司(德国)

例 3. Midland Bank 米兰银行(英国)

例 4. Nike Inc.耐克公司(美国)

**2. 意译法（free translation）**

意译就是不拘泥于原文的形式,把商号的内涵意义用再创性的译语表达出来。当遇到不适合音译或直译的商号时可以尝试意译法。意译法一般用来翻译以国名、地名和普通名词构成的公司或企业名称。

 **样例**

例 1. Consolidated Coal Company 联合煤炭公司（美国）

例 2. British Nuclear Associates 英国核子联合公司(英国)

例 3. Electronic Data Systems 电子数据系统公司（美国）

例 4. American International Underwriters Corporation 美国国际保险公司(美国)

**3. 音意结合法（transliteration combined with free translation）**

在商号翻译时,为了达到更佳的效果,有时需要采取音意相结合的办法。一般来讲是把商号中的专有名词按发音进行翻译,把普通名词按其意义进行翻译。这种翻译方法就是音意结合法,例如:

 **样例**

例 1. Boeing Commercial Airplane Group 波音商用飞机集团(美国)

例 2. Union Camp Corporation 友联坎普公司(美国)

例 3. Goldlion Holdings Limited 金利来集团有限公司(香港)

**4. 直接引用法（direct quoting）**

有些商号不好翻译,或者翻译出来没有意义,这时就可以直接使用原商号名。这种方法主要适用于一些以缩略词表示的商号,例如:

 **样例**

例 1. LG Corporation LG 公司(韩国)

例 2. CMS Energy Corp. CMS 能源公司(美国)

例 3. SBC Communications Inc. SBC 通讯公司（美国）

例 4. TCL Corporation TCL 公司（中国）

**5. 沿用法（using the old name）**

有些外国公司的汉语译名已由来已久，为人们所公认和接受，如果更换，会带来不必要的麻烦和误解，这时我们应该沿用约定俗成的译名，不应改动或重译，例如：

 **样例**

例 1. HSBC（The Hongkong & Shanghai Banking Corporation）Holdings plc.
汇丰控股有限公司（英国）

例 2. First National City Bank 花旗银行（美国）

例 3. Standard Chartered Bank 渣打银行（英国）

例 4. Cable & Wireless plc. 大东电报局（英国）

## （三）商号中表示"公司"的词语及译法

英文中表示公司的词很多，除了子公司、分公司、总公司之外，还有集团公司、有限公司、控股公司、联合公司等。尽管许多专家学者撰文阐释了公司名称翻译的诸多要点，但当我们真正动手翻译的时候，还是会遇到一些问题。下面，就看一看英语国家"公司"二字的表达方法，并从诸多例句中得到一些启示。

（1）Inc. 是个缩略词，全称为（incorporated），表示（股份）有限公司的意思。这是美国公司中用得最多的一个词，但英国公司用得较少，例如：

 **样例**

例 1. Coca-Cola Enterprises Inc. 可口可乐企业公司（美国）

例 2. United Airlines Inc. 联合航空公司（美国）

例 3. Dawson International Inc. 道森国际有限公司（美国）

（2）Corporation 是法人、集团公司或（股份）有限公司，经常缩写为 Corp. 它是除了 Inc. 之外，美国公司用得较多的一个词，但这个词英国公司用得较少，例如：

 **样例**

例 1. McDonnell-Douglas Corporation 麦道公司（美国）

例 2. Federal Express Corporation 联邦快递公司（美国）

例 3. Dell Computer Corporation 戴尔电脑公司（美国）

（3）Company（可以缩写成 Co.）一般指以营利为目的的社团或公司，这个词英国和美国公司都有使用。另外，Company 的后面还可以加上 Limited，缩写成 Co.,Ltd. 是"有限责任公司"的意思，例如：

 **样例**

例 1. Phillips Petroleum Company 菲利普石油公司（美国）

例 2. Ford Motor Company 福特汽车公司（美国）

例 3. Shell Oil Company 壳牌石油公司（美国）

（4）PLC.或 plc.是股份有限公司的意思,它是 Public Limited Company 的简称。这个词英国公司用得多,但美国公司很少使用,例如:

 **样例**

例 1. British Petroleum PLC. 英国石油公司（英国）

例 2. Cable & Wireless PLC. 大东电报局（英国）

例 3. Woolworths Group PLC. 沃尔沃斯有限公司（澳大利亚）

（5）Group 是集团或集团公司的意思,例如:

 **样例**

例 1. American International Group 美国国际集团

例 2. Royal & Sun Alliance Insurance Group 皇家太阳联合保险集团（英国）

例 3. New York Global Group 纽约国际集团

（6）Holdings 是指控股公司,例如:

 **样例**

例 1. Lehman Brothers Holdings 雷曼兄弟控股公司（美国）

例 2. MAI Holdings 麦安迪控股公司（美国）

例 3. UCBH Holdings Inc. 美国联合银行控股公司

（7）Air Lines,Airlines,Airways 指航空公司,例如:

 **样例**

例 1. Delta Air Lines 德尔塔航空公司（美国）

例 2. United Airlines 美国联合航空公司

例 3. South African Airways 南非航空公司

（8）Networks 特指网络公司,例如:

 **样例**

例 1. Fluke Networks 福禄克网络公司（美国）

例 2. A10 Networks Inc. A10 网络公司（美国）

例 3. Extreme Networks 极进网络公司（美国）

（9）Communications 特指通信(讯)公司,例如:

 **样例**

例 1. Verizon Communications 威瑞莱森通信公司（美国）

例 2. MRV Communications, Inc. MRV 通信公司（美国）

例 3. Transcend Communications, Inc. 卓越通信公司（美国）

（10）Associates 特指（联合）公司，例如：

**样例**

例 1. Wenzel Associates, Inc. 温泽联合公司（美国）

例 2. Manhattan Associates 曼哈顿联合公司（美国）

例 3. British Nuclear Associates 英国核子联合公司

（11）Son(s)或 Brothers 如果出现在公司名称中，分别表示"父子公司""兄弟公司"的意思，例如：

**样例**

例 1. Smith Brothers Inc. 史密斯兄弟公司（美国）

例 2. Toll Brothers Inc. 托尔兄弟公司（美国）

（12）在公司名称里，如果有 national、general、corporation、incorporation 等词可以表示总公司；而子公司、分公司，分支机构等用 subsidiary 和 branch 表示，办事处用 office 表示，例如：

**样例**

例 1. China National Machinery Import and Export Corporation 中国机械进出口总公司

例 2. General American Transportation Corp. 美国运输总公司

例 3. LG Electronics Beijing Sales Subsidiary LG 电子北京分公司

例 4. Medline Industries, Inc. Shanghai Office 美国美联实业有限公司上海代表处

（13）有些公司的名称中含有 united、consolidated、joint、associated、allied、integrated、joint、federated 等词，一般翻译成"联合公司"，例如：

**样例**

例 1. United Aircraft Corporation 联合飞机公司（美国）

例 2. Allied Chemical Corporation 联合化学公司（美国）

例 3. Federated Department Stores 联合百货（美国）

（14）还有一些公司企业的名称是由一些产品、服务或具有公司意义的普通名词构成的，如 Laboratories、Industries、Products、Enterprise(s)、Service(s)、System(s)、Works、Agency、Store、Steel、Machine、Motor、Insurance、Assurance、Telecom 等，例如：

**样例**

例 1. Fuji Heavy Industries 富士重工业（日本）

例 2. JM Family Enterprises JM 家庭企业公司（美国）

例 3. United Parcel Service, Inc. 联合包裹服务公司（美国）

例 4. American Mgmt. Systems Corporation 美国管理系统公司

例 5. P.A. Works P.A. 动画公司（日本）

例 6. International Business Machines Corporation IBM 公司（美国）

例 7. France Telecom 法国电信公司（法国）

例 8. Japan Ocean Shipping Agency 日本外轮代理公司

## 二、商务名片的翻译

### （一）商务名片的构成要素

商务名片英文为 Business Card 或 Visiting Card，它是众多管理人员、公关人员、涉外人员等在现代社会交往中一种必不可少的联络工具。由于对外交往的不断扩大，各行各业人士都希望在自己的名片上印制出中英文两种文字，这就涉及了名片的翻译问题。

一张正规的名片一般由四部分组成：

1. 持有人所在公司及部门；

2. 持有人的姓名；

3. 持有人的职位、职称、学位等内容；

4. 持有人的联络方式，包括地址、电话、传真、电子邮箱等。

一般来讲，公司的名称和持有人姓名、职位、职称等要置于名片的首要位置，并采取不同字体和字号，以此来突出持有人的身份，树立公司形象。另外，商务名片一般还需印有公司的标识（Logo），版面设计力求美观大方，能够体现持有者的个性。请看下面几张英文商务名片及中文对照：

**Sample 1**

LHP

**伦敦家庭用品公司**

**加尔文·R.贝克**
生产专员

地址：伦敦新桥大街19号
邮编：EC4 6DB
电话：02082 444 708
传真：02082 444 755
邮箱：CRBaker@MFP.com

LHP

**London Home Product**

**Calvin R. Baker**
Production Executive

19 New Bridge Street, London
EC4 6DB
Tel: 02082 444 708
Fax: 02082 444 755
e-mail: CRBaker@MFP.com

**Sample 2**

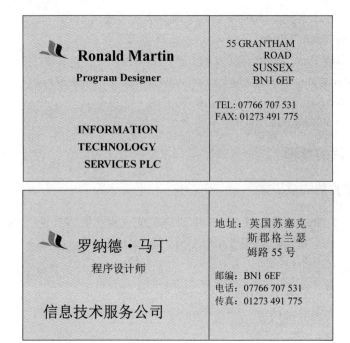

**（二）商务名片的翻译方法**

**1. 商务名片中姓名的翻译**

众所周知,中国人的姓名和英语国家人的姓名排列顺序是不同的,中国姓在前、名在后,英语国家则名在前、姓在后。英语国家人的姓名排列顺序是：First Name（名字）+Middle Name(名字)+Last Name（姓氏）。middle name 经常没有或缩写为第一个字母,如 Lisa Storm Nixon 可以写成 Lisa S. Nixon。

英语姓名汉译大多采取音译法,如 James Bond 詹姆斯·邦德,Patrick Henry 帕特里克·亨利,Anna Phelps 安娜·佩尔普斯,Mary D. Feldman,玛丽·D.菲尔德曼,William Henry Gates 威廉·亨利·盖茨,Steve Paul Jobs 史蒂夫·保罗·乔布斯等。翻译时要注意汉字的正确使用,拿不准是哪个汉字时,可以查阅《世界人名翻译辞典》。

把中文姓名译成英语时,一般是采取汉语拼音直译的方法,如李天骄 Li Tianjiao,柳如烟 Liu Ruyan,黄鑫 Huang Xin 等。复姓翻译时要把复姓的汉语拼音放在一起,如欧阳峰 Ouyang Feng,司马相如 Sima Xiangru,诸葛瑾 Zhuge Jin 等。中文姓名英译时,也有人按照英文习惯把名字放在姓氏之前,如钱美意 Meiyi Qian,吴笛 Di Wu,上官如雪 Ruxue Shangguan,但是这种翻译并非主流。在使用汉语拼音英译时,有时还需要使用隔音符号以防止音节的混淆,如吴承恩译为 Wu Cheng'en,黄狄傲译为 Huang Di'ao,上官婉儿 Shangguan Wan'er。

**2. 商务名片中地址的翻译**

英文地址是从小到大排列,这与中文习惯正好相反,所以把英文地址翻译成中文时一定要把地址的顺序调换过来。例如,25 9th Avenue,Greenwich Village,NY 10014 翻译成中文是：纽约格林威治村第九大道 25 号,邮编：10014。又如,68 Margaret Street,London W1W

8SR 伦敦玛格丽特大街 68 号,邮编:W1W 8SR。

在名片翻译时为了节省空间,有时会使用一些缩略语,如 Rd. (road),St. (street),Ave.
(avenue),Apt. (apartment),Sq. (square),Fl. (floor),Rm. (room),Dept. (department),N.E.
(northeast),Add. (address),Tel. (telephone),Prof. (professor),Dr. (doctor)等。

### 3. 商务名片中职位、职称的翻译

由于中西文化不同,有些职称、职务的名称及等级划分也不尽相同,有的虽然名称相同,
但内涵却有差异,因此在翻译时一定要字斟句酌,使名片的职位、职称翻译得准确规范。如
Chairman 董事长,President 总裁,Executive Director 执行董事,Advertising Manager 广告经理,
Associate Professor 副教授,Vice-Chancellor 副校长,Deputy Director 副主任,Assistant Engineer
助理工程师,Sales Representative 销售代表等。

在中译英时,要尽量采用国际化标准来翻译职位、职称及行政职务,能借用的则借用,如
注册会计师 Certified Public Accountant,律师 Lawyer,主任医师 Chief Physician,副总裁 Vice-
President,副经理 Vice-Manager,副研究员 Associate Research Fellow,经理助理 Assistant
Manager,审计员 Auditor 等。

但有时中方的某个职位在西方并不存在,这时就要根据具体情况进行处理。比如"办公
室主任"一职,在英美等国家没有相应的职务,在我国办公室主任的主要职责是协助本单位
领导处理日常事务,所以根据情况可以翻译成 Office Manager。还有我们常说的科长、副科
长、局长可以相应地翻译成 Section Chief,Deputy Section Chief,Director-general。

### 4. 商务名片中部门名称的翻译

在英语中部门名称的翻译常用的词有 department ( Dept. ) , office , service 等。如 Sales
Department 销售部,Personnel Department 人事部,Dispatch Dept. 发货部,Business Office 营业
部,Accounting Dept. 财务部,Public Relations Department 公关部,International Dept. 国际贸易
部,Logistics Dept. 物流部,Purchasing Dept. 采购部 Research and Development Department 研
发部等。

关于公司名称的翻译,在本章有关商号的翻译一节中已做了详细介绍,在此不再赘述。

## Section 4  Translating Strategies, Samples and Training

### Translating Strategies

### 一、形合与意合

形合(hypotaxis)和意合(parataxis)是英汉两种语言篇章组织的常用手段,也是两种语言
的重要区别。美国翻译理论家尤金·奈达在其 *Translating Meaning*(1983)一书中指出:"对
于汉语和英语来说,或许语言学上最重要的区别之一就是形合与意合的明显差异了。"形合
与意合是两种不同的句式安排,一般说来,前者注重形式上的衔接(cohesion),它通过连接
词、介词、关系代词、关系副词、非限定动词等将句子或语篇连接起来,多为显性衔接(overt
cohesion),以形显义。后者则注重行文上的连贯(coherence),它不借助语言形式手段,而借
助词语或句子的意义或逻辑关系实现彼此之间的连接,其特点是形隐意在。

英语重形合,汉语重意合,是对比语言学家普遍认同的特征。但是"重"是"偏重"或"侧重"的意思,不能简单理解为英语就是形合,汉语就是意合,使之绝对化。了解英汉形合和意合的区别,对于理解和翻译商务英语具有积极的指导作用。在英译汉翻译时,要由显变隐,要去掉那些没有必要的衔接词。在进行汉译英翻译时,要由隐变显,要注意加上那些十分必要的衔接词。请看下面几个英译汉的例子。

 **例句**

例 1. If winter comes, can spring be far behind?

冬天来了,春天还会远吗?

**分析**:该句中,英文用 if 表示条件,而译文则没有,这层意义已经蕴含在汉语句子之中。

例 2. The production cost is so high that we have to raise our prices.

生产成本太高,我们只能提价。

**分析**:该句英文使用了连接词"…so…that…"(太……以至于……)引导结果状语从句,但如果生硬译出,则译腔十足,反而失去了汉语的韵味。

例 3. Your claim doesn't hold water and we, therefore, disallow it on this point.

你方索赔不成立,我方不能接受。

**分析**:该句中使用了连接词"and"和"therefore",但是在汉语中并没有直接按字面意思翻译出来,这种逻辑关系隐含在译文的两个并列单句中。

在汉译英时,译者有时要根据具体情况添加适当的衔接词,以保持英文的形合。请看下面几个汉译英的例子。

 **例句**

例 1. 贵方的订单在履行中,可按约交货。

Your order is being carried out, and delivery will be made as instructed.

**分析**:在此例句中,汉语和英语几乎是一样的。但有一点区别,那就是英语译文中添加了连词 and。这个 and 很不起眼,你甚至感觉不到它的存在,但它却体现了英汉两种语言之间的差异,在汉译英时应特别引起译者的注意。

例 2. 这个款式在国际上享有盛誉,需求量很大。

Since this style enjoys high reputation in the world market, there is a great demand for it.

**分析**:通过分析不难看出该句含有因果逻辑关系,所以,在汉译英时添加了表示原因的连接词 since。

例 3. 价格再高我们也要订货。

No matter how high the price is, we will still place an order.

**分析**:该句汉语中含有"无论……我们也要……"的含义,在英语中属于让步状语从句,所以翻译时添加了连接词"no matter how",凸显英语的逻辑关系。

## 二、有灵主语与无灵主语

有灵主语(animate subject)是指用有生命的人称主体作为句子的主语,侧重"什么人怎么样啦",而无灵主语(inanimate subject)是指用无生命的名词或短语作句子的主语,主要表达"什么事情发生在什么人身上"。英语的无灵主语句(inanimate sentence)和汉语的有灵主语句(animate sentence)是英汉两种语言中的一个显著差异,究其原因主要是西方人的思维强调客体意识,而东方人更强调主观意识。无灵主语句是英语中独特的语言现象,具有表达客观、公正、生动、有力,语言简洁、凝练、庄重、含蓄等特点。

从翻译的角度来讲,在英译汉时,为了使译文更加符合中国人的习惯,宜将英语无灵主语句根据上下文变通为汉语的有灵主语句,将无灵主语转译成汉语句子的其他成分,如状语、谓语、宾语等,必要时还需要补充动作的执行者,请看下面几个英译汉的例子。

 **例句**

例1. The past few decades witnessed rapid development in Chinese foreign trade.

过去几十年来,中国的外贸有了迅速发展。

例2. Careful comparison of the two contracts will show you the differences.

你只要仔细比较一下,就会发现两份合同的差异。

例3. The name of the company escaped me for the moment.

我一时记不起这家公司的名字。

相反,在汉译英时,为了更符合西方人的习惯,有时可以将有灵主语句译成无灵主语句,请看下面几个汉译英的例子。

 **例句**

例1. 近年来,越来越多的外国公司来中国投资。

Recent years have seen more and more foreign companies come to invest in China.

例2. 他们对市场经济一无所知,因而公司受了很大的损失。

The ignorance of the market economy brought huge losses to their company.

例3. 现在许多人觉得,当时对他的任命是个严重的错误。

It is generally felt that his appointment was a grave mistake.

## 三、静态与动态

从英汉两种语言的用词来讲,也存在着一定的差异。英语倾向于使用名词、介词、形容词等静态性词类,是一种静态的(static)语言,而汉语多用动词,是一种动态性(dynamic)语言。应该特别提到的是英语的名词,由于英语中名词的频繁使用,因而具有"名词优于动词"(preponderance of nouns over verbs)的倾向,这种名词优势凸显了英语的静态特征。

在了解了英汉两种语言的用词差异之后,在翻译时就要特别注意词性的动静转换。请看下面这个句子:就价格和付款条件,我们双方达成了共识。

We are both **in agreement** on the points of price and terms of payment. 原句中的动词短语"达成了共识"在英译文中并没有按动词翻译,而是用了介词词组"in agreement",这是一种典型的动静转换,它是翻译中一种重要的变通手段。再请看下面的一些例子。

例句

例1. 职工强烈反对这项改革。

The staff members were strongly against the reform.

例2. 众所周知这家企业消耗了大量的自然资源。

It's known to all that the enterprise is a big drain on natural resources.

例3. 我相信本次交易会，也一定会与以往的交易会一样，取得圆满成功。

I'm sure that this trade fair, like the previous ones, will be a great success.

例4. 包装必须符合当地市场的喜好。

The packing must be in line with local market preference.

例5. 对你方要求担任代理商的申请，我们正在认真考虑。

Your application for sole agency is now under careful consideration.

## 四、重复与替代

一般来讲，除非有意强调或出于修辞的需要，英语总的倾向是尽量避免重复。在重复表达一个概念或思想时，英语往往采用词汇和语法手段来避免重复，这些手段主要包括替代法（substitution）、省略法（ellipsis）、换词法（variation）、保留介词法（retention of the preposition）等。相对来讲，汉语不怕重复，连续使用某个词语是常见的事。但是在汉译英时要尽量避免重复。请看下面的例句，特别注意英文的替代和汉语的重复。

 例句

例1. 雇员对公司作出了巨大贡献，管理层向雇员表示感谢。

The Management expressed their thanks to some of employees because they contributed a lot to the company. （替代法，they 替代了 employees）

例2. 野心不仅是罪恶的根源，也是毁灭的根源。

Ambition is the mother of destruction as well as (the mother) of evil. (省略法，省略了 the mother)

例3. 我们公司的产品质量相当高，不过价钱也很高。

The quality of our products is very high, but so are their prices. （替代法，so 替代了 very high）

例4. 交易会在9月11日开始，但是从开始的那刻起就麻烦不断。

The trade fair commenced on September 11. But from the moment it began, it was in constant trouble. （换词法，用 began 代替了 commenced）

例5. 这家公司不再重视产品质量，也不再重视产品数量和员工培训。

The company no longer focused on product quality, nor on quantity and staff training. （保留介词 on，回避重复动词 focused）

 **Translating Samples**

## 一、公司名称翻译案例

### （一）英译汉

1. Woolworths Group PLC.沃尔沃斯有限公司

2. Exxon Mobil Corporation 埃克森美孚公司

3. British Leyland Motor 英国利兰汽车公司

4. Corning Incorporated 康宁公司

5. Stanford Telecommunications Inc.斯坦福电信公司

6. L. M. Ericsson 爱立信公司

7. Hershey Foods Corp.好时食品公司

8. Pacific Container Line 太平洋集装箱航运公司

9. United Airlines Inc.联合航空公司

10. Imperial Chemical Industries PLC.帝国化学工业公司

### （二）汉译英

1. 中国精密机械公司 China National Precision Machinery Corporation

2. 中国机械进出口公司 China National Machinery Import and Export Corporation

3. 外国企业服务公司 Foreign Enterprises Service Corporation

4. 中国国际贸易促进会 China Council for the Promotion of International Trade

5. 对外贸易仲裁委员会 Foreign Trade Arbitration Commission

6. 广东科龙电器股份有限公司 Guangdong Kelon Electrical Holdings Co.,Ltd.

7. 保利科技有限公司 Poly Technologies Inc.

8. 国际招标公司 International Tendering Company

9. 青岛啤酒股份有限公司 Tsingtao Brewery Co.,Ltd.

10. 中国电信 China Telecom

## 二、地址翻译案例

### （一）英译汉

1. 425 Washington Ave.,Independence,MO 64052

密苏里州独立城华盛顿大道 425 号,邮编：64052

2. 55 Ladybrook Lane,Mansfield Nottinghamshire NG18 5JQ,England

英国诺丁汉郡曼斯菲尔德镇淑女巷 55 号,邮编：NG18 5JQ

3. Floor Five,Oliver Yard,48 City Road,London EC1Y 15P

伦敦市城市路 48 号奥利弗码头六层,邮编：EC1Y 15P

4. 8A Bellevue Road,Bellevue Hill,NSW 2012,Australia

澳大利亚新南威尔士州贝尔维尤山贝尔维尤路甲 8 号,邮编:2012

5. 2885 Cliveden Avenue,Delta,BC V3M 6P7 Canada

加拿大不列颠哥伦比亚省德尔塔市克里夫顿街 2885 号,邮编:V3M 6P7

## （二）汉译英

1. 北京市丰台区西三环中路 90 号通用技术大厦 23～28 层,邮政编码:100055。

F23-28,Genertec Plaza,No. 90,Xisanhuan Zhonglu,Fengtai District,Beijing 100055,China.

2. 北京朝阳区惠新东街 11 号紫光发展大厦 B3 座 6 层,邮编:100029

6/F, B3 Tower, Ziguang Building, No. 11 Huixin Dongjie, Chaoyang District, Beijing 100029,PRC.

3. 上海市虹口区临平路 20 弄 35 号 258 室,邮编:200086

Room 258,No. 35,Lane 20,Linping Road,Hongkou District,Shanghai 200086.

4. 广东省中山市东区汇桥花园 206 楼 5 单元 17 室,邮编:528403

Room 17, Entrance 5, Building 206, Huiqiao Garden, East District, Zhongshan 528403, Guangdong Province

5. 深圳市南山区科技园南区赋安大厦北座 15 楼,邮编:518052

15th Floor,North Bldg.,Fuan Mansion,Southern District,Scientific Park,Nanshan District, Shenzhen 518052.

### 🌑 Translating Training

**A：Translate the following departments of companies into English.**

| | |
|---|---|
| 1. 董事会 | 2. 总经理办公室 |
| 3. 行政部 | 4. 人力资源部 |
| 5. 人事部 | 6. 公关部 |
| 7. 销售部 | 8. 促销部 |
| 9. 产品开发部 | 10. 工程部 |
| 11. 研发部 | 12. 项目部 |
| 13. 发货部 | 14. 物流部 |
| 15. 进出口部 | 16. 广告部 |
| 17. 采购部 | 18. 企划部 |
| 19. 技术部 | 20. 售后服务部 |
| 21. 营业部 | 22. 财务部 |
| 23. 客户服务部 | 24. 质检部 |
| 25. 生产部 | |

**B：Translate the following company names into English.**

| | |
|---|---|
| 1. 英国航空公司 | 2. Adobe 系统公司 |
| 3. 联邦快递公司 | 4. 休斯敦广告公司 |
| 5. 美国电话电报公司 | 6. 联合健康集团公司 |

7. 金士顿科技公司                    8. 诺基亚(中国)投资有限公司

9. 美国友邦保险公司                  10. 联合百货公司

## C：Translate the following addresses into Chinese.

1. 508 King Ave., Odessa, TX 76514

2. 25 Hereford St., Mississauga, Ontario L5M 0H2, Canada

3. 20 Gordon St., Greater London, WC1H 0AJ, United Kingdom

4. No.2-6 Glenmore Street, Kelburn, Wellington, New Zealand

5. The National Gallery Trafalgar Square, London WC2N 5DN, England

6. Head office London 2012, One Churchill Place, Canary Wharf, London E14 5LN Tel：020 3 2010 000

7. TheBritish Library St Pancras, 96 Euston Road, London NW1 2DB

8. King's College London 49 Weston St., London SE1 3RB, United Kingdom 020 71880479

9. Caroline Black United Commercial Bank 56 Fillmore, Atlanta, GA 30325

10. 55 Bishop St., Glenfield NSW 2232, Australia Tel：61 2 9356 2375 Fax：61 2 9356 5687

## D：Translate the following addresses into English.

1. 中华人民共和国北京市东城区建国门内大街 19 号,邮编：100005

2. 北京市西城区复兴门内大街 45 号,邮编：100140

3. 北京市海淀区西三环北路 19 号外研社大厦,邮编：100089

4. 上海市宝山区上大路 99 号上海大学 邮编：200444

5. 河南省洛阳市西工区中州路 220 号,邮编：471000

6. 北京市东城区安定门东大街 28 号雍和大厦 D 座 1005 室

7. 上海静安富民路 197 弄 22 号 2 楼

8. 北京市朝阳区东三环北路 16 号盛厦商务楼 3 层

9. 上海市黄浦区西藏中路 268 号来福士广场办公楼 11 楼

10. 深圳市福田区深南中路 2018 号兴华大厦 A 座 8 楼

# Section 5   Extensive Expression

## 一、英语中表示"公司"和"工厂"的词语

| | |
|---|---|
| 1. Company( Co. ) | 公司,社团 |
| 2. Co., Ltd. | 有限责任公司 |
| 3. Corporation( Corp. ) | 法人、集团公司或(股份)有限公司 |
| 4. Inc.( incorporated ) | (股份)有限公司 |
| 5. PLC.( plc. ) ( Public Limited Company ) | 股份有限公司 |
| 6. Group | 集团,集团公司 |
| 7. Holdings | 控股公司 |
| 8. Networks | 网络公司 |
| 9. Communications | 通信(讯)公司 |

| 10. Insurance | 保险公司 |
|---|---|
| 11. Assurance | 保险公司 |
| 12. Department Stores | 百货公司 |
| 13. Brothers | 兄弟公司 |
| 14. Son(s) | 父子公司 |
| 15. Line(s) | 航空、航运公司 |
| 16. LLC(Limited Liability Company) | 有限责任公司 |
| 17. Airways | 航空公司 |
| 18. Industries | 实业公司,工业公司 |
| 19. Products | 产品公司 |
| 20. Service(s) | 服务公司 |
| 21. Telecom | 电信公司 |
| 22. System(s) | 系统公司 |
| 23. Laboratories | 制药公司 |
| 24. Associates | (联合)公司 |
| 25. Branch | 分公司 |
| 26. Factory | (各种)工厂 |
| 27. Plant | (大型)工厂 |
| 28. Works | (大型、重工业)工厂 |
| 29. Mill | (轻工业、手工业)工厂 |
| 30. Foundry | 铸造厂 |
| 31. Shipyard | 造船厂 |
| 32. Brewery | 酿酒厂 |
| 33. Winery | 酿酒厂 |
| 34. Mint | 造币厂 |
| 35. Arsenal | 兵工厂 |

## 二、商务英语中常见职位官衔

| 1. Managing Director | 执行总监 |
|---|---|
| 2. Marketing Director | 市场总监 |
| 3. Financial Director | 财务总监 |
| 4. Production Director | 生产总监 |
| 5. Director of Human Resources | 人力资源总监 |
| 6. Admin Manager | 行政经理 |
| 7. Sales Manager | 销售经理 |
| 8. Public Relations Manager | 公关经理 |
| 9. Purchasing Manager | 采购经理 |
| 10. Departmental Manager | 部门经理 |
| 11. Regional Sales Manager | 地区销售经理 |

| | |
|---|---|
| 12. Senior Customer Manager | 高级客户经理 |
| 13. Treasury Supervisor | 融资主管 |
| 14. Finance Supervisor | 财务主管 |
| 15. Project Supervisor | 项目主管 |
| 16. IT Supervisor | 信息技术主管 |
| 17. Certified Public Accountant | 注册会计师 |
| 18. Auctioneer | 拍卖师 |
| 19. Statistician | 统计师 |
| 20. Architect | 建筑师 |
| 21. Real Estate Appraiser | 房地产评估师 |
| 22. Training Specialist | 培训专员 |
| 23. Research Fellow | 研究员 |
| 24. Director-general | 局长 |
| 25. Secretary General | 秘书长 |

# Unit 4

# Brands and Trademarks

Unit Objectives

In this unit you should

➤ familiarize yourself with the format of business brands and trademarks.

➤ have a good command of the basic words and useful expressions of business brands and trademarks in this unit.

➤ enable yourself to acquire the translating skills of transliteration, free translation, the combination of transliteration and free translation and other ways of translation.

## ❓ Section 1   Theme Lead-in

**Read the following passage to gain a better understanding of this unit.**

A trademark, trade mark, or trade-mark is a recognizable sign, design, or expression which identifies products or services of a particular source from those of others, although trademarks used to identify services are usually called service marks. The trademark owner can be an individual, business organization, or any legal entity. A trademark may be located on a package, a label, a voucher, or on the product itself. For the sake of corporate identity, trademarks are also being displayed on company buildings.

A trademark identifies the brand owner of a particular product or service. Trademarks can be licensed to others, for example, Bullyland obtained a license to produce Smurf figurines; the Lego Group purchased a license from Lucas film in order to be allowed to launch Lego Star Wars; TT Toys Toys is a manufacturer of licensed ride-on replica cars for children. The unauthorized usage of trademarks by producing and trading counterfeit consumer goods is known as brand piracy.

The owner of a trademark may pursue legal action against trademark infringement. Most countries require formal registration of a trademark as a precondition for pursuing this type of action. The United States, Canada and other countries also recognize common law trademark rights, which means action can be taken to protect an unregistered trademark if it is in use. Still common law trademarks offer the holder in general less legal protection than registered trademarks.

In trademark treatises, it is usually reported that blacksmiths who made swords in the Roman Empire are thought of as being the first users of trademarks. Other notable trademarks that have been used for a long time include Löwenbräu, which claims use of its lion mark since 1383. The first trademark legislation was passed by the Parliament of England under the reign of King Henry III in 1266, which required all bakers to use a distinctive mark for the bread they sold.

The first modern trademark laws emerged in the late 19th century. In France, the first comprehensive trademark system in the world was passed into law in 1857 with the "Manufacture and Goods Mark Act". In Britain, the 1862 Merchandise Marks Act made it a criminal offense to imitate another's trade mark with intent to defraud or to enable another to defraud. In 1875, the Trade Marks Registration Act was passed which allowed formal registration of trade marks at the UK Patent Office for the first time. Registration was considered to comprise prima facie evidence of ownership of a trade mark and registration of marks began on 1st January, 1876. The 1875 Act defined a registrable trade mark as a device, or mark, or name of an individual or firm printed in some particular and distinctive manner; or a written signature or copy of a written signature of an individual or firm; or a distinctive label or ticket.

In the United States, Congress first attempted to establish a federal trademark regime in 1870. This statute purported to be an exercise of Congress Copyright Clause powers. However, the Supreme Court struck down the 1870 statute in the Trade-Mark Cases later on in the decade. In 1881, Congress passed a new trademark act, this time pursuant to its Commerce Clause powers. Congress revised the Trademark Act in 1905. The Lanham Act of 1946 updated the law and has served, with several amendments, as the primary federal law on trade marks.

The Trademarks Act of 1938 in the United Kingdom set up the first registration system based on the "intent-to-use" principle. The Act also established an application publishing procedure and expanded the rights of the trademark holder to include the barring of trademark use even in cases where confusion remained unlikely. This Act served as a model for similar legislation elsewhere.

## Section 2  Translation Warming-up

**A：Please match the Chinese translation in column B with the English expressions in column A.**

1. Sheraton          A. 贝亲
2. Sony             B. 雪碧
3. Fiyta            C. 皇冠
4. Philip           D. 飞利浦
5. Hazeline         E. 飞亚达
6. Pampers          F. 帮宝适
7. Sprite           G. 索尼
8. Pigeon           H. 喜来登
9. Crown            I. 夏士莲
10. Giant           J. 捷安特

**B：Translate the following brands or trademarks into English.**

1. 长虹（电视机）          2. 春兰（空调）
3. 凤凰（自行车）          4. 海信（电视）
5. 老板（电器）            6. 乐凯（胶卷）
7. 四通（电脑）            8. 联想（电脑）
9. 金威（啤酒）            10. 护舒宝（卫生巾）

## Section 3  Topic Features and Translation Principles

### 一、商标和品牌

商标又称牌子，是商品特定的标记。世界知识产权组织给商标下的定义是："商标是用来区别某一工业或商业、企业或企业集团的商品标志。"我国对商标的定义为："商标是企业、事业单位和个体工商业者对其生产、制造、加工、拣选或经销的商品所使用的标志。一般用文字、图形或其组合，注明在商品、商品包装、招牌、广告上面。"

商标的类型：

（1）按商标结构分类，分为文字商标、图形商标、字母商标、数字商标、三维标志商标、颜色组合商标、（上述的）组合商标、音响商标和气味商标。

（2）按商标使用者分类，分为商品商标、服务商标、集体商标、无主商标。

（3）按商标用途分类，分为营业商标、证明商标、等级商标、组集商标、亲族商标、备用商标、防御商标、联合商标和广告商标。

（4）按商标享誉程度分类，分为普通商标、知名商标、著名商标、驰名商标。

（5）按商标注册与否分类，分为注册商标、未注册商标。

（6）按商标的寓意分类，分为有含义商标和无含义商标。

品牌是指用于区分产品的名称、图案、设计等，是企业的一种无形资产。商标是品牌的一部分。品牌和商标翻译实际上只能对品牌和商标中可发音部分进行翻译,即品牌名、商标名的翻译。

## 二、商标和品牌的翻译的原则

商标和品牌的翻译必须以营销为目的,以有利于促进商品的营销为出发点,要遵循以下原则:

### 1. 译文要符合商品特性、体现商品特点

商标和品牌译文要符合商品特性、体现商品特点,使消费者一看到译文就知道商品的种类及特色。商标的作用就是让消费者一目了然地知道商品的种类及特色,商标本身就是最简洁、最有力的广告。一个精心设计的广告可以使消费者对商品产生一种有益的想象。比如,牙膏品牌"Colgate",其名称来源于创始人的名字,看不出与产品本身有什么联系,译成中文"高露洁",给人感觉干净、清爽,与牙膏的自身性质非常匹配。"可口可乐"可谓是经典中的经典。译文对"Coca-Cola"的渲染非常到位,使人觉得饮用这种饮料可以让人心旷神怡,确实有"味道好极了和好运相伴"的意义。

### 2. 既要注重商业效应,又要尊重译入语的民族文化

商标和品牌的译文既要注重商业效应,又要尊重译入语的民族文化;既要做到入乡随俗,又要自信地推广本民族独特的文化精髓,实现真正的中西文化交流。语言是文化的一部分,也是文化的载体,反映一个民族的心理特征。不同的民族有不同的价值观和消费观念。比如,上海"凤凰"自行车被直译为"Phoenix",在消费者心中容易产生不良的联想效果,不能起到商标的劝购作用。上海"白翎钢笔",意译为"white feather",正与英语"to show the white feather"接近,意思是临阵脱逃,白色羽毛在西方人心理上有胆小鬼的内涵。因此,这样的商品在西方消费者心理上肯定是难以接受的。而"Sheraton Hotel"的翻译就很合乎中国人的喜好。"喜来登"在读音上与原商标接近,而且选用的词符合中国人喜欢"喜事连连,鸿运当头"的意愿。

### 3. 译文和商标原语在语音、语义等方面要有直接的联系

英译汉时,尽量按字母的发音寻求意思良好、发音近似的词汇。世界著名的互联网搜索引擎"Yahoo!"被译为"雅虎",妙趣横生,吸引了消费者的眼球。"Yahoo!"与"雅虎"读音一致,而"虎"在中国人的心目中又象征着威严、吉祥。"虎"乃百兽之王,突出了"Yahoo!"在国际互联网中的地位。"雅"字更是体现出了小老虎的乖巧、可爱,消除了虎的凶性,使得品牌更贴近消费者,也赢得了消费者的喜爱。

### 4. 追求音韵美、奇特美、意境美

商标和品牌的译文不仅要准确翻译,追求音韵美,还要追求更高境界,达到奇特美和意境美。这个原则要求商标的译文不仅在拼写、读音方面接近,还要讲究选词的恰到好处。比如,照相机"Canon"译为"佳能",读音接近,而且体现"良好的性能"的意思,给消费者一种可靠的感觉,刺激了购买的欲望。钟表"Seiko"译为"精工",语音近似,而且恰如其分地体现了人们对手表的"做工精准,质量上乘"的希望。

"Revlon"化妆品名称取自公司创办者 Charles Revson 的姓 Revson 和其合伙人 C.

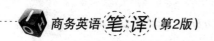

Lachman 的首字母"L"。汉译为"露华浓"则是源于李白的"云想衣裳花想容,春风拂槛露华浓"。除了发音相似,很容易使女性消费者联想到闭月羞花的杨贵妃,进而强化了该商品的高雅高贵品质,能够激发消费者的购买欲望。

**5. 译文要简短明快、易读易懂、易识易记**

商标作为最简短的广告,要选词简短明了,最好给人过目不忘的功效。尤其在使用音译法时,译文可以适当省译,力求简洁。比如照相机品牌"Kodak——柯达",若音译为"柯达克"也不妨碍商标意义的表达,但不如"柯达"更响亮,更易传诵。豪华车 Rolls-Royce 原译为"罗尔斯—罗伊斯",现译为"劳斯莱斯",简单易记,而且非常押韵。

# Section 4　Translating Strategies, Samples and Training

## Translating Strategies

在商标翻译原则的指导下,翻译方法多种多样,在商标和品牌翻译中常见的翻译方法有以下五种:音译法、半音半意法、意译法、转译法和不译法。

## 一、音译法

音译法是按照原语商标名称的发音,找到其发音相近的译名,主要适用于以人名、地名等以专有名词命名的商标名称。音译法一般又分为直接音译法、谐音译法和省音译法。直接音译法就是按照英语国际音标读音,把英语商标译为读音相同、相似或相近的汉语商标。谐音译法是指在翻译时不完全侧重语音上的对等、近似,更侧重语义上的近似,启发人的联想。省音译法就是在音译时把商标名简化省略,避免英文名过长导致汉语读起来拗口。

## 例句

例 1. 青岛啤酒 Tsingtao Beer

**分析**:直接音译法。可以让消费者立刻了解到该啤酒的名称源于地名,以地名命名,也必然是该地的特产,更具有吸引力。

例 2. Audi 奥迪

**分析**:直接音译法。中文名称与英文名称在读音上一致,而且所选的汉字组合忠于原标的呼唤功能,保留了原英文商标的音韵之美。

例 3. Motorola 摩托罗拉

**分析**:直接音译法。虽然不符合汉语词汇常规的组合模式,但是发音清晰响亮,而且平仄音节长短合适,新颖别致易于中国消费者接受。

例 4. Cadillac 凯迪拉克

**分析**:直接音译法。虽然不符合汉语词汇常规的组合模式,但是发音清晰响亮,而且平仄音节长短合适,新颖别致易于中国消费者接受。

例 5. Pierre Cardin 皮尔·卡丹

**分析**:直接音译法。原标来源于创始人的名字,译标完全符合发音规则,这样专有名词的翻译仍可以使消费者认识到创作者是谁。

例 6. Louis Cardy(皮具)路易·卡迪

**分析**：直接音译法。原标来源于创始人的名字,译标完全符合发音规则,这样专有名词的翻译仍可以使消费者认识到创作者是谁。

例 7. Benz 奔驰

**分析**：谐音译法。译标发音与原标近似,而且使人联想到"快速领先"的汽车性能。比原有的译法"奔丁茨""平治""朋驰"都有特色。

例 8. Contac(药品)康泰克

**分析**：谐音译法。译标与原标发音近似,而且选字恰到好处,"康""泰"都包含中国人对健康、平安的期望;"克"正好可以表达克除病患的感觉。这样的译标非常好地反映了药品的功能,比"元抬科"要更有意义。

例 9. McDonald's 麦当劳

**分析**：省音译法。"麦当劳"比完整翻译"麦克唐纳"更简短易记。

例 10. Solvil et Titus(瑞士名表)铁达时

**分析**：省音译法。对于手表来说,"铁达时"比译成"苏维利特·铁达时"更符合商标词易记易诵的标准。

## 二、半音半意法

半音半意法就是以原商标的音为基础,在译入语中找到发音与原文相同或相似的字,同时又反映出产品一定特性的词汇,这种译法往往独特生动,保留原文的风韵,最能体现商标设计者的意图。

 例句

例 1. Pentium Ⅲ 奔腾三代

**分析**：译标的读音与"P"和"t"的发音接近。原标英文词来源于希腊语"Pente",意思是"5"。在习惯上,人们把奔腾叫作"586"或"P5",是 Intel 公司于 1993 年推出的 80586 电脑芯片(CPU)的名称,译标"奔腾"使人联想到"骏马奔腾"的"迅捷、飘逸",反映了处理器的功能和特点。

例 2. Subway(食品)赛百味

**分析**：如果直译为"地铁",很难让人体会出该商品是一种美食,而译标恰好弥补了这一点,在读音上与原词接近,而且符合食品的特点。

例 3. Reebok(鞋)锐步

**分析**：原译为"雷宝",但不足以体现鞋的特性。"锐步"读音与原标接近,而且这个响亮的译名能帮助公司实现它对鞋品质的承诺——"只要合脚,就有办法让你穿上。"

例 4. Goldlion 金利来

**分析**：读音与原标接近。最初译为"金狮",是喜庆吉祥的象征,而且"狮"是百兽之王,喻在服装行业独占鳌头的意思。但是在粤语中"金狮"与"今输"谐音,消费者会对此产生顾忌。采用音意结合法,"Gold"意译为"金","lion"音译为"利来",合起来蕴含"金利滚滚来"的好兆头,符合消费者向往吉祥的心理。

例 5. Pantene 潘婷

**分析**：译标与原标读音接近。而且选字"婷"在汉字中能很好地体现女子的姣好，女性消费者会对这样的洗发产品产生好奇，有购买的动力。

例 6. Hazeline 夏士莲

**分析**：与上面的例子效果一样，"莲"在汉语中给人清新的感觉，恰当地体现了使用这种洗浴产品后的效果。

例 7. Clean-Clear 可伶可俐

**分析**：原标中的 clean 和 clear 就已经包含音韵美，首字母都是"C"。若是译为"干净清爽"或是"干净清洁"没有原标的音韵之美。若译为"可伶可俐"，头韵和尾韵齐压，形成了悦耳轻盈的读音。而且在意境上，"可"表示"可爱"，"伶俐"也能表示年轻女子俏皮可爱的样子。这样的翻译完美地体现了消费者使用护肤品后清新靓丽的模样。

例 8. Daily（按摩坐垫）得力

**分析**：译标与原标发音一致，没有翻译成与原标本身含义"日常的"相关的词，而是译成"得力"。这个名称用于按摩坐垫给人一种结实、舒适的感觉。

例 9. 乐百氏 Robust

**分析**：译标发音与中文名称接近，robust 英文意思是"强壮的"，体现饮用此水可强身健体的寓意。

例 10. 荣事达 Royalstar

**分析**：中文名称表达中国人对美好事物的向往，译名也模拟了汉字的发音特点，同时royal 的意思是"高贵、皇家"的意思，star 也符合英语国家用星状物做勋章的意思。译标充分显示了荣事达集团的档次和分量。

## 三、意译法

意译法是对商标常规翻译方法（音译、半音半意法等）的一种补充。它是根据商标的含义，译为意义相同或相近的词汇。意译法能较好地体现原商标确立者的初衷，并与商标图案在意蕴上达到和谐统一，达到在异国推销产品的目的。意译法可以分为直接翻译、择意翻译（在直接翻译的基础上，进行择意选词，构成理想商标）、还原择意（把缩写的英语商标首先还原为英语的全称，之后再用择意翻译的方法）。

 **例句**

例 1. 飞鸽（自行车）Flying Pigeon

**分析**：直接翻译。译标"Pigeon"是和平的象征，让人一见就心生喜欢。"Flying"更是把自行车"速度快"的特点表现得活灵活现。

例 2. 熊猫（彩电）Panda

**分析**：直接翻译。译标直接采用对应的英文 panda，这个名称对于西方人来说也不陌生，是众所周知的中国国宝，以国宝的名字来命名电视机，有先入为主的效果，提高了消费者对电视机的信赖程度。

例 3. 好孩子(童车)Goodbaby

**分析**：直接翻译。译标与原标在发音上没有相近之处，但是都表达了该童车品牌对孩子的呵护之情。

例 4. 永久牌 Forever

**分析**：直接翻译。译标与原标在发音上没有相近之处，而对应的 forever 英文意思恰好是"永远"的意思，符合各国消费者的心理需求。

例 5. 小护士 Mini Nurse

**分析**：直接翻译。译文与原名没有发音相关之处，但是意思完全对等，给人一种亲近、可爱的感觉，符合消费者购买化妆品的心理。

例 6. Crown(汽车)皇冠

**分析**：直接翻译。译标直接采用 crown 的中文意思，正好反映了此款汽车的尊贵品质，提升了它在消费者心目中的地位。

例 7. Rejoice 飘柔

**分析**：择意翻译。译标与原标读音没有联系，"rejoice"的含义是"感到欣喜的"，翻译为"飘柔"的译法令人想象到秀发柔美、随风飘动的突出效果。

例 8. Dutch Lady(奶粉)子母

**分析**：择意翻译。译标没有拘泥于字面的意思，另辟蹊径，重新组织，使之与原标神韵相同，也很好地说明了奶粉的消费群体。

例 9. NEC(彩电)日电

**分析**：还原择意。译标是将其英语的缩写字母还原为全称"Nippon Electric Company"之后译为"日电"。

例 10. HSBC 汇丰银行

**分析**：还原择意。译标是将英语的缩写字母还原为全称"The Hongkong and Shanghai Banking Corporation Limited"之后择意翻译为"汇丰"，寓意财源滚滚、殷实丰厚。

## 四、转译法

转译法主要应用于日本商标的翻译，即将英语译为日语，然后从相应的日语汉字转译成中文。

 样例

| | | | |
|---|---|---|---|
| TOYOTA | 丰田 | ISUZU | 五十铃 |
| SUZUKI | 铃木 | HONDA | 本田 |
| SANYO | 三洋 | HITACHI | 日立 |
| TOSHIBA | 东芝 | HINO | 日野 |

## 五、不译法

不译法用于有些不可翻译或翻译后很不自然的商标，遇到这种情况，可以不翻译或者只是翻译其中的部分内容。

**样例**

例1. 不可翻译

IBM（International Business Machines Corporation）国际商业机器公司

**分析**：人们对"国际商业机器公司"这个名称不是很熟悉，但是提到其英文简称IBM，应该是家喻户晓，这样的表达方法非常自然。

3M（Minnesota Mining and Manufacturing Company）明尼苏达矿业及制造公司（美国）

**分析**：直接称呼美国3M公司的简称比起烦琐的中文翻译更方便人们记忆。

WST（World Satellite Terminal）世界卫星终端公司

**分析**：业内人士谈到WST就知道是世界卫星终端公司，这样称呼比较方便。

NEC（Nippon Electric Company）日本电气公司

**分析**：直接称呼日本电器公司为NEC，简便，易于传播企业名称。

RCA（Radio Cotporation of America）美国无线电公司

**分析**：直接称呼美国无线电公司为RCA，简便，企业名称易于传播。

例2. 部分翻译

Remy Martin X.O　人头马XO

**分析**：前半部分Remy Martin采用半音半意法翻译，体现它是具有高贵品质的酒类的含义。后半部分采用不译法，直接用简单字母组合形式出现在人们面前反而体现出它的独特之处。

L-hoe　L形平炉

**分析**：L本身已不能做任何翻译，该商标只翻译后面的实意词，这样的组合恰到好处地体现出商品的功能和特征。

Java Tea　Java茶

**分析**：Java Tea是印尼生产的"爪哇茶"，如果直接翻译为"爪哇茶"，虽然能帮助顾客了解产品的性质、产地，但是不符合商标翻译的"形美"原则。Java采取英文原文，tea意译为"茶"，这样的结合可以给人音美、形美和意美兼有的感觉。

## Translating Samples

### 一、音译法

1. Bausch & Lomb 博士伦

2. Chevron 雪佛龙

3. Decis 敌杀死

4. Dell 戴尔（计算机）

5. Electrolux 伊莱克斯

6. Johnson & Johnson 强生

7. Kentucky Fried Chicken 肯德基

8. Kroger 克罗格（食品、药品店）

9. Marathon Oil 马拉松石油

10. Morgan Stanley 摩根士丹利（证券投资）

11. Nike 耐克

12. Nokia 诺基亚（手机）

13. Ordram 禾大壮

14. Pepsi-Cola 百事可乐

15. Quick 快克

16. Saturn 杀草丹

17. Tide 汰渍

18. Hewlett-Packard（HP）惠普(计算机)

19. 苏泊尔 Supor

20. 李宁牌 Li-Ning

21. 美的 Midea

22. 九阳 Joyung

23. 国美 Gome

24. 万科 Vanke

25. 奇瑞 Chery

## 二、意译法

1. Apple 苹果(计算机)

2. Ariel 碧浪

3. Arrow"箭"牌衬衫

4. Camel 骆驼(香烟)

5. Citigroup 花旗银行

6. Comfort 金纺

7. Continental 欧陆(汽车)

8. Diamond 钻石(手表)

9. Elegance 雅致(女装)

10. Kleenex 舒洁

11. Ivory 象牙(香皂)

12. Joy 喜悦(香水)

13. Nestle 雀巢

14. JVC 胜利

15. Orient 东方(手表)

16. Rock 滚石唱片

17. Pioneer(音响)先锋

18. Shell 壳牌(汽油)

19. Universal 环球(影业)

20. 长城(电器、红酒)Great Wall

21. 葵花牌(电扇)Sunflower

22. 七匹狼 Septwolves

23. 小天鹅 Little Swan

24. 皇朝(葡萄酒)Dynasty

25. 海鸥(照相机)Sea-gull

## 三、半音半意法

1. Mystere(法国化妆品)蜜雪儿

2. Arche(化妆品)雅倩

3. Best Buy 百思买(消费电子零售)

4. Buick 别克(汽车)

5. Budweiser 百威(啤酒)

6. Canon 佳能(照相机)

7. Carrefour 家乐福

8. Coca-Cola 可口可乐(饮料)

9. Coldrex(感冒药)可立治

10. Crest 佳洁士(牙膏)

11. Costco Wholesale 好市多(专业零售)

12. Extra 益达(口香糖)

13. Goldman Sachs Group 高盛(证券经纪)

14. Heineken 喜力啤酒

15. Home Depot 家得宝(专业零售)

16. Lowe's 劳氏(专业零售)

17. OMO 奥妙(洗衣粉)

18. Ricoh(相机)理光

19. Safeguard 舒肤佳

20. Wells Fargo 富国银行

21. 海尔 Haier(电器)

22. 回力 Warrior(运动鞋)

23. 乐凯 Lucky(胶卷)

24. 新科 Shinco(电器)

25. 雅戈尔 Youngor

### Translating Training

**A：Translate the following brands or trademarks into Chinese.**

1. NewBalance(运动鞋)

2. Puma(运动产品)

3. Time Warner（娱乐）    4. Mitsubishi

5. Suzuki    6. Oracle（数据库软件公司）

7. Acer（电脑品牌）    8. Xerox（软件公司）

9. Cisco Systems（互联网）    10. Leica（相机品牌）

11. Bentley（汽车）    12. Chevrolet（汽车）

13. Chrysler（汽车）    14. Renault（汽车公司）

15. Porsche（汽车）    16. Fiat（汽车）

17. Volkswagen（汽车）    18. Rover（汽车）

19. Opel（汽车）    20. Jaguar（汽车）

21. Longines（手表）    22. Burberry

23. Versace（时尚品牌）    24. Patek-philippe

25. Lincoln（汽车）    26. Adidas

27. Peak    28. X-Tep

29. Dove    30. Lexus

31. Abbott（奶粉）    32. Dumex（奶粉）

33. Wyethbb（奶粉）    34. Meiji（奶粉）

35. Friso（奶粉）    36. Lego（积木玩具）

37. Combi（婴儿用品）    38. Fisher Price（玩具）

39. BrainBox（玩具）    40. Columbia（服装）

41. Converse（服装）    42. Ellassay（服装）

43. Esprit（服装）    44. Fila（服装）

45. Guess（服装）    46. Gucci（服装）

47. Kappa（服装）    48. Kenzo（服装）

49. Lotto（服装）    50. Louis Vuitton（箱包）

51. Metersbonwe（服装）    52. Mizuno（服装）

53. Ochirly（服装）    54. Old Navy（服装）

55. Only（服装）    56. Prada（箱包）

57. Paul Frank（服装）    58. Rapido（服装）

59. Snoopy（服装）    60. Timberland（服装）

**B：Translate the following brands or trademarks into English.**

1. 非常可乐（饮料）    2. 苏泊尔（家电）

3. 格力（空调）    4. 中华啤酒

5. 丽臣（洗衣粉）    6. 安琪儿（自行车）

7. 雄山（内衣）    8. 昂立一号（保健品）

9. 金纺（柔顺剂）    10. 回力（运动鞋）

11. 联邦快递    12. 迪士尼

13. 州立农业保险    14. 红苹果（家具）

15. 星巴克    16. 亚马逊（网络）

17. 维基百科                     18. 马自达

19. 电子港湾(网站)               20. 波导(手机)

21. 阿桑娜                       22. 真美诗

23. 唯尔福(纸业)                24. 冰纯(化妆品)

25. 宝姿(服装)                  26. 安踏

27. 杜邦                        28. 立邦

29. 美标                        30. 舒蕾

31. 统一                        32. 洁婷

33. 猴王                        34. 瑞幸

35. 七喜                        36. 蒙牛

37. 昆仑                        38. 明一

39. 羽西                        40. 虎牌

41. 飒拉                        42. 梦特娇

43. 万耐特(刀具)                44. 日立(刀具)

45. 山高(刀具)                  46. 住友电工(刀具)

47. 百年灵(钟表)                48. 宝齐来(钟表)

49. 绰美(钟表)                  50. 爱马仕

51. 帅奇                        52. 豪华表

53. 梅花                        54. 帝舵

55. 派格                        56. 土拨鼠

57. 哥伦布                      58. 诺诗兰

59. 探路者                      60. 奥索卡

## Section 5   Extensive Expression

### 一、商标

| | |
|---|---|
| 1. word mark | 文字商标 |
| 2. figurative mark | 图形商标 |
| 3. associated mark | 组合商标 |
| 4. certification mark | 保证商标 |
| 5. collective mark | 集体商标 |
| 6. well-known mark | 驰名商标 |
| 7. famous mark | 著名商标 |
| 8. similar mark | 近似商标 |
| 9. defensive mark | 防御商标 |
| 10. service mark | 服务商标 |
| 11. certificate mark | 证明商标 |
| 12. visual mark | 视觉商标 |
| 13. sound mark | 声音商标 |

| | |
|---|---|
| 14. taste mark | 味觉商标 |
| 15. single color mark | 单色商标 |
| 16. registered mark | 注册商标 |
| 17. collective marks | 集体商标 |
| 18. collective membership mark | 集体成员商标 |
| 19. collective service mark | 集体服务商标 |
| 20. collective trademark | 集体商标 |

## 二、商标法词汇

| | |
|---|---|
| 1. marks consisting of multiple words | 多词商标 |
| 2. aesthetic functionality | 美学功能 |
| 3. alternative designs | 替代设计 |
| 4. ancillary services | 辅助性服务 |
| 5. application for use of trademark | 基于使用商标申请注册 |
| 6. asserted trademark | 申请商标 |
| 7. assignee of registrant | 注册商标受让人 |
| 8. commercial impression | 商业印象 |
| 9. companion application | 姊妹申请 |
| 10. concurrent registration | 并存注册 |
| 11. concurrent use | 并存使用 |
| 12. duplicate registration | 注册相同商标 |
| 13. foreign equivalents | 外语对应词 |
| 14. parody marks | 滑稽模仿商标 |
| 15. pending application | 未决申请 |
| 16. period of use | 使用期限 |
| 17. phonetic equivalent | 同音词 |
| 18. reference mark | 引证商标 |
| 19. trademark operation | 商标部 |
| 20. trade name | 字号 |
| 21. trade mark registration certificate | 商标注册证 |
| 22. trade mark registration number | 商标注册号 |
| 23. trade mark registration date | 商标注册日 |
| 24. trade mark registration book | 商标注册簿 |
| 25. the term of validity | 注册有效期 |
| 26. trade mark enquires | 注册查询 |
| 27. renewal of trade mark | 注册续展 |
| 28. separate application | 分别申请 |
| 29. new registration | 重新申请 |
| 30. application regarding changes | 变更申请 |

| | | |
|---|---|---|
| 31. | trade mark agency | 注册代理 |
| 32. | trade mark publication | 注册公告 |
| 33. | application for registration | 申请注册 |
| 34. | renewal of registration | 续展注册 |
| 35. | registration of assignment | 转让注册 |
| 36. | patent specification | 专利说明书 |
| 37. | patent claim | 专利要求书 |
| 38. | letter of patent | 专利证书 |
| 39. | intellectual property | 知识产权 |
| 40. | industrial property | 工业产权 |

# Unit 5

# Business Advertisement

Unit Objectives

In this unit you should

➤ familiarize yourself with the format of business advertisement.

➤ have a good command of the basic words and useful expressions of business advertisement in this unit.

➤ enable yourself to acquire the translating skills of literal translation, free translation, creative translation, supplementary translation, concentrated translation and no translation.

## ❓ Section 1   Theme Lead-in

**Read the following passage to gain a better understanding of this unit.**

In the ancient and medieval world such advertising as existed was conducted by word of mouth. The first step toward modern advertising came with the development of printing in the 15th and 16th centuries. In the 17th century, weekly newspapers in London began to carry advertisements, and by the 18th century such advertising flourishing.

The great expansion of business in the 19th century was accompanied by the growth of an advertising industry; it was that century, primarily in the United States, that was the establishment of the advertising agencies. The first agencies were, in essence, brokers for space in newspapers. But by the early 20th century, agencies became involved in producing the massage itself, including copy and artwork, and by 1920s agencies had come into being that could plan and execute complete advertising campaigns, from initial research to copy preparation to placement in various media.

In the 21st century, with an intensely competitive consumer market, advertisers increasingly used digital technology to call greater attention to products. In 2009, for example, the world's first video advertisements to be embedded in a print publication appeared in *Entertainment Weekly* magazine. The thin battery-powered screen implanted in the page could store up to 40 minutes of video via chip technology and automatically began to play when the reader opened the page.

For an advertisement to be effective, its production and placement must be based on a knowledge of the public and a skilled use of the media. Advertising agencies serve to orchestrate complex campaigns whose strategies of media use are based on research into consumer behavior and demographic analysis of the market area. A strategy will combine creativity in the production of the advertising messages with canny scheduling and placement, so that the messages are seen by, and will have an effect on, the people the advertiser most wants to address.

There are eight principal media for advertising. Perhaps the most basic medium is the newspaper, which offers advertisers large circulations, a readership located close to the advertiser's place of business. Magazines, the other chief print medium, may be of general interest or they may be aimed at specific audiences. The most pervasive media are television and radio. The other advertising media include direct mail, which can make a highly detailed and personalized appeal; outdoor billboards and posters; transit advertising, which can reach the millions of users of mass-transit systems; and miscellaneous media, including dealer displays and promotional items such as matchbook or calendars.

## Section 2  Translation Warming-up

**A: Please match the Chinese translation in column B with the English expressions in column A.**

| | |
|---|---|
| 1. we take customers as our Gods | A. 规格齐全 |
| 2. selling well all over the world | B. 美观大方 |
| 3. elegant and graceful | C. 使用方便 |
| 4. durable in use | D. 顾客是我们的上帝 |
| 5. choice materials | E. 畅销全球 |
| 6. easy to use | F. 经久耐用 |
| 7. complete in specifications | G. 选料考究 |
| 8. quality and quantity assured | H. 价廉物美 |
| 9. high quality and inexpensive | I. 方便顾客 |

10. making things convenient for customers      J. 保质保量

**B：Translate the following advertisements into English.**

1. 滴滴香浓,意犹未尽。（麦斯威尔咖啡）

2. 昨日锋芒,今日辉煌。（保时捷）

3. 掌中乾坤,梦之灵魂。（微软）

4. 光临风韵之境——万宝路世界。

5. 饮可口可乐,万事如意。（可口可乐）

6. 天长地久。（斯沃琪手表）

7. 动态的诗,向我舞近。（丰田）

8. 钻石恒久远,一颗永流传。（戴·比尔斯）

9. 人类精神的动力。（梅赛德斯-奔驰）

10. 玉兰油晚霜无油脂,轻柔、舒适,让皮肤一面自然呼吸,一面吸收玉兰油晚霜的特殊营养。（玉兰油晚霜广告）

## Section 3　Topic Features and Translation Principles

### 一、商务广告

商务广告又称营利性广告或经济广告,是以盈利为主要目的的广告,通过大众传播媒介所进行的有关商品、劳务、观念等信息的有说服力的销售促进活动。

商务广告的类型:

（1）商品广告又称产品广告,是以销售为导向,介绍商品的质量、功能、价格、品牌、生产厂家、销售地点以及该商品的独到之处等有关商品本身的一切信息,追求近期效益和经济效益。

（2）劳务广告是服务广告的一种,比如介绍银行、保险、旅游、饭店、车辆出租、家电维修、房屋搬迁等内容的广告。

（3）声誉广告又称公关广告、形象广告,是指通过一定的媒介,把企业有关的信息有计划地传播给公众的广告。这类广告的目的是引起公众对企业的注意、好感和合作,从而提高知名度和美誉度,树立良好的企业形象。

（4）招聘广告又叫招聘人才广告,此类广告着重宣传招聘方的各种优势,并写明所招聘的项目和应聘人员条件以及联系期限和方式。

### 二、商务广告的翻译原则

商务广告翻译的关键是使广告译文对读者产生与原文同样的感染力,同时符合读者所在国家的风俗,被读者接受并喜欢,一般遵循以下标准:

（1）广告译文要充分体现广告的信息功能和劝说功能,精练易懂、生动形象、唤起兴趣、激发欲望;

（2）广告译文要有美感。译者在深刻体会原文信息实质的基础上,运用翻译技巧,译出原文中的拟声和韵类,使译文产生音乐美感;

（3）广告译文要遵循忠实、统一的原则,译者尽可能体现原文的文体特点,用相应的文体体现原文语言的感染力;

（4）译者要准确把握中西方文化异同,遵循社会文化习惯,注意大众的心理接受程度,进行适当的文化转化,最大限度地实现广告的功能。

要翻译好商务广告,译者要注意以下几个方面:

### （一）广告英语的用词特点

商务广告英语用词要富有情感色彩和感染力,以便吸引人们的视听关注、留下深刻印象。

#### 1. 简明、通俗、易记

广告文字一般都简单通俗,易懂易记。具体而言,就是使用生活中出现频率高的、大众化的、有时代感和引申义的词汇。

（1）常用的动词有：make、come、get、go、know、have、keep、look、see、need、buy、love、use、take、feel、like、start、taste、save、choose 等。

 **例句**

例 1. Mosquito Bye Bye Bye. 蚊虫杀杀杀。

**分析**：在英语中,单音节动词的语义既灵活又准确,"Bye"是非常口语化的动词,在这里重复使用三次,以诙谐俏皮的方式表达了人们对蚊虫的厌恶和消灭它们的决心,读起来朗朗上口,又起到让人过目不忘的作用。此类例子还有：

例 2. We bring high technology home. （日本 NEC 电器广告语）我们把高科技带回家。

例 3. Start Ahead. （飘柔洗发液）成功之路,从头开始。

（2）常用的形容词有：new、good、better、best、free、fresh、delicious、full、sure、clean、wonderful、special、crisp、fine、big、great、real、easy、bright、extra、safe、rich 等。

 **例句**

例 1. There's never been a better Time.（《时代》周刊广告）从未有过的好时代。

**分析**："better"是生活中出现频率很高的形容词,在这里"better Time"一语双关,表面上是说人们现在过着最"美好的生活",实际是说《时代》周刊是本好杂志,在取悦读者的同时,达到非常好的广告效果。此类例子还有：

例 2. Minolta,finest to put you finest. （照相机广告）第一流的美能达,第一流的你。

例 3. Good to the last drop.（雀巢咖啡广告）滴滴香浓,意犹未尽。

#### 2. 新奇与创意

广告独具个性是消费者被吸引的秘诀。广告语新奇感的创造,一般从微观入手,注重词语的选择和锤炼,还要善于创造,创造新词和新的表达方法,例如：

**例句**

例 1. Give a Timex to all, and to all a good time.（手表广告）

拥有一块天美时表，拥有一段美好时光。

**分析**："Timex"是由"Time + Excellent"构成的，是厂家创造的一个新词。"Excellent"意思是卓越的、优等的，用以充分强调手表的一流品质。此类例子还有：

例 2. The Orange mostest Drink in the world.（饮料广告）（mostest＝most + -est）

这款橙汁是世界上最棒的饮料。

例 3. Drink a Pinta Milka Day.（牛奶广告）（a Pinta＝a pnit of；Milka Day＝milk a day）

每天一杯牛奶。

**3. 强烈的针对性**

商务广告应该抓住产品最主要的特点，根据消费者的特殊心理需求，有的放矢，例如：

 **例句**

例 1. Tide's In. Dirt's Out.（汰渍洗衣粉广告） 汰渍放进去，污垢洗出来。

**分析**：本广告语用一个"In"和一个"Out"构成的对称语言，生动形象地表达了汰渍洗衣粉的优点，满足了消费者对洗衣粉的最大心理期待。此类例子还有：

例 2. Not all cars are created equal.（轿车广告）

并非所有的车都生来平等。（套用《美国独立宣言》中"that all men are created equal."的句子来表明此车品质非凡。）

例 3. To smoke or not, that's a question.（香烟广告）

要不要抽烟，的确是个问题。（套用莎士比亚名剧《哈姆雷特》中经典对白"To be or not to be, that's a question."来引起人们注意。）

## （二）广告英语的句法特点

**1. 使用单词或短语代替整句**

为达到短小精练的效果，商务广告英语经常使用包括名词短语、分词短语和介词短语等来表达思想和意蕴，以达到令人思索、玩味的效果，例如：

 **例句**

例 1. A World of Comfort.（日本航空公司广告） 充满舒适与温馨的世界。

**分析**：广告语只有一个短语，显得语句短小精悍。"Comfort"一词抓住人们乘飞机出行时，希望旅途舒服的心理期待。此类例子还有：

例 2. A work of art.（苏格兰威士忌酒广告）艺术精品。

例 3. Without all taste, without all fat and cholesterol.（食品广告）

没有异味，不含脂肪，不含胆固醇。

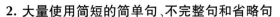
**2. 大量使用简短的简单句、不完整句和省略句**

广告受篇幅和时间的限制,在语言结构上常使用短小精练的简单句、不完整句、无动词句和省略句,例如:

 **例句**

例 1. No caffeine. Virtually no calories. Just a unique, sparkling citrus taste. (饮料广告)

不含咖啡因,不含卡路里。独特的柠檬味碳酸饮料。

**分析**: 广告语只有三个简单句构成,无主谓结构,行文紧凑明快,把人们喝饮料时最关注的问题一目了然地呈现在消费者眼前。此类例子还有:

例 2. Going East, Staying Westin. (Westin 宾馆广告)

游在东方,住在"西方"。

例 3. We're not in the computer business. We're in the results business. (IBM 电脑广告)

唯我电脑,成效更高。

**3. 大量使用祈使句**

广告的目的是劝说和促成消费者采取行动,而这恰恰是祈使句的功能,所以在广告英语中会大量使用祈使句,例如:

 **例句**

例 1. Catch that Pepsi spirit. Drink it in. (百事可乐广告)

喝百事饮料,感受百事精神。

**分析**: 这句广告语中使用了祈使句,起到带动消费者的作用。此类例子还有:

例 2. Show your true colors. (柯达胶卷广告)

秀出你的真彩。

例 3. Ask for More. (摩尔香烟广告)

再来一支,还吸"摩尔"。

**4. 使用各式疑问句**

疑问句往往能让听众积极做出反应,引起听众的共鸣,所以特殊疑问句、设问句、反问句和一般疑问句在广告英语中备受青睐,以鼓励消费者采取消费行动,例如:

 **例句**

例 1. Are you going gray too early? (染发剂广告)  您的头发是否白得太早?

**分析**: 这个广告疑问句的使用,提醒消费者关注自己的头发是否过早变白,是否与年龄相配,引起心理上对衰老的恐慌,产生通过染头发变年轻的念头。此类例子还有:

例 2. Isn't it good to know that walking is good exercise? (步行健身器广告)

了解步行是一项有益的运动,难道不是件好事儿吗?

例 3. You will buy this special gift to your darling, don't you ?

难道你就不打算买一个特别的礼物送给你心爱的人吗?

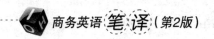
## Section 4   Translating Strategies, Samples and Training

### Translating Strategies

翻译方法多种多样,在广告翻译中常见的翻译方法有以下六种。

### 一、直译法

直译(literal translation)是把原文的语法结构转换为译文中最近似的对应结构,词汇一一对译,不过多考虑上下文。直译法主要用于原文意思明确,结构简单,按字面意思翻译就可以把句子表层意思和深层意思表达清楚的广告词。

 例句

例 1. Challenge the limits. (三星电子广告) 挑战极限。

例 2. Take TOSHIBA, take the world. (东芝电子广告) 拥有东芝,拥有世界。

例 3. We lead. Others copy. (理光复印机广告) 我们领先,他人效仿。

例 4. Hand in hand, future in your hand. (太平人寿广告)

伴你同行,齐握未来。

例 5. For your reference, we're enclosing few copies of leaflets and will send you samples under separate cover.

兹随函附上几份说明书并另寄样品,供你方参考。

### 二、意译法

意译(free translation)是注重表达原文内容,忽略其形式的翻译方法,更多地考虑译文读者因文化差异而产生的阅读和理解上的差异。

 例句

例 1. Start Ahead. (飘柔洗发水广告) 成功之路,从头开始。

例 2. Intelligence everywhere. (摩托罗拉手机广告) 智慧演绎,无处不在。

例 3. For next generation. (百事可乐广告) 新一代的选择。

例 4. Every time a good time. (麦当劳广告) 分分秒秒欢聚欢笑。

例 5. 关起门来搞建设不成,中国的发展离不开世界。

China can't develop in isolation from the rest of the world.

### 三、创译法

创译(creative translation)是把原文的直译摈弃,进行重新创造,与原文的表层意思相去甚远,但比直译境界更高,感染力更强。

例句

例 1. Music makes us. (香港康乐及文化事务署广告) 生有趣, 乐无穷。

例 2. Take time to indulge. (雀巢冰激凌广告) 尽情享受吧!

例 3. Things go better with Coca-Cola. (可乐广告) 可口可乐, 让你更快乐。

例 4. It happens at the Hilton. (希尔顿酒店广告) 希尔顿酒店有求必应。

例 5. Quality services for quality life. (香港康乐及文化事务署广告)

凝聚新动力, 文康展新姿。

## 四、增补法

增补 (supplementary translation) 有两种, 一种是对原文某些关键词的词义进行挖掘、引申或扩充, 将原文的深层意思加以发挥, 或使其隐含的意思突显, 因此, 译文的意义明显超出原文, 是典型的超额翻译。例如:

 例句

例 1. Elegance is an attitude. (浪琴表广告) 优雅态度, 真我性格。

例 2. Any shape and size to Europe. (联邦快递广告)

不同大小各种形状, 火速直飞欧洲。

例 3. Beyond your imagination. (大韩航空广告) 意想不到的天空。

例 4. Be good to yourself. Fly emirates. (阿联酋航空广告) 纵爱自己, 纵横万里。

例 5. You're at 35,000 feet. Your head is in New York. Your heart is in Paris. Your Rolex can be in both places at once. (劳力士表广告)

身在 35,000 英尺高空的纽约上空, 巴黎的浪漫仍系心中, 唯有你的劳力士可两地相容。

另一种增补源于对中文习惯表达的考虑。汉语里的四字词语言简意赅, 寓意深长, 能表达丰富的内涵, 所以译者往往在完成语义上已经完美的译文后, 再增加一个四字词语来锦上添花, 使之符合中国人对用词的习惯, 例如:

 例句

例 1. Anytime (快递公司广告) 随时随地, 准确无误。

例 2. Live with focus. (福特汽车广告) 专注生活, 享受人生。

例 3. Straight talk smart deals (东亚兴业有限公司) 真言实干, 称心方案。

例 4. Prepare to want one. (现代汽车广告) 众望所归, 翘首以待。

例 5. Your future is our future. (香港汇丰银行广告) 与您并肩, 迈向明天。

## 五、浓缩法

对于写得不够精练、信息过剩的广告原文, 可以采用浓缩 (concentrated translation) 法作为翻译策略, 相对于上文提到的"超额翻译", 我们称之为"欠额翻译"。这种译文比较少见。

**例句**

例 1. Overseas. Time set free Overseas. (江诗丹顿表广告) 自由真义。

例 2. Wherever you are. Whatever you do. The Allianz Group is always on your side. (安联集团广告) 安联集团,永远站在你身边。

例 3. From set time to any time. From one place to a million places. (康博电脑广告) 不再有时间的界限。

例 4. Clean your breath while it clean your teeth. (高露洁牙膏广告) 洁齿清气。

例 5. If you leave "managing money" alone, money will manage to leave you alone. 你不理财,财不理你。

## 六、零译法

在翻译中有种零译(no translation)现象。如果广告口号的原文短小精悍,译者很难找到同样惟妙惟肖的对应句,就可以采取零译法,即把原文原封不动地移入译文。

 **例句**

例 1. Open your eyes to the world. (Slogan:) The world's news leader. (国际新闻网)
让您放眼看世界。(口号:)The world's news leader.

例 2. Use the American Express Card to reflect your classic style. (Slogan:) do more. (美国运通)
使用美国运通卡,配衬经典性格。(口号:)do more

例 3. How would you know which one handles better? (Slogan:) The ultimate driving machine (BMW 宝马)
好不好,自己掌握。(口号:)登峰造极

例 4. My way, this is what I create. (Slogan:) for life(沃尔沃越野车广告)
路,由我出来。(口号:)for life

例 5. Currently taking on all projects. Large. Small. Impossible(Slogan:)Never stop thinking. (英飞凌科技公司广告)
无论任务大小,即使是不可能,我们必都全力以赴。(口号:)Never stop thinking.

 **Translating Samples**

## 一、商品广告

**案例**

**例 1**

### 北 京 烤 鸭

北京烤鸭是一种风味独特的中国传统名菜,已有三百多年的历史。最早是从金陵(今南京)王府膳房流传出来的。北京烤鸭以北京填鸭为原料,经特殊加工而成。烤鸭色泽枣红、鲜艳油亮、皮脆肉嫩、味美适口、风味独特、久吃不腻、营养丰富。

译文：

## Beijing Roast Duck

Beijing Roast Duck is a special traditional Chinese recipe which has a history of more than 300 years, from the Imperial Kitchen originating in Nanjing. Beijing Roast Duck is prepared from Beijing duck. The color of Beijing Roast Duck is purplish red and shiny bright. Its skin is crisp and the meat is tender. Its taste is delicious and has a special aroma which one never gets tired of eating. It is also very nutritious.

**例 2**

## Running Shoes Sale

$50—$80 Off normal retail

3 Days Only—Fri/Sat/Sun, Finishes 4th Sept 2021

4 Margaret St. Lower Hutt. Tel：5102-9453

Open Time：9am—8pm

译文：

### 让利出售跑鞋

按正常零售价降低 50~80 美元出售

仅此 3 天：周五、周六、周日，到 2021 年 9 月 4 日结束

玛格丽特大街 4 号，电话：5102-9453

营业时间：上午 9:00—下午 8:00

## 二、劳务广告

 **案例**

### 财产主人的责任

在明细表规定的保险期内发生的下列意外事故中，对于完全由您拥有某住宅及土地或由您曾拥有并居住某私人住宅而应负法律责任的，我们将支付全部款项：①任何人的意外死亡或身体伤害，②资产的意外损失或损坏；但不包括下列责任：

1. 您的任何家庭成员或家务人员的死亡或身体伤害；

2. 属于您、您的家人或家务人员或在您、您的家人或家务人员的保管或控制下的财产的损坏由于下列原因发生的：

（1）任何职业、商业或雇佣关系；

（2）某项协议，除非该责任在该协议不存在的情况下也成立。

对于一次事故带来的索赔金额一次不超过 50 万美元。

我们还将支付凡经过我们书面许可而产生的必要的费用、支出及法律费用。

译文：

### Your Liability As Property Owner

We will pay all sums for which you become legally liable arising solely from your ownership of your home and its land or from any private dwelling previously owned and occupied by you for accidental：① death of or bodily injury to any person, or ② loss of or damage to material property occurring during the period of insurance shown in the schedule, but not liability for

1. death or bodily injuring to any member of your family or domestic staff;

2. damage to property belong to or in the custody or control of you, your family or domestic arising from

(1) any profession, business or employment, or

(2) an agreement unless that liability would have existed otherwise.

Any claim payment resulting from one incident will not be more than $50,000.

We will also pay costs, expenses and legal fees necessarily incurred with our written consent.

## 三、招聘广告

 案例

例 1

### Wanted

Project Management Assistant

Responsibility：

• Provide service for the project in Beijing

• Provide assistance to the project manager for everyday work

Requirements：

• College degree and above

• Good English and computer skills

• Related working experience in the international organization

• Patient and careful, and has strong team work spirit.

译文：

### 诚　　聘

工程管理助理

责任：

——为北京的工程提供服务

——日常工作中为工程经理提供帮助

要求：

——大学学历或以上程度

——英语和计算机技能良好

——在国际机构中有过相关工作经验

——耐心仔细, 具有强烈团队工作精神

### 例 2

因发展需要,本公司诚聘一名销售助理。工作内容:根据公司的指示负责管理本地的销售活动;收集相关信息,发送到总公司;发展同本地媒体和用户的关系。要求:大学学历或以上程度,英语良好;具有销售和营销的基本理念,有相关经验者优先;在跨国机构和组织中有相关工作经验;具备良好的沟通和表达能力。联系电话:13987654321。

**译文:**

For development, our company needs a marketing assistant. Responsibility: responsible for the local management of the marketing sales activities according to the instruction from the head office; collect the information to the head office; building the relationship with the local media and customers. Requirements: college degree and above with good English; with basic idea of sales and marketing, related experience is preferred; working experience in the international organization is a must; good communication and presentation skills. Tel: 13987654321.

## 四、声誉广告

 **案例**

### 例 1

本公司主营文教用品、纸张及纸制品,体育及健身器械用具、运动服装及包袋、旅游用品、玩具、乐器,以及各类海外用户适销的有关商品。本公司竭诚与国内外新老朋友和伙伴加强合作,在"平等互利"的宗旨下,开展各类国际间的进出口贸易,还可以来料加工、来样生产、来料装配、补偿贸易、对销贸易、定牌生产、咨询邮购、代理进出口业务、各类合资或合作经营等贸易方式。

**译文:**

We deal with a variety of goods including stationary and paper products, sports and fitness equipment, sportswear and daily wear items, travel necessities, toys, musical instruments, and a variety of salable commodities that appeal to overseas clients. Our company now is seeking to establish an equitable and mutually beneficial partnership with old and new friends both at home and abroad. Apart from import and export, we also engage in the following business: processing on order, sample manufacturing, assembling on provided parts, compensation trade, counter trade, manufacturing brand-name goods, mail-order consulting, import and export procurement, joint-venture planning and cooperation.

### 例 2

凭着训练有素的外贸专业人才、科学的管理体系、高质量的商品、优质的服务和可靠的信誉,40余年来,我公司与国内20多个省市千余家厂商建有销购关系,与世界100多个国家和地区的上万家贸易商开展了进出口业务,年进出口额已达8000万美元,跻身于中国500家最大进出口企业。我公司将不断增强自身活力,在世界贸易海洋中显示蓬勃的生命力。

**译文：**

Our high-quality products and service have helped us develop a reliable reputation during our forty-plus years in business. We employ a well-trained staff of professionals specializing in foreign trade, which, combined with our state-of-the-trained management system, has helped our corporation to establish a productive trading relationship with more than 1,000 manufacturers from more than 20 provinces and municipalities in China and more than 10,000 traders from in 100-plus countries and regions throughout the world. Our volume of the trade has amounted to US $ 80 million annually, hence securing our company's position among the top 500 import-export enterprises in China.

## Translating Training

**A：Translate the following advertisements into Chinese.**

1. Maxam erases years off from your skin.

2. Only your time is more precious than this watch.

3. Once tasted, always loved.

4. Cleans your breath while it cleans your teeth.

5. Volvos have always forced other cars to be safer. This one will force them to be better.

6. On women and children's wear as well as on men's shirts, our label says—quietly but persuasively—all there is to say about our good quality and your good taste.

7. Unlike me, my Rolex never needs a rest.

8. No dream is too big.

9. No more sore feet, no more crowded stores, no more endless shopping lists. With just one call, you can wrap up all your holiday shopping by giving Newsweek as a gift to your family and friends.

10. She's the nimblest girl around. Nimble is the way she goes. Nimble is the bread he eats. Light, Delicious, Nimble.

**B：Translate the following advertisements into English.**

1. 城乡路万千，路路有航天。

2. 天然药材，纯正蜂蜜。

3. 要想皮肤好，早晚用大宝。

4. 我是女生，我优先。伊利优酸乳。

5. 体积虽小，颇具功效。

6. "雪山"牌羊绒衫色泽鲜艳、手感柔滑、穿着舒适、轻软保暖。

7. 愿集财富、吉祥、艺术、智慧于一身的北京牙雕成为您的镇库之宝！

8. 我们的克力架选用上乘原料，由独特秘方精制而成，如此轻巧松脆，带给您全家新鲜美味。

9. 烤鸭色泽枣红、鲜艳油亮、皮脆肉嫩、味美适口、风味独特、久吃不腻、营养丰富。

10. 西凤酒清澈透明、香气浓郁、醇厚圆满、回味悠长、别具一格。

## Section 5   Extensive Expression

### 一、广告(Advertisements/ads)

| | | |
|---|---|---|
| 1. account service | 客户服务 |
| 2. advertising agency | 广告代理 |
| 3. advertising campaign | 广告活动 |
| 4. advertising department | 广告部 |
| 5. airport advertising | 机场广告 |
| 6. appeal | 诉求 |
| 7. area sampling | 区域抽样 |
| 8. audience | 受众 |
| 9. audio-visual advertising | 视听广告 |
| 10. book ads | 图书广告 |
| 11. bill board | 路牌广告 |
| 12. classified ads | 分类广告 |
| 13. direct mail ads | 直邮广告 |
| 14. handbill ads | 传单广告 |
| 15. magazine ads | 杂志广告 |
| 16. network ads | 网络广告 |
| 17. neo-light ads | 霓虹灯广告 |
| 18. outdoor ads | 户外广告 |
| 19. packaging ads | 包装广告 |
| 20. posters | 招贴广告 |
| 21. public service ads | 公益广告 |
| 22. radio ads | 广播广告 |
| 23. recruit ads | 招聘广告 |
| 24. transportation ads | 交通广告 |
| 25. TV commercials | 电视广告 |

### 二、网络广告(Network Advertisements/ads)

| | | |
|---|---|---|
| 1. ad news | 广告浏览 |
| 2. banner | 横幅广告 |
| 3. button ads | 按钮式广告 |
| 4. click rate | 点击率 |
| 5. click troughs | 点击次数 |
| 6. cost per click | 点击成本 |
| 7. demographics | 人口统计特征 |
| 8. e-mail ads | 电子邮件广告 |

| 9. floating ads | 浮动广告 |
| 10. hit | 点击 |
| 11. impression | 印象数 |
| 12. log file | 访客流量、统计流量 |
| 13. page view | 浏览量 |
| 14. pop-up ads | 弹出式广告 |
| 15. reach | 到达率 |
| 16. text links ads | 文字链接广告 |
| 17. traffic | 流量 |
| 18. vist | 访问 |
| 19. unique user | 唯一用户 |
| 20. media buying | 媒介购买 |
| 21. media mix | 媒介组合 |
| 22. media objectives | 媒介目标 |
| 23. media research | 媒介调查 |
| 24. media service | 媒介服务 |
| 25. media recommendations | 媒介介绍 |

# Unit 6

# Commodity Specifications

Unit Objectives

In this unit you should

➤ familiarize yourself with the format of business advertisement.

➤ have a good command of the basic words and useful expressions of the business advertisement in this unit.

➤ enable yourself to acquire the translating skills of idioms and slangs.

## ❷ Section 1 Theme Lead-in

**Read the following passage to gain a better understanding of this unit.**

With the advancement of the process of globalization, especially after China's entrance into WTO, the international trade is in a prosperous and quickly-developing period. Chinese commodities are facing both opportunities and challenges in export activities. Commodity instruction plays quite an important role in international communication and co-operation. It helps foreign consumers to get to know and apply the commodities; and through detailed introduction and

evaluation, it can arouse consumers' interest in purchase, further achieve the purpose of publicity and promotion. Commodity instruction is the literal material which introduces the information such as usage, specification, function, composition, application and maintenance of commodity to consumers. Commodity instructions not only offer information to readers but undertake the burden of promoting commercial sales and companies' reputation. An excellent and successful commodity instruction contains three aspects of function: informative function, aesthetic function and vocative function.

When a product is marketed to another country, usually the original commodity instruction is translated with appropriate adaption to cater to the needs of the new market. Translation becomes a commercial activity with more participants involved. The translator's choice of translation strategy is dependent on the power balance between the agents of translation, including not only translator, but initiators, the target-text receivers and on the cultural, historical and economic situation in which translation takes place.

In the translating process, the manufacturer or the trader plays the key role of translation initiator by outlining the objectives for the translator to fulfill; receivers are differently vulnerable to particular persuasion strategies, and the content and linguistic choices in commodity instructions vary cross-culturally. So the main task of the translator is to reach target text's functional adequacy, at times by making cultural transportation or adaptation inevitably in this type of translation, which is not only legitimate, but also necessary, in the attainment of the objectives. This necessity of giving the translator the power his expert status deserves if the target text is not only to offer information but appeal to English consumers' preferences and potential needs. Considering the difference between Chinese and English and readers on both sides, the translator should adopt flexible translation strategies on lexical level, syntactic level and textual level to entirely reveal the functions of commodity instructions.

But now in domestic market, there exist serious problems about the translation of commodity instructions with mistranslation and word-for-word translation printed on various packages or manuals. The reason consists of the translator's inefficiency and various external factors, including underdevelopment of Chinese current translation circle, business eagerness for instant profit and domestic consumers' misunderstanding about medium languages.

## Section 2  Translation Warming-up

**A: Translate the following commodity specifications into Chinese.**

1. Complete the whole treatment course even if the condition seems to be improved.

2. Press the center button to pause a song or video; press again to resume playback.

3. After the engine started, it is not permissible to turn the key from the switch-on position to the starting position.

4. The most serious side-effect is damage to the bone marrow. Because of this, the white blood cell count should be controlled often enough during the treatment.

5. Remove the AC supply lead before servicing or cleaning heads, rolers, etc.

6. When frying, take particular care to prevent oil and grease from catching fire.

7. Regular use of the cream results in the increase of skin cell vitality and improvement of metabolism to restore youthful fairness of the skin.

8. In addition, you can connect it to any telephone line so that you can send and receive e-mail and faxes and get on the Internet.

9. Connect the blue connector of the video cable to the blue video connector on the back of your computer.

10. Store in a dry place at room temperature. Protect from light and in an airtight container.

**B：Translate the following commodity specifications into English.**

1. 建议饮法：取 3~5 朵菊花用沸水直接冲泡，可根据自己的喜好添加其他辅料。

2. 本品特点：富含人体必需的多种维生素、矿物质及各种氨基酸，有动植物蛋白互补作用，促进营养的合理平衡。

3. 本品采摘当地的鲜桂花用祖传工艺加工成桂花干，保持原有的色香味形，已有上百年历史。

4. 本品色泽自然、汁水清香、味甘爽口、花形完美，是常饮不厌口、四季皆宜的高级饮料。

5. 该空调广泛用于各种场合，如宾馆、饭店、医院、托儿所、住宅等，为您创造舒适的生活环境。

6. 该面膜富含高效美白滋养精华，淡化斑点，使皮肤再现净白与柔皙。

7. 本品为黄色糖衣片，除去糖衣后显棕褐色；味苦。

8. 经先进的科学方法精制而成，既保持了酱香浓郁、典雅细致、协调丰满、回味悠长等特点，又具有加水、加冰后不浑浊，风格不变等特点，深受国内外各界人士的欢迎。

9. 接电源时必须先检查插座是否带有地线插孔，电源电压是否与该电器内部参数标牌上所标电压相匹配。

10. 切勿将插座、插头浸水或溅湿，防止漏电，严禁将壶体浸入水中。

## Section 3　Topic Features and Translation Principles

### 一、商品说明书

商品说明书有时也叫使用说明书，是一种以说明为主要表达方式，用平易、朴实、易懂的语言向用户通俗地介绍商品（包括服务等）的性能、特征、用途、使用和保养方法等知识的文书材料。

### 二、商品说明书的种类

由于商品的种类涉及较广泛，各类说明书性能和用途不同。按所要说明的事物来分，可以分为以下几种：

（1）产品说明书：主要指那些关于日常生产、生活产品的说明书。主要是对某一产品的所有情况的介绍，诸如其组成材料、性能、存储方式、注意事项、主要用途等。这类说明书可以是生产消费品的，如生产设备、农业机械；也可以是生活消费品的，如食品、药品等；

（2）使用说明书：是向人们介绍具体的关于某产品的使用方法和步骤的说明书；

（3）安装说明书：主要介绍如何将一堆分散的产品零件安装成一个可以使用的完整的产品。

## 三、商品说明书的内容

商品说明书包括标题、正文和落款。标题通常为"××产品说明"。正文是核心部分，用来说明商品的用法、功能、构造，成分等（例如食品说明书重在说明其成分、使用方法及保质期限；药物说明书重在说明其构成成分、基本效用及用量；电器说明书重在说明其使用和保养方法等），一般包括以下几个方面的内容：产品的概况（如名称、产地、规格、发展史、制作方法等）；产品的性能、规格、用途；安装和使用方法；保养和维修方法；附件、备件及其他需要说明的内容。落款要写明产品的制造厂家的名称、地址、邮编、E-mail 地址、电话、传真及产品的批号、生产日期、优质级别等。

## 四、商品说明书的翻译原则

### 1. 说明书词汇相对固定和专业

说明书通常具有固定的结构要素，例如成分（ingredients），有效期（period of validity），注意事项（precautions），功能（functions），规格（specifications），净含量（net content），保质期（shelf life）等。此外，某一技术领域中特有的"土话""行话"或"俚语"也会频繁使用。

 **案例**

**例 1**

胖胖瓜子仁（Plump Shelled Pumpkin Seeds）说明书中的部分内容：

配料：天然无壳南瓜子、食盐、天然调味品

贮藏：低温、干燥

保质期：7 个月

生产日期：见封口处

译文：

Ingredients：shell-less pumpkin seeds，salt，natural flavoring

Storage：in a cool and dry place

Shelf life：7 months

Production：see the seal

**例 2**

途锐豪华运动型全能车（Touareg：off-road，on-road a class act）说明书的部分内容：

最大爬坡度：100%　45 度

涉水深度：580 毫米

安全侧倾角度：35 度（静止时 45 度）

译文：

Hill climbs capacity：100 percent or 45 degrees

Fording depth：up to 580 mm(with air suspension)

Overhang title：up to 35 degrees (static 45 degrees)

**2. 说明书语言简洁、通俗易懂**

说明书的句子经常被浓缩为名词(或词组)，被动句、祈使句、省略句、分词(介词)＋名词、(情态动词) be ＋介词短语、be ＋形容词＋介词短语等句式经常被使用。

(情态动词) be ＋形容词(或过去分词)＋目的状语，句子主语往往是产品名称，来突出产品的特性、功能或注意事项。

 **例句**

例1. 本装置仅限由接受过导管插入诊断及治疗培训的医生使用。

The device should be used only by physicians trained in diagnostic and therapeutic catheter procedures.

现在分词(介词)＋名词(非谓语动词形式较多)往往用于解说维护或操作程序，常伴有图解。

例2. 使用本产品时须注意遵守定期消毒规定。

Observe sterile technique at regular intervals when using this product.

祈使句，常用来表示强调、命令、警告。

例3. 早晚刷牙后含漱2~5分钟。

Gargle with the product 2-5 minutes after brushing in the morning and evening.

省略句使说明书简洁明了。

例4. 禁忌症：尚未发现。

Contraindications：None known.

被动语态使消费者更加关注说明对象。

例5. 产品可根据用户需要采用柜式、立架式、卧式、地面摆放及与其他电源柜内置式使用等各种形式。

The products can be installed in several types such as cabinet, vertical racks, horizontal racks, ground placement and installed with other kinds of power supply cabinet according to user's requirements.

**3. 翻译商品说明书时，应重点突出其解释说明的功能、定义准确无误，力求言简意赅、通俗易懂，语言风格与原文一致，确保原文的技术性特点。**

 **案例**

**例1**

如广电DVD影碟机特点的说明：

高清晰度：采用MPEG2编码格式，使水平清晰度达到500线以上。

时间搜索：可快速寻找到碟片上某一点的内容，尤其适合武打故事片的欣赏。

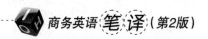

内容显示：采用彩色荧光显示及电视屏中英文显示，碟片信息一目了然。

译文：

High definition：this unit adopts MPEG2 coding format and brings the horizontal resolution over 500 lines.

Time search：it can quickly search a specific part on a disc，especially agreeable for playing action movies.

Content display：TFT LCD and Chinese/English OSD make disc contents clearer.

**例 2**

威莱(Valle)家庭影院智能音频功率放大器的说明书内容：

常见故障及排除方法：如果障碍是按动开关却没有任何声响，请检查是否(1)已接电源；(2)选择了正确的输入；(3)音量开到最小；(4)音箱已正确接驳；(5)主机处于静音状态。

译文：

Troubles and troubleshooting：if the unit makes no response when power button is pressed，please check if (1) the power supple is already turned on；(2) the correct input is chosen；(3) the volume is turned to its minimum level；(4) the speakers are correctly connected；and (5) the main unit is set at the "mute" mode.

# Section 4   Translating Strategies, Samples and Training

## Translating Strategies

### 一、习语

习语(idiom)是语言发展中长期积淀的精华，是人类长期习用、形式简洁、含义精辟的定型词组或短句。英语词汇量极为丰富，习语也纷繁多姿，洋溢着浓郁的西方文化气息。

**1. 习语对等的翻译方法**

**例句**

例 1. 他们坚持要以眼还眼，以牙还牙地向对手报复。

They insist on an eye for an eye，a tooth for a tooth.

例 2. 他对我们的联合请愿置之不理、充耳不闻。

He shut his eyes to our joint petition.

例 3. 彼得的财产在他投资的企业倒闭后损失得精光。

Peter lost his shirt when that business he had invested in failed.

例 4. 那些喜欢无理取闹的人永远讨不到什么便宜。

Those who like to make a scene will never get advantage.

例 5. To requite like for like is a common practice.

一报还一报，是人们通常的做法。

**2. 形神兼顾法**

 例句

例 1. 他们经过碰头商量,最后决定购买那批商品。

They put their heads together and decided to buy the products.

例 2. It was in the cards for the son to succeed his father as head of the business.

子承父业顺理成章,他后来成了他父亲创办的企业的老板。

例 3. 因为一个错误的投资,他一生的积蓄全部化为乌有。

His life savings went down the drain in a bad investment.

例 4. 老板总是装腔作势,以饱学之士自矜。

Our boss always puts on high airs with his learning.

例 5. 听说产品全部卖光,员工们兴奋到了极点。

Hearing all products were sold out, the staff were enjoying themselves to the top of their heads.

**3. 意译改造法**

 例句

例 1. 因为对环境不熟悉,新员工在这里感到不自在。

The new employee is here like a fish out of water.

例 2. 年轻人养成了见物就买的坏习惯。

The young people have a bad habit of buying a pig in the poke.

例 3. 经理的表扬使他飘飘欲仙。

The manager's praise carries him off his feet.

例 4. 他被解雇了,因为他不能处理突发事件。

He got the sack, because he could not deal with a great rush of business.

例 5. 他头脑清醒,做事绝不糊涂。

He keeps his memory green in doing things.

**4. 优势互补翻译法**

 例句

例 1. 你不要浪费时间了,我们已经决定坚持到底、绝不投降。

Don't waste your time, we have already decided to nail our colors to the mast.

例 2. 老板的话使我羞愧难当、无地自容。

The boss's words bowed me to the earth.

例 3. 他努力经营生意,可是几乎血本无归。

He worked hard on a business, but brought his pigs to the wrong market.

例 4. 他无论到哪里工作,总能得到上司的照顾。

Wherever he works, he always wins his chief's ears.

例 5. 你无须再解释什么,我知道你是在指桑骂槐。

You don't have to explain it anymore. I see you just fit the cap on me.

## 二、俚语

俚语(slang)数量很大,其中大多数都与西方英语和非英语国家的地域文化有着密切的关系。翻译英语俚语时,一般都要借助有关词典,才能较准确地理解俚语的基本意思,并根据词语的上下文准确判断出具体词条的确切含义。

### 1. 以俚语译俚语

 例句

例 1. 麦克什么都不懂,他就是一个呆瓜。

Mike can't understand anything, he is such an airbrain.

例 2. 这家饭店才开张半年就关门倒闭了。

This restaurant went belly up after being open for only six months.

例 3. 这个理论对我来说简直太玄妙了。

This theory is too far out for me.

例 4. 这部电影是个大热门,观众都非常喜欢。

This film is a hit! The audience loved it very much.

例 5. 我们主任总是在纠正别人,他觉得自己简直是个万事通。

Our director is always correcting other people, he thinks he is just a know-it-all.

### 2. 以俗语译俚语

 例句

例 1. 这个花瓶花了我一大笔钱,不过还是值得的。

This vase cost me an arm and a leg, but it was worth it.

例 2. 自从他向她借了 1,000 美元不还之后,他们之间就有了隔阂。

Ever since he borrowed 1,000 dollars from her and never paid her back, there has been bad blood between them.

例 3. 他们一见面就很投缘,从此成了好朋友。

They hit it off instantly and have been good friends ever since.

例 4. 彼得是个爱占小便宜的人,他一直住在史蒂夫家里白吃白喝。

Peter is a real freeloader. He has been staying with Steve and eating all his food.

例 5. 别去烦他,经理不喜欢工作时被人打扰。

Don't get in his hair. He doesn't like to be bothered when he's working.

### 3. 以习语译俚语

 **例句**

例 1. 约翰上班时总是神采奕奕。

John always shows up at work bright-eyed and bushy-tailed.

例 2. 别大惊小怪,公司会赔偿你损失的。

Don't have a cow! The company will pay for the damages.

例 3. 约翰逊先生买一辆新劳斯莱斯的钱和他的年薪相比只不过九牛一毛。

The amount of money Mr. Jonson spent on a new Rolls-Royce was just a drop in the bucket compared to his annual salary.

例 4. 他并未尽全力,却依旧轻松取胜。

He didn't put in his full effort and he still won hands down.

例 5. 今天是安的大好日子,他跟一个重要客户做成了一笔大生意。

This is a red-letter day for Anne, she made a big sale to a very important client.

### 4. 以四字格译俚语

 **例句**

例 1. 让我们咬紧牙关完成工作吧。

Let's bite the bullet and get over with the work.

例 2. 中国出现了一批雄心勃勃、受过高等教育的新生代年轻企业家。

China is experiencing a new breed of ambitious and educated, young businessmen.

例 3. 虽然我辛苦工作,老板只给我一点微不足道的报酬。

The boss gave me diddly squat for all my hard work.

例 4. 保持冷静,他并非要有意触犯你。

Keep your shirt on, He didn't mean to offend you.

例 5. 公司准备的丰盛大餐让员工们大呼过瘾。

The company knocked the staff out with the delicious meal.

## Translating Samples

## 一、产品说明书

 **案例**

　　乐陵金丝小枣位于全国三大枣子产区之首,以优质的品质和丰富的营养闻名于世。乐陵金丝小枣体形小、色红、皮薄、核小、肉质丰满,含有果胶维生素、蛋白质、脂肪,丰富的铁、钙、磷和维生素 AP 等营养物质,对人身增热补血、滋肝健脾、益气养肾、润肤延寿有明显功能。本品是历史悠久、中外驰名的高级补品。

译文：

Leling Small Sweet Dates are of the best quality in China's three big date-growing areas. They are well-known for their small bodies, rich pulp, tiny pits, thin skin, good quality and rich nutrients. The dates contain various nutritious elements such as pectin vitamins, protein and fat and are rich in ferrum, calcium, phosphorus and vitamin AP. They serve to improve your health by enriching the blood to promote the production of heat, nourishing the liver and invigorating the spleen, supplementing qi and the kidney, to prolong your life. It is a high-grade tonic with long, well-known both at home and abroad.

## 二、使用说明书

 **案例**

**例1**

### 如何使用推拿按摩机

1. 检查开关是否处于"OFF"挡。

2. 首先将电源插头插入插座,启动按钮向顺时针方向转动,此时电源显示灯打开。按摩器开始工作。按加热按钮使其打开,此时加热功能也启动。当推拿工作进行时,调节"调速器",按顺时针方向旋转,推拿速度由快到慢。如果按递时针方向旋转,推拿速度由慢到快。

3. 使用后,将调速器拨至"OFF"挡。

译文：

### How to Use a Massor

1. Make sure that the power is on the "off".

2. Put the plug in the socket and turn the button clockwise. When the power light is on, the massor starts to work. Turn the button of heating on, and the function of heating also starts to work. When it is on the move, adjust the speeding governor. If adjusted clockwise, it will speed down. If turned counterclockwise, it will speed up.

3. After use, set the governor on the "off".

**例2**

### 清音丸说明书

［药品名称］通用名：清音丸;汉语拼音：Qingyin Wan

［成分］诃子肉、乌梅肉、川贝母、葛根、天花粉、茯苓、百药煎、甘草。

［性状］本品为褐色的大蜜丸;味甘,微酸涩。

［功能主治］清热利咽,生津润燥。用于肺热津亏,咽喉不利,口舌干燥,声哑失音。

［用法用量］口服,温开水送服或嚼化。一次一丸,一日 2 次。

［注意事项］服用前应除去蜡皮、塑料球壳;本品不可整丸吞服;忌服辛辣食物。

［规格］每丸重 3g。

［贮藏］密封。

［包装］塑料球壳,10 丸/盒。

［有效期］5 年。

［批准文号］国药准字 Z11020173。

［生产企业］企业名称：北京同仁堂股份有限公司同仁堂制药厂

地址：北京市东城区西打磨厂 46 号

电话号码：（010）67025631

传真号码：（010）67018048

译文：

## Qingyin Wan

Ingredient：Fructus Chebulae；Fructus Mume；Bulbus Fritillariae Cirrhosae；Radix Puerariae；Radix Trichosanthis；Poria；Massala；Radix Glycyrrhizae.

Description：Brown big honeyed pills；tastes sweet，slightly sour and astringent.

Action：To remove heat and relieve sore-throat and promote production of body fluid and moisten for dryness. Loss of body fluid due to lung heat，discomfort in pharynx，dryness of the throat and mouth，celostomia and aphonia.

Usage and dosage：1 pill each time，twice a day，to be swallowed with warm boiled water or kept in mouth to dissolve gradually.

Notice：Remove the waxen shell and the plastic shell before taking it；do not swallow in the whole pill. Contraindicated with pungent and spicy foods.

Specification：3g per pill.

Shortage：To be preserved in tightly closed containers

Package：Plastic shell，10 pills per package

Validity：5 years.

Approval No.：GUO YAO ZHUN ZI Z11020173

BEIJING TONG REN TANG LIMITED COMPANY

TONG REN TANG PHARMACEUTICAL FACTORY

Add. 46，Xidamochang Street，Dongcheng District，Beijing

Tel：（010）67025631

Fax：（010）67018048

## 例 3

### Develop Lesson

Vegetable & Fruits Residue Scavenger

**Product Characteristics**

Richly containing Nacocoyl special effective ingredient extracted from coconut oil via high-tech method，it can rapidly dissolve the soluble oil component in pesticides so as to quickly separate the pesticides from vegetables and fruits. It contains especially IMAZALIL special effect sterilizing component，fast killing pathogenic bacteria with 99.9% effective rate. Vegetables and fruits keep their freshness and nice taste. The active ingredient in this product I approved by

WHO, EU and US-EPA and complies with FAO specifications. With edible standardized component and low foaming.

**Usage**

Put several drops of product per liter of water to rinse the fruits or vegetables. Leave the fruit or vegetable in the rinsing water for 5 minutes. Before eating，rinse them with clean water.

**Caution**

Do not drink this product；keep away from children. If having swallowed by accident，drink lots of water.

译文：

**德利邦立鲜**

蔬果残留清洗剂

**产品特点**：富含用高科技手段从椰果中提取的椰油两性醋酸（Nacocoyl）特效成分，能快速溶解农药中的乳油成分，使农药和果蔬迅速剥离。富含 IMAZALIL 特效杀菌消毒成分，快速杀灭致病菌。杀菌率99.9%，持久保持蔬果新鲜美味。本品所含活性成分经世界卫生组织、欧盟和美国环保署批准，符合联合国粮农组织标准，含有可使用标准成分。本品为低泡型。

**使用方法**：清洗蔬菜瓜果时，每公升水加入本品数滴，浸泡5分钟后，用清水冲洗干净即可食用。

**注意事项**：本品为非饮用品，请避免儿童触及。不慎误食，需多饮水。

## 三、安装说明书

 **案例**

**Safety Precautions and Maintenance**

1. Unplug the monitor if you are not going to use it for an extended period of time.

2. Unplug the monitor before cleaning. Clean with a slightly damp cloth. Wiping the screen with a dry cloth is okay when the power is off. However，never use alcohol or ammonia-based liquids.

3. If the monitor does not operate normally when you have followed the instructions in this manual，consult a service technician.

4. The back cover should be removed only by qualified service personnel.

5. Keep the monitor out of direct sunlight and away from stoves or other heat sources.

译文：

**安全预防与维护**

1. 如果您长时间不使用该显示器，请拔下插头。

2. 如果需要清洁，请拔下显示器插头，用微湿的织物清洁。当电源关闭时，可用干织物擦拭。但切勿使用酒精或氨水溶液。

3. 按此手册中的说明安装后，如果显示器仍不工作，请咨询提供服务的技术人员。

4. 后盖应该仅由有资格的服务人员打开。

5. 不要让阳光直射显示器，并要远离炉子或其他热源。

## Translating Training

**A: Translate the following commodity specifications into Chinese.**

1. If you answer no to this message, you are prompted to terminate the Auto install.

2. This is an e-dictionary made in Hong Kong, China. It is the latest product of Hongda Company Ltd.

3. There is a large vocabulary of 1 million words and phrases stored in it. You can look up any word you meet in your senior period.

4. If the needle points towards the minus(-)sign of the scale when the switch is turned on, the battery is being discharged.

5. Do not disassemble, install backward, or expose batteries to liquid, moisture, fire or extreme temperature.

6. Wash the face with warm boiled water and evenly rub a little amount all over, twice daily, one in the morning and the other in the evening, and the satisfactory effect will soon be obtained. An additional rub before bedtime would be more effective due to the full intake of various nutritious elements by the skin.

7. Unfamiliarity with the equipment, poor fault judgment or lack of proper training may cause injury to both the operator and others.

8. The dosage should be determined individually. In severe cases up to 4 dragees may be taken as a single dose.

9. If the battery contacts touch metal objects, the battery may short-circuit, discharge energy, become hot or leak.

10. Eye Contact eye shadow applies smoothly and even with the new velvety formula, provides an unforgettable look with eye-opening colors and lightweight feel.

11. Read and follow warnings and instructions supplied by the battery manufacturer.

12. For unresponsive dry skin, try mixing equal parts Skin Recovery Hydrating Mask with nonirritating plant oil such as olive, apricot or sesame. Leave the mixture on skin for 30 minutes or longer then gently remove the excess with a warm washcloth.

13. basic operations

Switch the Phone on/off

Press and hold the power key. The phone will display the power-on/off animation. If the Power-on Code function is active, after switching on the phone, enter the Security Code (with each input displayed as * ) and press the left soft key (OK). If correct, the power-on animation will be displayed; otherwise Code Error will be displayed.

14.

—Protects and softens chapped lips.

—Contains the antioxidants of Vitamin C&E. Helps delay aging and maintain healthy lips.

—Gives natural and lovely colors with a glossy shine.

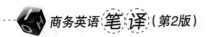

—Apply directly on lips or use with other color lip balm.

15. For standard bleaching：

Machine washing：

（1）For top-loading machine：5 bottle caps of Bleach（approx. 70g）per load.

（2）For front-loading machine：3 bottle caps of Bleach（approx. 40g）.

Hand washing：Dilute 1 bottle cap of Bleach with 5 liters of water.

For extra large bleaching：Dilute 3 bottle caps of Bleach with 5 liters of water.

Precautionary statements：

（1）Do not use on silk, wool, nylon, textile or leather easy to fade.

（2）Do not use or mix with acidic cleaner. Wear rubber gloves when using this product.

（3）Avoid direct contact with clothes；otherwise, it will change the color of clothes.

（4）Keep out of children's reach.

**B：Translate the following commodity specifications into English.**

1. 如误饮本清洁剂，请立即饮用大量清水，并就医治疗。

2. 此词典内部由尖端电脑科技控制，而此电脑科技是由本公司研究了 20 年所获得的成果。

3. 电子词典的外壳由轻金属制造，体积小，携带方便；操作简单，价格优惠，是英语学习者的理想选择。

4. 一周使用一次，深层长效，美白修护，肌肤水嫩白皙。

5. 如果你准备在寒冷的室外待几个小时的话，在用日霜之前，抹一些补水修复面膜在脸上，可以帮助你抵御寒流对皮肤造成的伤害。

6. 补水修复面膜可当作晚上的高级滋润品，只要在清洁后的脸上抹上厚厚的一层，美美地睡一觉，第二天一早洗去即可。

7. 这款眼部卸妆啫喱能柔和地去除眼部的所有妆容，它柔和、不含刺激的配方，十分适合眼部的敏感肌肤以及隐形眼镜佩戴者。

8. SPF10 蕴含维他命 E 及独特的防护成分，在皮肤表面形成一层透气的保护膜，有效隔离脏空气，避免污染物伤害肌肤，隔离彩妆，为健康肌肤提供一年四季的完美呵护。

9. 潘婷 Pro-V 营养洗发露含有更多维他命原 B5，营养能由发根彻底渗透至发尖，补充养分，令头发健康、亮泽。潘婷 Pro-V 洗发露兼含护发素，能够做到洗发同时护发。

10. 本品采用新疆薰衣草之乡天然薰衣草花穗蒸馏提取精华，含有芳樟脂和萜族化合物，具有消毒抗毒、消炎杀菌作用。

11. 成人：通常每天两片，早晨及中午各 1 片。严重病例早晨的剂量可加至 2 片。老年病人通常每天 1 片，早晨口服。对失眠或严重不安的病例，建议在急性期加服镇静剂。

12. 若维修需要替换零部件，则这些零部件可以是翻新过的，或含有翻新过的材料。如有必要替换整个产品，则可用翻新产品替换。

13. 不得在抽油烟机附近使用任何易燃物；清洗除油烟过滤网罩和油垢时务必遵照操作说明。

14. 本厂生产的电热水壶，是最新流行的快速煮沸开水及饮料的家用电器产品。适用于家庭、机关、企事业等单位。其结构合理，工艺先进，并具有热效高、耗电少、性能可靠、安全卫生等优点。本品愿竭诚为广大消费者服务。

15. 本型号空调器装有四通换向阀及高低两挡风量和新风装置,因此可供冬暖夏凉之用。室内通风时能不断补充新鲜空气,过滤空气中的尘埃并吸收湿气,可提供一个较理想的生活与工作环境。该机采用自行设计制造的全封闭压缩机,整机结构紧凑,外形美观,效率高,噪声低,使用方便,性能稳定可靠。

##  Section 5　Extensive Expression

### 一、商品描述词汇

| | | |
|---|---|---|
| 1. sale manual | 推销说明书 |
| 2. uses & features | 用途和特点 |
| 3. at home and abroad | 国内外 |
| 4. parameters & specifications | 参数与规格 |
| 5. technical specifications | 技术规格 |
| 6. power source | 电源 |
| 7. exterior measurements | 外形尺寸 |
| 8. electrocaloric power | 电热功率 |
| 9. total weight | 总重 |
| 10. controllable temperature | 可控温度 |
| 11. main products | 主要产品 |
| 12. dimensions of body | 外形尺寸 |
| 13. format and presentation | 格式和表达 |
| 14. development skills required | 开发能力要求 |
| 15. quality criteria | 质量标准 |
| 16. quality tolerances | 质量公差 |
| 17. in short supply | 供不应求 |
| 18. quality skills required | 质量技术要求 |
| 19. quality responsibilities | 质量责任 |
| 20. scope of application | 适用范围 |
| 21. pleasant in after-taste | 回味隽永 |
| 22. pure biological agents | 纯生物制剂 |
| 23. evident effect | 疗效显著 |
| 24. selling well all over the world | 畅销全球 |
| 25. elegant and graceful | 典雅大方 |
| 26. durable modeling | 定型耐久 |
| 27. convenience goods | 方便商品 |
| 28. large assortment | 各式俱全 |
| 29. customers first | 顾客第一 |
| 30. a great variety of models | 款式多样 |

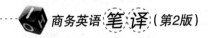

## 二、商品涉及的技术词汇

产品说明书常用词汇和日常生活常用词汇对照举例。

| 产品说明书常用词汇 | 日常生活常用词汇 | 汉 语 译 文 |
|---|---|---|
| application | use | 应用 |
| construction | structure，building | 结构、建造 |
| commission | experiment and adjustment | 调试 |
| hazard | danger | 危险 |
| prior to | before | 在……之前 |
| terminate | end | 结束，终止 |
| assume | take | 承担 |
| vary | differ，change | 与……不同，改变 |
| dismantle/dissemble | take apart | 拆卸 |

## 三、商品涉及的缩略词

缩略词和完整词表达法及其对应的汉语译文。

| 缩 略 词 | 完 整 词 | 汉 语 译 文 |
|---|---|---|
| AC | alternating current | 交流电 |
| Ad. | adjustment | 调节 |
| Cal. | calibration | 校准 |
| DC | direct current | 直流电 |
| Dia. | diameter | 直径 |
| Eff. | efficiency | 效率 |
| GP | gauge pressure | 表压 |
| I/O | input and output | 输入和输出 |
| ipm | inches per minute | 英寸/每分钟 |
| rpm | revolutions per minute | 转数/每分钟 |
| Max | maximum | 最大 |
| Min | minimum | 最小 |
| Reg. | regulator | 调整器 |
| tem. | temperature | 温度 |
| L×W×H | Length×Width×Height | 长×宽×高 |

# Unit 7

# Ceremonial Address

Unit Objectives

In this unit you should

➢ familiarize yourself with the format of ceremonial address.

➢ have a good command of the basic words and useful expressions of ceremonial address in this unit.

➢ enable yourself to acquire the translating skills of the comparative sentences.

## ❓ Section 1   Theme Lead-in

**Read the following passage to gain a better understanding of this unit.**

A ceremony is an event of ritual significance, performed on a special occasion.

Ceremonial occasions: A ceremony may mark a rite of passage in a human life, marking the significance of, for example: birth (birthday), initiation (college orientation week), puberty, social adulthood (Bar (or Bat) Mitzvah), graduation, marriage, retirement, death (Day of the Dead), burial (funeral), spiritual (baptism, communion).

Government ceremonies: Sometimes, a ceremony may only be performed by a person with

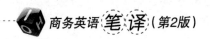

certain authority. For example, the opening of the United Kingdom Parliament is presided over by the Sovereign (Her Majesty Queen Elizabeth Ⅱ). A captain or a higher-ranked naval officer usually supervises the naming and launching of a warship. A wedding is performed by a priest or a Civil Celebrant, as in Australia. The President of the United States is customarily sworn in by the Chief Justice of the United States, and the British sovereign is always crowned by the Archbishop of Canterbury.

Celebration of events: Other, society-wide ceremonies may mark annual or seasonal or recurrent events such as: vernalequinox, winter solstice and other annual astronomical positions; weekly Sabbath day; inauguration of an elected office-holder; occasions in a liturgical year or "feasts" in a calendar of saints. Other ceremonies underscore the importance of non-regular special occasions, such as the coronation of a monarch; victory in battle. In some Asian cultures, ceremonies also play an important social role, for example the tea ceremony.

Process (Ceremonies may have a physical display or the atrical component): dance, a procession, the laying on of hands. A declaratory verbal pronouncement may explain or cap the occasion, for instance:

I now pronounce you man and wife.

I swear to serve and defend the nation...

I declare open the games of...

I/We dedicate this...to...

Both physical and verbal components of a ceremony may become part of a liturgy.

Address may refer to public speaking. It is the process of speaking to a group of people in a structured, deliberate manner intended to inform, influence, or entertain the listeners. It is closely allied to "presenting", although the latter has more of a commercial connotation.

## Section 2  Translation Warming-up

**A: Translate the following phrases and sentences into Chinese.**

1. look back on

2. I feel honored to...

3. last but not least

4. propose a toast

5. make joint efforts

6. on the occasion of

7. enduring friendship

8. look ahead/look into the future

9. It is with great pleasure that I extend a warm welcome to...

10. It is my great honor to declare the commencement of...

**B: Translate the following sentences into English.**

1. 为我们的友谊干杯!

2. 展望前程,我们信心百倍。

3. 祝各位来宾在中国生活愉快。

4. 为了我们的事业成功,干杯!

5. 愿你俩福星高照,幸福与日俱增。

6. 感谢大家在过去一年里对我工作的支持,我敬大家一杯。

7. 此时此刻,最能引起人们回顾既往,展望前程。

8. 现在,我愉快地宣布第二十二届万国邮政联盟大会开幕。

9. 首先,我谨代表中国政府,并以我个人的名义,对各位朋友的到来表示诚挚的欢迎!

10. 晚上好! 在这个美好的夜晚,很高兴同大家在这里相聚,参加 2021 年北京《财富》全球论坛开幕式。

## Section 3　Topic Features and Translation Principles

### 一、商务礼仪致词

商务礼仪,即商务人员在其商务交往中所应恪守的行为规范。商务礼仪的核心是一种行为的准则,用来约束日常商务活动的方方面面。商务礼仪的作用是为了体现人与人之间的相互尊重。

商务礼仪致词,是人们在社交场合用来表示礼节,以维系和发展人与人之间,人与组织群体之间,组织与组织之间相互关系的文书。

商务礼仪致词的类型:

(1) 欢迎词(客人在光临时,主人为表示热烈欢迎,在座谈会、宴会及酒会等发表的热情友好的讲话。)和欢送词(指行政机关、企事业单位、社会团体或个人在公共场合欢送友好团体回归或亲友出行时的致词。)

(2) 开幕词(指一些大型会议开始时由主持人或主要领导人所作的开宗明义的讲话。)和闭幕词(指大型会议在结束时由有关领导人或德高望重者所作的讲话。)

(3) 祝酒词(一般是指在开宴前说的一些调节气氛,诚挚敬祝的话语。不同场合有不同场合的祝酒词。)

(4) 贺词(指祝贺的词语。)

### 二、商务礼仪致词的翻译原则

商务礼仪致词的翻译要求译者有较强驾驭汉英两种语言的能力,有较为丰富的中外文化知识,同时掌握一些特定表达方式。翻译要遵循以下原则:

(1) 忠实原文、语言通顺、用词规范、简练、信息传递的等值准确是商务英语翻译所要遵循的基本标准。商务礼仪致词的翻译在大多数情况下做到准确、通白即可,有时根据不同的交流对象可将"信、达、雅"结合起来。

(2) 商务礼仪致词的译文选词要具有国际通用性,此外,商务礼仪致词属于商务范畴,有专业化特点,应尽量使用客观性语言和专用术语。比如,general average(共同海损),remittance(发票),foreign bill(国外汇票)和 inland bill(国内汇票)等。

对于致词中的各种组织名词也不要随意杜撰,最好遵从国际惯例名称。比如:World

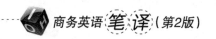
Trade Organization 世界贸易组织，World Intellectual Property Organization 世界知识产权组织，World Customs Organization 世界海关组织，World Business Council for Sustainable Development 促进可持续发展世界商业理事会，United Nations Information Centre 联合国新闻中心，United Nations Children's Fund 联合国儿童基金会。

（3）商务礼仪致词的译文根据不同类型的致词采用不同的规范用语，并做到简单易懂。比如，称呼的正确使用：Ladies and gentlemen 女士们、先生们；Distinguished/Honorable Guests 尊敬的各位来宾；Your /His/Her Majesty 陛下。

还要注意称呼语的翻译顺序，英语习惯上将重要人物的翻译放在前面。比如：Your Excellency Vice President and Mrs. Williams，Our distinguished guests，Ladies and gentlemen. 威廉副总统阁下及夫人，贵宾们、女士们、先生们。Honorable Leaders，Distinguished Guests，Dear Friends，Ladies and Gentlemen. 尊敬的各位领导、各位来宾、女士们、先生们、朋友们。

（4）商务礼仪致词可以采用一些套用句型进行翻译，这样更加规范和正式，体现商务礼仪致词的庄重性、典雅性、礼貌性和正式性。商务礼仪致词发表的场合多为正式会议和聚会，因而常规的套语较多，而且多用程式化的翻译。比如：It is my great honor to declare the commencement of...我非常荣幸地宣布……会议现在开始！On behalf of...and in my own name I would like to extend my warmest welcome to all the delegates and guests. I would also like to express my congratulations on the successful opening of the commencement of...我代表……，并以我个人的名义，向所有与会代表和来宾表示热烈的欢迎。祝贺这次……胜利召开。

（5）商务礼仪致词的译文要考虑中西文化差异，既要尊重译入语的民族文化，又要注重传递本民族独特的文化精髓信息，实现真正的中西文化交流，帮助推进商务活动。如，"爱屋及乌"不能译成"Love me，love my raven"，其中，"raven"应译为"dog"，因为"dog"比"raven"更受欢迎。

（6）礼仪致词中常用经典名句，尽量采用惯用的经典翻译。如若需要翻译，要注意：

① 以习语翻译习语。英语、汉语中有大量的习语，许多是形同意合或形虽异但意却相似的习语，这时采用以习语翻译习语的方法。如：谋事在人，成事在天。Man proposes，God disposes.

② 当无法找到对应习语时，采用直译法或意译法等翻译。如：独在异乡为异客，每逢佳节倍思亲。A lonely stranger in a strange land I am cast，I miss my family all the more on every festival day.

## Section 4　Translating Strategies, Samples and Training

### Translating Strategies

商务礼仪致词翻译常用到"比较句式"（the comparative sentences）的翻译。比较句是英语中比较普遍的句式。比较级的基本结构是"形容词或副词比较级＋than"，一般译为"比……更……"，在不同语境中大致存在以下几种主要含义和功能：

### 一、比较级表示差异

比较句式中最常见句式，表示比较双方的区别或差异。

**例句**

例 1. He can do a better job than his predecessor in controlling inflation.

在控制通货膨胀方面,他的工作比他的前任做得好。

例 2. We feel that culture is often a better solvent than state-to-state negotiations.

文化往往能够成为国家之间更好的融合剂。

例 3. The wise man draws more advantages from his enemies, than a fool from his friends.

智者从敌人处得利,多于愚人从朋友处获益。

例 4. Many dealers face the future with more confidences than they have exhibited in the past years.

许多经销商对未来的信心比过去几年更强了。

例 5. When foreign executives speak of their American counterparts, they are apt to be more scornful than awestruck.

当国外的经理们谈到他们的美国同行时,往往是轻蔑多于敬畏。

## 二、比较级表示同等

比较级与否定词搭配表示同一性,含义相当于原级比较。一般应用于"no+形容词(副词)比较级+than",可以翻译为"……一样+形容词(副词)的反义词(原级)"。

 **例句**

例 1. Mary is no more beautiful than her younger sister.

玛丽和她妹妹一样都不漂亮。

例 2. This opening ceremony is no more attractive than that one.

这次开幕式和那次的一样让人提不起兴趣来。

例 3. Nations are not to be judged by their size any more than individuals.

国家不能以大小而论,如同个人不能以大小而论一样。

例 4. The remainder of my schooldays were no more auspicious than the first.

后来在学校的日子跟第一天一样不顺心。

例 5. Nobody with any sense expects to find the whole truth in an advertisement any more than he expects a man applying for a job to describe his short-coming and more serious faults.

有头脑的人谁也不会指望广告里说的都是真的,同样也不指望申请工作的人会说出自己的缺点和严重过失。

## 三、比较级表示倾向

这种比较级通常是"more+形容词原级+than"结构或"less than"翻译为"与其说……不如说……"。

 **例句**

例 1. The president's speech is more encouraging than instructive to his people.

总统的致词对于人民来说与其说是一番教育，不如说是一种鼓励。

例 2. The audiences were less shocked than attracted by the speaker's speech.

观众们与其说对演讲感到吃惊，不如说是被演讲吸引了。

例 3. The greeting is not given so much for the public in the party as for the leaders at present.

这番祝词与其说是致参加晚会的所有人，倒不如说是致在场的领导。

例 4. Many difficulties in the country were due less to any ideology reasons than to nationalistic feelings.

那个国家的许多纠纷与其说是由意识形态造成的，不如说是由民族主义感情造成的。

例 5. The second reason for the amorphous nature of political parties in the United States is that each party is more interested in winning elections than in putting across a particular policy or law.

美国政党成分复杂的第二个原因是，每个政党所关心的与其说是要推行一项特定的政策或法律，不如说是要争取在选举中获胜。

## 四、比较级表示强调

这种比较级具有强调的意味。通常是 more than 放在一起表示"很"。

 例句

例 1. Medals will more than bring your honor.
奖牌不仅仅给人带来荣誉。

例 2. We are more than happy to hear of your visit to China next year.
听说您明年来华访问，我们无比高兴。

例 3. Reagan was more than cordial to Ford as they met for 65 minutes.
在六十五分钟的会谈中，里根对福特表现得格外亲切。

例 4. The excellent greeting by the president will more than excite the public.
总统的精彩祝词令在场民众无比兴奋。

例 5. May each hour be happy one on this special day. May the day ahead be more than happy, too, as all your dreams and plans work out just right for you.
祝你在这特殊的日子里，时时刻刻都充满快乐，祝你来日多福，捷报频传！

### Translating Samples

## 一、欢迎词

欢迎词，是指客人光临时，主人为表示热烈的欢迎，在座谈会、宴会、酒会等场合发表的热情友好的讲话。

例句

例 1. Your Excellency Vice President and Mrs Williams, Our distinguished guests, ladies and gentlemen.

威廉斯副总统阁下及夫人，贵宾们、女士们、先生们。

例 2. Honorable Leaders, Distinguished Guests, Dear Friends, Ladies and Gentlemen.

尊敬的各位领导、各位来宾、女士们、先生们、朋友们。

例 3. Toast by Chinese President Xi Jinping at the Welcoming Banquet of the Olympic Winter Games Beijing 2022：

It gives me great pleasure to meet so many old and new friends in Beijing as the Chinese people celebrate the Spring Festival, the start of the lunar new year. Let me begin by extending, on behalf of the Chinese government and people, and in the name of my wife and myself, a warm welcome to all the distinguished guests travelling to China and attending the Olympic Winter Games Beijing 2022.

习近平主席在北京 2022 年冬奥会欢迎宴会上的致词：

在中国人民欢度新春佳节的喜庆日子里，同各位新老朋友在北京相聚，我感到十分高兴。首先，我代表中国政府和中国人民，代表我的夫人，并以我个人的名义，对来华出席北京冬奥会的各位嘉宾，表示热烈的欢迎！

例 4. Welcoming Remarks by President Richard C. Levin of Yale University to Chinese President Hu Jintao：

Mr. President, it is my pleasure to extend a warm welcome to you and Mrs. Liu on behalf of our entire community. We are deeply honored that you have chosen to visit Yale.

耶鲁大学理查德·莱文校长对胡锦涛所作的欢迎词：

主席先生，我高兴地代表耶鲁大学的全体师生向您表示热烈欢迎。对您特意造访耶鲁，我们深感荣幸。

## 二、开幕词

开幕词是在重要会议或重大活动开始时，为会议主持人或主要领导人讲话所用的文稿。开幕词的主要特点是宣告性和引导性。不论召开什么重要会议，或开展什么重要活动，按照惯例，一般都要由主持人或主要领导人致开幕词，这是一个必不可少的程序，标志着会议或活动的正式开始。开幕词通常要阐明会议或活动的性质、宗旨、任务、要求和议程安排等，集中体现了大会或活动的指导思想，起着定调的作用，对引导会议或活动朝着既定的正确方向顺利进行，保证会议或活动的圆满成功，有着重要的意义。

 例句

例 1. In this beautiful spring season, the Eighth Investment and Trade Forum for Cooperation between East and West China is grandly opened today.

在这春意盎然的美好时节，第八届中国东西部合作与投资贸易洽谈会于今天隆重开幕了。

例 2. Let us wish the Eighth Investment and Trade Forum for Cooperation between East and West China a complete success! Thank you all!

让我们共同预祝第八届中国东西部合作与投资洽谈会取得圆满成功！谢谢大家！

例 3. It is my great honor to declare the commencement of... I would also like to express my congratulations on the successful opening of the conference in Beijing... I wish the conference a complete success.

我非常荣幸地宣布……会议现在开幕！祝贺这次会议在北京胜利召开。……预祝大会圆满成功！

例 4. Remarks at the Opening Ceremony of the 17th China-ASEAN Expo and China-ASEAN Business and Investment Summit：

As the 17th China-ASEAN Expo（CAEXPO）and China-ASEAN Business and Investment Summit（CABIS）open today，I wish to extend，on behalf of the Chinese government and people and also in my own name，a hearty welcome and warm greetings to all the guests attending in person or via the Internet.

习近平主席在 2020 年第十七届中国—东盟博览会开幕式上致词：

值此第十七届中国—东盟博览会、中国—东盟商务与投资峰会开幕之际，我谨代表中国政府和中国人民，并以我个人的名义，对参加本次大会的线上线下所有嘉宾，表示热烈的欢迎和诚挚的问候！

## 三、闭幕词

闭幕词与开幕词一样，具有简明性和口语化两个共同特点，其种类与开幕词相同。凡重要会议或重要活动，与开幕词相对应，一般都有闭幕词，这是一道必不可少的程序，标志着整个会议或活动的结束。闭幕词通常要对会议或活动作出正确的评估和总结，充分肯定会议或活动所取得的成果，强调会议或活动的主要精神和深远影响，激励有关人员宣传会议或活动的精神实质和贯彻落实有关的决议或倡议。

 例句

例 1. And now I have to mark the end of this unforgettable Olympic experience：I declare the 24th Olympic Winter Games Beijing 2022 closed.

In accordance with tradition，I call upon the youth of the world to assemble four years from now in Milano Cortina，Italy，to celebrate with all of us，the 25th Olympic Winter Games.

现在我不得不为这段令人难忘的奥运经历画上句号。我宣布北京 2022 年第二十四届冬季奥林匹克运动会闭幕。

按照奥林匹克传统，我号召全世界青年四年之后在意大利米兰-科尔蒂纳丹佩佐相聚，与我们一起参加第二十五届冬季奥林匹克运动会。

例 2. It gives me great pleasure to attend the Conference Marking the 60th Anniversary of the China-Russia Diplomatic Relations and the Closing Ceremony of the "Year of the Russian Language" in China together with my old friend Prime Minister Putin.

很高兴同老朋友普京总理一起,出席中俄建交 60 周年庆祝大会暨中国"俄语年"闭幕式。

例 3. President Obama's Closing Remarks at the Nuclear Security Summit：

Good afternoon, everybody. We have just concluded an enormously productive day.

I said this morning that today would be an opportunity for our nations, both individually and collectively, to make concrete commitments and take tangible steps to secure nuclear materials so they never fall into the hands of terrorists who would surely use them.

This evening, I can report that we have seized this opportunity, and because of the steps we've taken—as individual nations and as an international community —the American people will be safer and the world will be more secure.

美国总统奥巴马发表核峰会闭幕词：

大家好。我们刚刚结束了成就斐然的一天。

我在上午说过,今天我们各国面临一个机会,可以分别和共同作出具体承诺和采取明确措施,确保核材料的安全,防止核材料落入那些无疑会利用它们的恐怖主义分子手中。

今晚,我可以这么说,我们成功地把握了这一机遇,作为具体的国家和国际社会,我们已经采取了措施,美国人民将因此更安全,世界将更稳定。

例 4. Speech by International Olympic Committee（IOC）President Thomas Bach at the Closing Ceremony of the Olympic Winter Games Beijing 2022：

Over the past 16 days, we admired your outstanding performances.

Each and every one of you strived to achieve your personal best. We were deeply touched how you were wishing and cheering for your competitors to achieve their best as well.

You not only respected each other. You supported each other. You embraced each other, even if your countries are divided by conflict.

国际奥委会主席巴赫在 2022 年北京冬奥会闭幕式上的致词：

在过去 16 天里,我对你们的出色表现钦佩不已。

你们每一个人都力争取得最佳成绩,但你们也希望竞争对手取得最佳成绩,并为他们加油。我们为此深受感动。

你们不仅彼此尊重,还相互支持,即使有的地方因为冲突而对立,但你们彼此拥抱。

## 四、祝酒词

祝酒词是在酒席宴会的开始,主人表示热烈欢迎、亲切问候、诚挚感谢,客人进行答谢并表示衷心的祝愿的应酬之词。是招待宾客的一种礼仪形式。祝酒词其内容以叙述友谊为主,一般篇幅短小,文辞庄重、热情、得体、大方,是很流行的一种演讲文体。

 例句

例 1. I now propose a toast to the friendship between our two people—to our friendship.

现在,我提议为我们两国人民的友谊干杯！

例 2. On the occasion of the New Year, may my wife and I extend to you and yours our

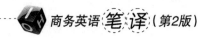

warmest greetings, wishing you a happy New Year, your career greater success and your family happiness.

在此新年之际，我同夫人向你及你的家人致以节日的问候，并祝你们新年快乐、事业有成、家庭幸福。

例3. In that spirit, I ask all of you present to join me in raising your glasses to Chairman Mao, to Prime Minister Chou, and to the friendship of the Chinese and American people which can lead to friendship and peace for all people in the world.

本着这种精神，我请求诸位同我一起举杯，为毛主席，为周总理，为能够带来全世界所有人民的友谊与和平的中国人民和美国人民之间的友谊，干杯。（美国尼克松总统1972年访华时的一次祝酒词）

例4. Toast by Chinese President Xi Jinping at the Welcoming Banquet of the Olympic Winter Games Beijing 2022：

Ladies and Gentlemen,

Friends,

To borrow a Chinese poetic line, "Out goes the old year with the sound of firecrackers; in comes the new with the warmth of wine and spring breeze." China has just entered the Year of the Tiger according to the lunar calendar. Tiger is a symbol of strength, courage and fearlessness. I wish all Olympic athletes excellent performance with the strength of the tiger. I am confident that with the joint efforts of us all, Beijing 2022 will surely go down in history as a streamlined, safe and splendid Olympic Games.

To conclude, I propose a toast：

To the dynamic development of the Olympic Movement；

To humanity's noble cause of peace and development； and

To the health of all distinguished guests and your families.

Cheers！

习近平在北京2022年冬奥会欢迎宴会上的致词：

女士们、先生们、朋友们！

"爆竹声中一岁除，春风送暖入屠苏。"中国刚刚迎来农历虎年。虎象征着力量、勇敢、无畏，祝愿奥运健儿像虎一样充满力量、创造佳绩。我相信，在大家共同努力下，北京冬奥会一定会成为简约、安全、精彩的奥运盛会而载入史册。

最后，我提议，大家共同举杯，

为国际奥林匹克运动蓬勃发展，

为人类和平与发展的崇高事业，

为各位嘉宾和家人的健康，

干杯！

## 五、贺词

单位、团体或个人应邀参加某一重大会议或活动时，常常要即时发表讲话，表达对主人的祝贺、感谢之意，这番话就称为贺词。贺词是祝贺喜庆之事的一类应用文。以函件形式送达的贺词通常叫作贺信,借助电报发出的贺词通常称作贺电。贺信、贺电都是贺词,贺年片也属贺词范畴。

 **例句**

例 1. I want to send my best wishes to people in China, the United Kingdom and around the world who are celebrating the Chinese New Year.

我想对在中国、英国以及全世界正要欢度中国农历春节的人们致以我最美好的祝福。(英国首相卡梅伦 2011 年中国农历春节致词)

例 2. I wish you all, wherever you may be, a very happy Christmas.

不论你们现时身在何处,我都祝愿你们圣诞快乐。

例 3. Statement by Secretary Clinton on Anniversary of the Founding of People's Republic of China:

I would like to extend warm wishes and congratulations to the People's Republic of China on the 60th anniversary of its founding on October 1. In the last 30 years, China has undergone an extraordinary economic transformation, lifting millions of people out of poverty. This is truly an historic accomplishment.

希拉里·克林顿庆祝新中国成立 60 周年贺词:

值此 10 月 1 日中华人民共和国成立 60 周年之际,我谨向中华人民共和国致以热诚的祝愿和道贺。近 30 年来,中国经历了不凡的经济转型,千百万人民摆脱了贫困。这简直是具有历史意义的成就。

例 4. Xi Jinping's 2021 New Year address:

Comrades, friends, ladies and gentlemen, greetings to you all!

The year 2021 is arriving. From China's capital Beijing, I extend my New Year wishes to you all!

2020 was an extraordinary year. Facing the sudden coronavirus pandemic, we put people and their lives first to interpret the great love among humans. With solidarity and resilience, we wrote the epic of our fight against the pandemic.

国家主席习近平发表二〇二一年新年贺词:

大家好! 2021 年的脚步越来越近,我在北京向大家致以新年的美好祝福!

2020 年是极不平凡的一年。面对突如其来的新冠肺炎疫情,我们以人民至上、生命至上诠释了人间大爱,用众志成城、坚忍不拔书写了抗疫史诗。

## Translating Training

**A: Translate the following ceremonial address into Chinese.**

1. When the great way is followed, all under heaven will be equal.

2. Xi'an was perhaps the most open and culturally advanced city in the entire world.

3. I look forward to seeing the Terracotta Warriors, the old city walls, and the Muslim quarter.

4. Here in this city of your magnificent history we must always remember that we too are

ancestors.

5. The steps we take over the next week can lead to far greater strides for our people in the years ahead.

6. Distinguished guests, Ladies and gentlemen, Friends, It gives me great pleasure to meet friends, both old and new, at the Boao Forum for Asia Annual Conference 2019 in Hainan. I would like to extend, on behalf of the Chinese government, warm congratulations on the opening of the conference and sincere welcome to all the guests coming from afar. (李克强总理 2019 年在博鳌亚洲论坛年会开幕式上的主旨演讲)

7. I am pleased to join you online for the 19th Meeting of the Council of Heads of Government of Member States of the Shanghai Cooperation Organization (SCO). I wish to thank our host for the preparations it has made for this meeting. [李克强总理 2020 年在上合组织成员国政府首脑(总理)理事会第 19 次会议上的讲话]

8. I want to close by once again expressing my sincere appreciation to President Hu and Premier Wen and to the Chinese delegation for their leadership and hospitality. (美国财政部长盖特纳在中美战略与经济对话闭幕式上的讲话)

9. It gives me great pleasure to attend this meeting. I thank Prime Minister Ardern and the New Zealand government for their great efforts to make the meeting possible. (习近平 2021 年在亚太经合组织领导人非正式会议上的讲话)

10. On the occasion of this New Year's Eve of national celebration, and on behalf of all my colleagues of the company, I wish to thank all the guests here for their gracious presence at this Spring Festival gathering.

11. Thank you. Good morning. It is a great honor to welcome you to the first meeting of the Strategic Economic Dialogue between the United States and China. This is an essential step in advancing a positive, constructive, and comprehensive relationship between our countries. (奥巴马在美中战略与经济对话上致开幕词)

12. Sustained stability and development in East Asia has not come easy, and must be cherished and preserved by all of us. China will enhance mutual trust, maintain candid dialogue and deepen cooperation with EAS participating countries and work tirelessly for a bright future of the region and for the well-being of our peoples. (2020 年李克强总理在第 15 届东亚峰会上的讲话)

13. I'm pleased to congratulate China on the opening of the Shanghai Expo, a major event in the world this year and one that will allow Americans and Chinese to continue to get to know each other on the deeper and broader basis. (美国驻中国大使发表电视致词祝贺上海世博会开幕)

14. Spanning five-plus months from balmy spring to golden autumn, the International Horticultural Exhibition 2019 Beijing China is now drawing to a successful close. On behalf of the Chinese government and people, I wish to express warm congratulations on the success of the Expo and heartfelt appreciation to friends from across the world for their support and participation. (李克强总理在 2019 年北京世园会闭幕式上的讲话)

15. Today, I'm very pleased to be with my new and old friends to attend the Sino-European

Economic Forum jointly hosted by the University of International Business and Economics and the China Association of International Trade…Hereby, I'd like to wish this Sino-EU Economic Forum a complete success.(中欧经济论坛开幕词)

**B：Translate the following ceremonial address into English.**

1. 朋友们,让我们共同努力,开创新世纪中欧经贸合作的美好未来。

2. 我非常高兴有机会出席这次欧中贸协与比中经贸理事会联合举行的午餐报告会。

3. 加入世界贸易组织,是中国对外开放和现代化建设进程中具有历史性意义的一件大事。

4. 近年来,面对世界经济贸易增长缓慢,中国政府继续实施积极的财政政策和稳健的货币政策。

5. 谢谢德威特主席热情洋溢的欢迎词,感谢欧中贸协和比中经贸理事会的盛情邀请和热情款待。

6. 首先,我谨代表中国政府和中国人民,并以我个人的名义,对远道而来的各位嘉宾,表示热烈的欢迎! 对支持和参与北京世界园艺博览会的各国朋友,表示衷心的感谢! （习近平在 2019 年北京世界园艺博览会开幕式上的讲话）

7. 很高兴与各位专家学者再次相聚,共同盘点今年的国际形势与中国外交。首先,我要对大家长期以来对外交工作的关心支持表示感谢,也真诚欢迎大家继续为中国外交提出真知灼见。（王毅在 2021 年国际形势与中国外交研讨会上的演讲）

8. 祝贺参加 2022 年冬奥会、冬残奥会的每一位奥运选手和残奥选手! 奥林匹克精神包含着热爱和平、相互尊重、相互理解。年轻的参赛者们就体现了这些品质,你们激励着我们所有人。我热切希望这种精神远远超越本届冬奥会、冬残奥会,提醒包括参赛者和观众在内的每一个人：我们同属于人类大家庭! （古特雷斯 2022 年北京冬奥会致词）

9. 值此联合国亚太经社会成立 75 周年之际,很高兴出席今天的会议,同大家一起回顾亚太经社会走过的不平凡道路,共同展望亚太地区未来前景。（2022 年王毅在联合国亚太经社会第 78 届年会开幕式上的讲话）

10. 现在,我提议：为举办一届成功、精彩、难忘的世博会,为世界各国人民的团结和友谊,为人类文明发展进步,为各位嘉宾和家人身体健康,干杯! （胡锦涛在上海世博会欢迎晚宴上的祝酒词）

11. 今天,我们怀着喜悦的心情,在这里隆重集会,庆祝香港回归祖国 20 周年,举行香港特别行政区第五届政府就职典礼。（习近平主席在庆祝香港回归祖国 20 周年大会暨香港特别行政区第五届政府就职典礼上的讲话）

12. 很高兴参加青海藏毯国际展览会开幕式,在此,我代表中国商务部,对展览会的召开表示热烈的祝贺,对参展参会的国内外客商表示诚挚的欢迎! ……最后,祝青海藏毯国际展览会圆满成功! （青海藏毯国际展览会开幕式致词）

13. 很高兴与大家再次相聚在美丽的大连。首先,我谨代表中国政府,对第十三届夏季达沃斯论坛的召开,表示热烈祝贺! 对远道而来的各位嘉宾和媒体界朋友,表示诚挚欢迎! （李克强在 2019 第十三届夏季达沃斯论坛开幕式上的致词）

14. 我在联合国,和大家一起迎接新年。我们带着不确定性和不安全感进入 2020 年。

不平等持续存在,仇恨情绪日益高涨。世界在交战,地球在变暖。气候变化既是长期问题,更是实实在在的近期危险。气候变化不断加剧,我们不能事不关己高高挂起。但是,我们也要看到希望。(联合国秘书长古特雷斯 2020 年新年致词)

15. 很高兴应邀出席伊斯兰合作组织外长会开幕式并致词,这是中国外长首次参加伊斯兰合作组织外长会,充分体现了中国和伊斯兰世界加强交流合作的真诚愿望,必将推动双方关系迈上新台阶。(王毅在 2022 年伊斯兰合作组织外长会开幕式上的致词)

## Section 5　Extensive Expression

### 一、礼仪祝词

| | |
|---|---|
| 1. address of welcome/greeting | 欢迎词 |
| 2. opening speech/address | 开幕词 |
| 3. closing speech/address | 闭幕词 |
| 4. toast | 祝酒词 |
| 5. congratulatory address/speech of congratulation | 贺词 |

### 二、称谓

| | |
|---|---|
| 1. ladies and gentlemen | 女士们,先生们 |
| 2. distinguished guests | 贵宾们 |
| 3. Your Majesty | 陛下 |
| 4. Your Majesty Queen | 女王殿下 |
| 5. Excellency/Honor | 阁下 |
| 6. Your Excellency President | 总统阁下 |
| 7. Your Excellency Mr. Ambassador | 大使先生阁下 |
| 8. Your Honor Mr. Mayor | 市长先生阁下 |
| 9. Respected/Respectable/Honorable | 尊敬的 |
| 10. Respected Mr. Minister | 尊敬的部长先生 |

### 三、会议

| | |
|---|---|
| 1. ministerial meeting | 部长级会议 |
| 2. Senior Officials Meeting（SOM） | 高官会 |
| 3. forum | 论坛 |
| 4. annual | 年会 |
| 5. fair | 洽谈会 |
| 6. celebration | 庆典 |
| 7. summit（meeting） | 首脑会议 |
| 8. trade fair | 商品交易会 |
| 9. world expo | 世博会 |
| 10. tea party | 茶会 |

| 11. state banquet | 国宴 |
| 12. welcoming banquet | 欢迎宴会 |
| 13. farewell meeting | 欢送会 |
| 14. wedding reception | 结婚宴会 |
| 15. cocktail party | 鸡尾酒会 |

## 四、惯用短语

| 1. exchange views | 交换意见 |
| 2. reach consensus | 达成共识 |
| 3. frequent exchange of visits | 频繁互访 |
| 4. a wonderful time | 良辰佳时 |
| 5. all my colleagues | 全体同仁 |
| 6. bilateral relationships | 双边关系 |
| 7. official invitation | 正式邀请 |
| 8. envoy of friendship | 友好使者 |
| 9. renew one's old friendships | 再叙旧情 |
| 10. establish new contacts | 结交新朋 |
| 11. feel reluctant to part | 恋恋不舍 |
| 12. in the common interest of | 符合……共同利益 |
| 13. remain in my memory forever | 永远留在我心中 |
| 14. cutting the ribbon at an opening ceremony | 开幕式剪彩 |
| 15. in a cordial and friendly atmosphere | 在热情友好的气氛中 |
| 16. take the time off one's busy schedule | 拨冗光临 |
| 17. promote understanding and friendship | 增进理解与友谊 |
| 18. friends from a distant | 远道而来的朋友 |
| 19. establishment of diplomatic relations between | 建交 |
| 20. in the persistent pursuit of | 一贯奉行 |

# Unit *8*

# Business Correspondence (I)

Unit Objectives

In this unit you should

➢ familiarize yourself with the format of business correspondence.

➢ master the basic words and useful expressions of business correspondence.

➢ have a good command of the translating skills of the transformation of parts of speech.

## ❷ Section 1   Theme Lead-in

**Read the following passage to gain a better understanding of this unit.**

Despite the constant use and popularity of the telephone, telex, short messages on the mobile phones, chatting on the Internet, letters continue to be written in millions. Why is this so? Why have letters retained their importance in an age of electrical and electronic communication? We shall find the answers if we study some ideas that we associate with letters as a means of communication in business.

1. A letter gives the writer time for reflection. The writer has time to work out exactly what he

wishes to say and to make a draft of his letter. While looking at his draft or his final letter the writer sees precisely what the reader will see and he has time to consider the impression that his words will make on the reader. On the other hand, when people contact on the phone, they may expect an immediate or at least a quick response, thus putting both parties under pressure.

2. A letter gives the writer an opportunity to state things at length. Although we should avoid wordiness in writing letters, we are justified in giving full details and even in repeating ourselves in order to assist the reader in contract to compressing our message to avoid some details while using the phone.

3. A letter has the advantage over a telephone call that it can be read an unlimited number of times. It is, moreover, the sender's own words and not the recipient's record of the sender's words that are read again and again. By contrast, while making a telephone call, we may ask the speaker to repeat some certain words or sentences, but asking a person to repeat many words would provoke embarrassment.

4. Letters provide both the sender and the addressee with a definite permanent record of what has been communicated.

5. Letters have a degree of authority that telephone messages do not have. Whether people are making or receiving a telephone call, they feel that what is said on the telephone has not the weight that it would have if it were put into writing. They feel that something "in black and white" with a signature attached to it has more weight and authority than spoken words have.

6. Letters can be sent to small businesses, householders and other private correspondents that have no telex machines.

7. A letter is read when the recipient decides that it is convenient to read it.

8. A letter may reach a "difficult" person who will not accept a telephone call or a visit by the writer.

9. Letters provide a degree of confidentiality that the telephone and the telex cannot provide.

10. Statements of account and length tables of statistics are not things that can be sent conveniently or confidentially by telephone or by telex but they can be sent easily as part of a letter or as an enclosure.

11. Letters provide a means of promoting goodwill.

12. Letters may be cheaper than international telephone call and telex messages.

## Section 2   Translation Warming-up

A: Translate the following sentences into Chinese, paying attention to the underlined parts.

1. No <u>admittance</u> except on business.

2. Some new workshops are under <u>construction</u>.

3. No <u>violation</u> of this principle can be tolerated.

4. He is a <u>stranger</u> to international trade in this area.

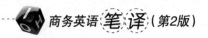

5. We have much <u>pleasure</u> in enclosing a quotation sheet for our products.

6. We place the <u>highest</u> value on our friendly relationship with your company.

7. The 30-year long cooperation between the two companies is <u>over</u> due to the war.

8. Be <u>through</u> with the discussion about all the details before the contract is signed.

9. Your quotation should be <u>attractive</u> to the buyers if you want to push the sale of your skirts successfully.

10. As our market is now somewhat <u>dull</u> and prices are generally low, you are very fortunate in making purchases at this time.

**B：Translate the following sentences into English，paying attention to the underlined parts.**

1. 这家公司<u>由于</u>管理不善而<u>破产</u>。

2. 他们<u>满足于</u>去年的进出口统计数据。

3. 他们说他们不敢<u>肯定</u>能按时发货。

4. 我们在工作中非常<u>注意</u>理论联系实际。

5. 经济指数显示，30 余年的改革至今是<u>成功</u>的。

6. 只有研究这些材料的特性才能<u>更好地</u>利用它们。

7. 设计的<u>目</u>的在于<u>自动操作</u>、<u>调节方便</u>、<u>维护容易</u>。

8. 认真<u>研究</u>目标市场将给我们的生意带来巨大的好处。

9. 价格<u>不变</u>，则一类商品的供应数量与其所获利润<u>成正比例</u>。

10. 有关不合格材料的索赔问题必须在<u>货到</u>后 60 天内予以解决。

## Section 3　Topic Features and Translation Principles

### 一、商务信函的类型

**1. 与销售有关的信函（Sales Related Letters）**

（1）建立客户关系；（2）询盘、报盘、还盘；（3）订单；（4）订单确认函；（5）销售函；（6）催款函；（7）筹款函；（8）涨价/降价通知；（9）确定支付方式函；（10）信用证；（11）包装要求；（12）装运指示；（13）保险；（14）投诉、索赔和理赔；（15）合同；（16）促销推广函

**2. 与职业相关的信函（Employment Related Letters）**

（1）推荐信；（2）求职信；（3）简历；（4）简历的附件；（5）面试通知；（6）录用通知；（7）工作拒收函；（8）加薪请求函；（9）辞职信；（10）接受辞职函

**3. 其他商务信函（Other Business Letters）**

（1）邀请函；（2）贺信；（3）感谢信；（4）道歉信；（5）备忘录；（6）会议通知；（7）会议记录；（8）日程表；（9）电子邮件

### 二、商务信函的句式特点

**1. 句子类型特点**

在四种句式(陈述句、疑问句、祈使句和感叹句)当中，商务信函主要使用陈述句。祈使

句表示请求、劝告、命令等,用祈使句可避免生硬刻板,比陈述句更有礼貌。

 **例句**

例 1. Please look into the matter at once and let us have your definite reply by cable without any further delay.

请立即调查此事,并尽快电告确切答复。

疑问句也可用来表达写信人的观点或向对方提议,疑问句给对方留有更大的余地,更有礼貌,它的使用频率比祈使句相对要多,如:

例 2. Would you please send us a copy of your catalogue?

能否向我公司邮寄一份贵公司的产品目录?

感叹句虽然可以渲染气氛、增强语势,但与商务函电讲求客观、严谨的文体不符,因此感叹句在商务函电中极少使用。

**2. 句子结构特点**

在简单句、并列句和复合句中,商务函电中采用大量的并列句和复合句。

简单句结构简单、简洁明快;复合句则结构复杂,表达完备周密。为了保证考究的句式和严密的逻辑性,英语函电往往需要将连续的短句结合成一个独立的主从复合句或并列句。商务函电对严谨和简洁都有要求,目的在于追求准确严谨的语言风格,因此复合句的使用虽普遍,但不排斥简单句的使用。

常用并列结构:用 and 连接并列结构,使表达更精确。

 **例句**

例 3. This contract is made by and between the two parties.

双方签订本合同。

也常用 or 引导的选择性并列结构,使内容更严谨全面。

 **例句**

例 4. Any dispute arising from the execution of, or in connection with the agreement, shall be settled through friendly consultations between the two parties.

在本合同执行中引起的或与本合同有关的争议应由双方通过友好协商解决。

状语位置独特:商务函电中,由 if,when,in case 等引导的较长的状语经常出现在主谓语之间,一般文体的主谓语间不放长状语。

 **例句**

例 5. The Contractor shall, if called upon to do so, enter into and execute the Contract, to be prepared and completed at the cost of the employer, in the form annexed to these conditions with such modification as may be necessary.

在被邀签约时,承包人应同意签订并履行合同,该合同由业主按照本合同条件所附格式拟定,如有必要可对其进行修改。该合同的拟定和签订费用由业主承担。

### 3. 句子语气特点

在陈述语气、祈使语气和虚拟语气中,除了普遍使用的陈述语气之外,商务函电中还大量地使用虚拟语气。

虚拟语气可表示主观愿望和假想虚拟的情况,并可使语气委婉,谓语由 should,would,could,might 等加动词原形构成。在英语函电中,大量使用情态动词,可以准确表达写信人的预测、能力、允诺等语气和态度,也可以表现出写信人的礼貌。

 **例句**

例 6. We sincerely hope that the incident would not do harm to the friendly relationship between us and hope that this matter might be settled satisfactorily.

我方真诚地希望此事件不会影响我们之间的友好关系,并希望此事能得到圆满的解决。

## 三、商务信函翻译的原则

商务英语信函翻译的原则——准确规范、功能对等。准确不仅指用词、用句和语言结构上的准确,还包括对信函内容的准确把握;规范指译文必须符合本行业的专业规范。

（1）准确理解各种术语、外来词汇、套语和习惯表达的专业含义和固定译法,尽量保留原文风格,译成符合译入语商务语言规范的术语或套语。

 **例句**

例 1. The duplicate shipping documents including bill of lading, invoice, packing list and inspection certification were airmailed to you today.

包括提货单、发票、装箱单和检验证书在内的装运单证副本今日已航邮贵处。

例 2. We are looking forward to a favorable reply.

静候贵方佳音。

（2）了解词汇的特定含义,如: discharge 可作名词或动词,一般为"卸货",但要分场合,试看下面几个句子当中 discharge 的不同翻译。

 **例句**

例 3. Party A agrees that the expiration of this license shall not discharge party B from its obligation.

甲方同意在许可证到期时并不免除乙方应尽的义务。

例 4. Party B shall check the quality of each discharge in accordance with the contract.

乙方应按合同规定检查发出的每批货物的质量。

（3）正确理解原文结构,厘清全文的句法结构和逻辑关系。

例句

例 5. Routine duties of the Joint Venture Company are to be discharged by the general manager appointed by the Board of Directors.

董事会任命的总经理负责履行合资公司的日常职权。

例 6. The goods we received contrary to our instructions are packed in wooden cases without iron hoops.

收到的货物是包装在没有铁箍的木箱里,而这种包装和我们的指示不符。

## Section 4   Translating Strategies, Samples and Training

### ✔ Translating Strategies

#### 词类转换

词类转换(transformation of parts of speech)是商务信函翻译中的重要手段之一,其最显著的作用就是使译文更加通顺、流畅、自然,符合译入语在语言结构和表达上的习惯。因此,在翻译商务信函时,应该按照上下文意念的表达需要,进行词类性质的转换。商务信函互译中常见的此类转换现象包括:名词与动词的转换,介词与动词的转换,形容词与动词的转换,以及名词与副词、名词与形容词、副词与形容词之间的转换等。

汉语是一种动词显著的语言,在汉语句式中动词的使用频率大大超过英语,因此,英译汉的词类转换最重要的一项就是将英语的各种词类转换成汉语的动词;相反,在汉译英中,为了使译文符合英语的表达习惯,就要将汉语中的大量动词转换为名词、形容词、介词、副词等。当然,在英汉互译中也有反过来的情况,即英语的动词转译成汉语的名词等。

#### 一、动词与名词的转换

这种转换包括:(1)英语的名词转译成汉语的动词;(2)英语作名词用的不定式短语转译成汉语的动词短语;(3)英语作名词用的动名词转译成汉语的动词短语。

 例句

例 1. The operation of a machine needs some knowledge of its performance.
操作机器需要懂得机器的一些性能。

例 2. To sum up experience in the international trade with other countries consciously is of great importance.
认真总结与他国国际贸易中的经验十分重要。

例 3. We should appreciate your paying the bill without delay.
如从速结清货款,当不胜感激。

英语中的动词也有被转译成汉语名词的情况。

例 4. Our company has prepared meticulously for the coming negotiation.

我们公司已经为即将举行的谈判做了周密的准备。

例 5. This product differs from that one in that the former is of better quality.

这个产品与那个产品的不同点在于前者的质量好一些。

## 二、介词与动词的转换

介词在英语中使用非常多,是一种异常活跃的词类。有些介词本身就具有动词的特性,这就是翻译中英语介词和汉语动词经常发生转换的原因。

 **例句**

例 1. Your ad in today's *China Daily* interests us.

对你们刊登在今天《中国日报》上的广告,我们很感兴趣。

例 2. We are in hope of some allowance on your quoted prices.

我方希望贵方能对你方的报价做些减让。

例 3. The irregularly shaped parts of that machine can be washed very clean by ultrasonic waves.

用超声波把这台机器中形状不规则的部件洗得十分干净。

例 4. We learn from the Internet that your firm is in the line of silk dresses, and would like to establish a business relationship with you.

从网络获悉贵公司经营真丝裙,现愿与贵公司建立业务关系。

例 5. We usually pack each piece of men's T-shirt in a poly bag, a dozen to a box and 10 boxes to a wooden case.

我方通常把一件男 T 恤衫装入一个塑料袋内,一打装入一盒,十盒装入一个木箱子。

## 三、形容词与动词的转换

英语中许多形容词,尤其是表示心理状态的形容词用作表语时,往往转译成汉语动词;同样,汉语中表示知觉、情感等心理状态的动词,往往可以转译成英语的形容词,构成英语的系表结构。

 **例句**

例 1. We are grateful to you for having offered us the information about your local market.
对于贵方所提供当地市场之信息,我方深表谢意。

例 2. We are willing to make you a firm offer at this price.
我方愿意以此价格向贵方报实盘。

例 3. 他们不知道包装上有破损。
They are not aware of the damage in the packing.

例 4. 我方为货物的安全运输担忧。
We are anxious about the shipping safety of the goods.

例 5. This offer is based on an <u>expanding</u> market and is <u>competitive</u>.

此报盘着眼于<u>扩大</u>销路而且<u>有竞争性</u>。

## 四、名词与副词、形容词之间的转换

英语中的有些名词,尤其是抽象名词,汉译时常转译为形容词或副词;汉译英时,由于语法结构和修辞上的需要,也常把汉语的一些形容词或副词转译成英语的名词。

 例句

例 1. It is our great <u>pleasure</u> to note that your company is developing vigorously.

我们十分<u>高兴</u>地注意到贵公司正在蓬勃地发展。

例 2. You should consider the <u>safety</u> of sending the goods by sea.

贵方应考虑海运这批货物是否<u>安全</u>。

例 3. We have found <u>difficulty</u> in entertaining your claim.

我们发现<u>难</u>以满足贵方的索赔。

例 4. 产品的价格具有竞争力是十分<u>必要的</u>。

The competitiveness in the prices of the products is of vital <u>necessity</u>.

例 5. 我们觉得解决这个问题非常<u>重要</u>。

We felt great <u>importance</u> in solving this problem.

## 五、形容词与副词之间的转换

形容词与副词之间的转译多与其他词类转译同时进行,比如名词转译成动词后,原来修饰名词的形容词即转译成副词;动词(或形容词)转译成名词后,原修饰动词(或形容词)的副词即转译成形容词。

 例句

例 1. Your performance at the negotiation impressed us <u>deeply</u>.

贵方在谈判中的表现给我方留下了<u>深刻的</u>印象。

例 2. The new products of your company interested us <u>tremendously</u>.

我方对贵公司的新产品有<u>浓厚的</u>兴趣。

例 3. This washing machine is <u>mainly</u> characterized by its water-saving design and elegant appearance.

这台洗衣机的<u>主要</u>特点是它的节水设计和优雅的外观。

例 4. 如该产品符合我方的标准,我方将<u>大量</u>订货。

If this product is of the standard we require, we will place a <u>substantial</u> order.

例 5. 中国出口贸易额<u>持续</u>增加已导致了一些主要的发达国家<u>不断</u>要求中国货币升值。

A <u>continuous</u> increase in the trade volume of China's exports has led to a <u>continuous</u> demand from some major developed countries of the increase in the value of China's currency.

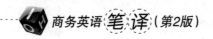 

 **Translating Samples**

## 一、建立业务关系函

 **案例**

Dear Sirs,

Having obtained your name and address from China Council for the Promotion of International Trade, we are writing you in the hope of establishing business relations with you.

We have been importers of Arts & Crafts for many years. At present, we are interested in various kinds of Chinese Arts and Crafts and should appreciate your catalogues and quotations. If your prices are in line, we trust important business can materialize.

We are looking forward to receiving your early reply.

Yours faithfully,<br>×××

**译文:**

敬启者:

我方从中国国际贸易促进会得知贵公司的名字和地址,给您去信希望能同贵方建立业务关系。

我方作为手工艺品进口商已有多年了。目前,我方对各种各样的中国手工艺品都很感兴趣,如蒙报价并赐商品目录将不胜感激。如贵方价格与市场相符,我方相信会成交大笔生意。

敬盼收到贵方的早日回复。

谨上

## 二、询盘、报盘、还盘

 **案例**

询　　盘

Dear Sirs,

We have learned from Smith Company of Birmingham that you manufacture a range of high-fashion leather handbags in a variety.

We operate a quality retail business and although our sales volume is not large, we obtain high prices for our quality goods. Would you please send us a copy of your handbag catalogue with details of your prices and payment terms? We would find it most helpful if you could also supply samples of the various leather from which the handbags are made.

Yours faithfully,<br>×××

**译文:**

敬启者:

从伯明翰史密斯公司获悉贵公司制作了一系列款式新颖的皮革手提包。

本公司经营高档零售业务,虽然销量不多,但货品属优质高档。现恳请惠寄货品目录、价格表和付款方式细则。此外,如蒙提供各类皮革样本,不胜感激。

谨上

## 三、订单

 **案例**

敬启者:

贵公司 11 月 20 日所寄样品及价目表收悉,我方在此深表谢意。我方欣喜地发现贵方材料质量上乘。

兹欣订 150 条 L/#123 之蓝色裤子料,并以此小量订单试购。请务必使待运货物与贵公司之样品一致。

请参见随寄第 106 号订单之详情。本公司急于购买该批货,请以电报告知贵公司接受此订单。一俟收到该电报,我方即通过美国世界银行开立不可撤销信用证。

倘首次订货令人满意,我方将于近期大宗订购。

谨上

**译文**：

Dear Sirs,

Thank you for your samples and price list of November 20. We are pleased to find that your material appears to be of fine quality.

As trial we are delighted to place you a small order for cloth of 150 pieces of blue trousers L/#123. Please note that the goods to be shipped are in accordance with your samples.

The particulars are detailed in the enclosed Order Sheet No. 106. We are in a hurry to obtain the goods, so please cable your acceptance upon receipt, of which we will open an irrevocable L/C through the World Bank in the United States.

If this initial order turns out satisfactory, we shall be able to give you a large order in the near future.

Yours faithfully,<br>×××

## 四、确定支付方式函

 **案例**

要求以 D/A 作为支付方式

Dear Sirs,

Thanks for your support and offer for 150 pairs of leather boots. The original designs and superior quality will definitely find a promising market in our local market.

We notice your requirement of payment is by irrevocable letter of credit, which is also our usual practice. As the leather boots we are purchasing are just for the coming trade exhibition at the end of next month, the purchase value is well below the usual contracted figure. For such a small volume of business, it is impractical to have a letter of credit opened because the resulting charges would leave a big gap to balance the profit margin for us. What is more, the time schedule does not allow us to have the work done at your request. Therefore, we feel it necessary to insist that you draw on us at 60 days on documents against acceptance. For business larger than this in the future we will be prepared to accept payment by letter of credit.

We hope you will understand our position. If the sales for promotion at the coming trade exhibition prove profitable, hopefully you can rely on our growing import lists of more leather boots.

Yours faithfully,<br>×××

**译文：**

敬启者：

非常感谢贵方的大力支持及 150 双皮靴。贵方皮靴的新颖设计和优越的质量在本地定会有好的市场前景。

贵方要求以不可撤销的信用证作为支付方式，这也是我方一贯的做法。我方所订购的皮靴准备在下个月末的商品交易博览会上做展品用，因此这批订单的价值远低于一般合同规定的数字，像这样的小业务，无利润可赚，开信用证是不实际的。更重要的是由于时间的关系，我方满足不了贵方的要求。因此，我方认为应以 60 天的承兑交单作为支付方式，等将来业务量大了，我方定以信用证作为支付方式。

希望贵方能理解我方的处境，如果这次商品促销成功，我方定会向贵方发出越来越多的皮靴进口订单。

谨上

## 五、投诉、索赔和理赔

 **案例**

投　诉

Dear Sirs,

Thank you for your delivery of the working clothes which we ordered on November 6. To our regret, on inspection, we found that the color of the goods does not conform to the original sample.

We are returning two of these by separate mail and would like you to replace all of them in correct color immediately, as we are in urgent need of them. Concerning the airfreight, we may pay the extra costs for airfreight. However, your costs for packing and insurance must have been lower for air cargo and we request you to take this fact into consideration and bear some part of the airfreight charges.

Above are our suggestions to dispose of the goods and await your reply as to whether you agree to our proposal.

Yours faithfully,<br>×××

**译文：**

敬启者：

我方 11 月 6 日所订工作服已收到，谢谢。很遗憾，经检查，我方发现货物的颜色和样品不符。

我方现另寄出其中的两件。因我方急需此批货物,希望贵方能立即调换所有的工作服。至于额外的空邮费用,我方可以支付。但是,空运货物包装及保险费用更低,同时敬请贵方考虑并分担部分空运费用。

以上是我方对此事的处理建议,是否同意,敬请来信告知。

敬启

## Translating Training

**A：Translate the following sentences about business correspondence into Chinese.**

1. We will keep your enquiry before us and as soon as we are in a position to accept new orders, we will contact you by cable.

2. Our cartons of canned food are not only seaworthy, but also strong enough to protect the goods from possible damage.

3. Unfortunately, the recent rush of orders for our goods has made it impossible to promise shipment earlier than November 1.

4. We believe our prices are so realistic that no suppliers will possibly offer the makes of the same quality at a lower level than ours.

5. We are glad to send you this introductory letter, hoping that it will be the prelude to mutually beneficial relations between us.

6. The quality and prices of the commodities to be exchanged between the ex-importers in the two countries shall be acceptable to both sides.

7. The Seller shall not be responsible for the delay of shipment or non delivery of the goods due to Force Majeure, which might occur during the process of manufacturing or in the course of loading or transit.

8. The Buyer may, within 15 days after arrival of the goods at the destination, lodge a claim against the Seller for short-weight being supported by Inspection Certificate issued by a reputable public surveyor.

9. On the transfer date New Company shall transfer to B, free from any lien or encumbrance created by New Company and without the payment of any compensation, all its right, title to and interest in the infrastructure project, unless otherwise specified in the Agreement or any supplementary agreement.

10. If a Party breaches any of the representations or warranties given by it in Articles 18.1 or repeated in 18.2, then in addition to any other remedies available to the other Party under this contract or under Applicable Laws, it shall indemnify and keep indemnified the other Party and the company against any losses, damages, costs, expenses, liabilities and claims that such Party or the Company may suffer as a result of such breach.

**B：Translate the following sentences about business correspondence into English.**

1. 包装必须坚固,经得住粗暴装卸。

2. 经过对照发票核查之后，我们发现数量少了许多。

3. 我们有幸自荐，盼望能有机会与贵方合作，扩展业务。

4. 如果本月底前收到贵方的订单，我方打算给贵方5%的折扣。

5. 因货物在运输途中受损，我方已向保险商提出索赔450美元。

6. 我方可以让步，但赔偿不得超过300美元，否则将提交仲裁。

7. 很遗憾地通知贵方，我方未能接受贵方的还盘。

8. 由于卖货太多，抱歉我方不能再接受标题项下货物的任何新订单。

9. 我方愿意在平等互利、互通有无的基础上与贵公司建立业务关系。

10. 我方已把价格降到底线，因此很遗憾不能按照贵方的要求再降价了。

**C：Translate the following business letters into Chinese.**

1. Dear Sirs,

We are interested in buying large quantities of steel screws in all sizes. We would be obliged if you would give us a quotation per kilogram C&F Liverpool, England. It would also be appreciated if you could forward samples and your price-list to us.

We used to purchase these products from other sources. We may now prefer to buy from your company because we understand that you are able to supply larger quantities at more attractive prices for products of superior quality.

We look forward to hearing from you by return E-mail.

Yours sincerely,

×××

2. Dear Sirs,

We note from your letter dated November 20 that the price quoted by us for the silk dresses is found to be on the high side.

While we appreciate your cooperation in giving us the information about the Indian supply in your market, we are regretful that we are unable to reduce our price to the level you indicated. We have to point out that your counteroffer is obviously out of line with the price ruling in the present market, as other buyers in your neighboring cities are buying freely at our quoted price. Moreover, the market is firm with an upward tendency, and there is very little likelihood of the goods remaining unsold once this particular offer has lapsed. In view of the above, we would suggest in your interest that you take full advantage of the market.

Faithfully yours,

×××

3. Dear Sirs,

Thanks a lot for your order of March 20. We shall make it sure to dispatch the goods immediately on receiving your payment. We regret very much that we can only do business on basis of cash. As the prices have been cut so low, they do not permit credit terms.

We'd like to assure that you are always of our best attention.

Yours faithfully,

×××

4. Dear Sirs,

Please be advised that the shipment of MP4 under your L/C 30036 was carried by the S.S. "Princess" sailing for your port on October 29. As special care has been taken by our Shipping Department, we trust that the goods will reach you in good order and turn out to your entire satisfaction. Enclosed you will find the relative shipping documents listed below.

| | |
|---|---|
| 1. Invoice | 2 copies |
| 2. Bill of Lading | 1 copy |
| 3. Marine Risk note No. T/B29/33 | 1 copy |

5. Dear Sirs,

We have received your goods covering our order No. 336 of November 3. Upon opening the cases we found case No. 77 contained completely different articles.

As we are in urgent need of the goods, we request you to arrange for the dispatch of the replacement immediately. A list of the contents of the wrongly dispatched case is attached. Please let us know what you are going to do with them.

Yours sincerely,

×××

**D：Translate the following business letters into English.**

1. 敬启者：

我方收到贵方 11 月 24 日的报价,很遗憾贵方拒绝了我方的还盘。

由于我方急需这批真丝裙并渴望与贵方达成交易,我方已经尽最大的努力说服我方的客户接受贵方每件 60 美元的报价。幸好,我方的加利福尼亚客户已经改变主意并重新同我方接洽,按照贵方条款订购上述货物 2 000 打。

我方很高兴能够在长时间的信件往来之后同贵方达成交易,期待着贵方的销售合同,一经接到,我方将及时开出相关的信用证。

谨上

2. 敬启者：

贵方订购产品的出口许可证已核准。产品即将于 2 周内制作完成,特此奉告。我方建议,以见到中国银行开出的以我方为收款人的不可撤销的信用证时付款。

我方一俟接到贵方信用证已确立的确认书,就起运发货,并将文件寄出,作为向银行结账凭据。

谨上

3. 敬启者：

感谢贵方 12 月 12 日来函,兹欣然奉告,我方接受贵方的包装条件。

贵方在来函中谈及:"羊毛衫必须一件装一个聚乙烯(polythene)塑料袋,内衬坚固防水材料,然后装入硬纸盒,10 打装一纸箱。每一纸板箱均衬一层塑料布,并用带子完全捆扎加固。"兹复,我方严格按照贵方指示包装,并确保货物安全完好地到达贵方港口。但因此需要额外的劳务和费用,我方需对指定包装加收劳务费用,总计达 100 美元。

敬候佳音。

谨上

4. 敬启者：

感谢贵方 12 月 6 日来函。兹奉告，按惯例，以 CIF 成交的交易，我方一般根据 1981 年 1 月 1 日中国保险条款向中国人民保险公司按发票面额的 110% 投保一切险。而为了满足贵方的要求，我方可以按发票面值的 150% 投保，但现在 150% 与 110% 间保险费的差额要由贵方来负担。

请告知贵方可否接受此项条件。盼复。

谨上

5. 敬启者：

我方已收到贵方来函，对 30 箱浸湿的红糖提出申诉。

但是，很遗憾，我方不能接受贵方提出的申诉，因为在包装以前，我方已对货物进行了严格的检查，而且装船时货物的状态良好。该损失应该是在航程中造成的，因此，依我方看，贵方遭受的损失应该由船运公司来承担。

兹对此深表遗憾，并希望此事不会损害我们之间的友好关系，只愿此事能得到圆满的解决。

谨上

## Section 5  Extensive Expression

### 一、建立业务关系、询盘、报盘、还盘

| | |
|---|---|
| 1. business relations | 业务关系 |
| 2. self-introduction | 自我介绍 |
| 3. quotation | 报价 |
| 4. quote | 报价 |
| 5. catalogue | 目录 |
| 6. enquiry | 询盘 |
| 7. offer | 报盘 |
| 8. firm offer | 实盘 |
| 9. non-firm offer | 虚盘 |
| 10. under/on offer | 在出售中 |
| 11. bid | 递价,出价 |
| 12. voluntary offer | 出盘 |
| 13. counter offer | 还盘 |
| 14. covering letter | 附函 |
| 15. discount | 折扣 |
| 16. special discount | 特别折扣 |
| 17. exceptional discount | 额外折扣 |
| 18. quantity discount | 数量折扣 |
| 19. trade discount | 同业折扣 |
| 20. cash discount | 现金折扣 |
| 21. decline price reduction | 拒绝降价 |

| | |
|---|---|
| 22. concession on price | 价格让步 |
| 23. accept the offer | 接受报盘 |
| 24. be on the low side | (价格)偏低 |
| 25. be on the high side | (价格)偏高 |
| 26. order(form) | 订单 |
| 27. place an order | 下订单 |
| 28. decline the order | 拒绝订单 |
| 29. D/P at sight | 即期付款交单 |
| 30. D/P after sight | 远期付款交单 |
| 31. acknowledgement of order | 接受订单 |
| 32. discontinued line | 中断/停止(生产/使用/供应等)的货物 |
| 33. terms of payment | 支付方式 |
| 34. D/A(documents against acceptance) | 承兑交单 |
| 35. D/P(documents against payment) | 付款交单 |

## 二、包装及运输要求

| | |
|---|---|
| 1. packing | 包装 |
| 2. packing requirements | 包装要求 |
| 3. packing instructions | 包装须知 |
| 4. packing list | 包装单 |
| 5. packing charge | 包装费用 |
| 6. inner packing | 内包装 |
| 7. outer packing | 外包装 |
| 8. neutral packing | 中性包装 |
| 9. cardboard packing | 硬纸盒包装 |
| 10. plastic packing | 塑料包装 |
| 11. paper packing | 纸包装 |
| 12. waterproof packing | 防水包装 |
| 13. seaworthy packing | 海运包装 |
| 14. customary packing | 普通包装 |
| 15. Handle with care | 小心轻放 |
| 16. No hook | 请勿用钩 |
| 17. To be kept upright | 竖立安放 |
| 18. Keep flat | 注意平放 |
| 19. This side up | 此面朝上 |
| 20. Explosive | 易爆货物 |
| 21. Poison | 小心有毒 |
| 22. Perishable | 易坏货物 |
| 23. Inflammable | 易燃货物 |
| 24. Fusible | 易熔货物 |

| | |
|---|---|
| 25. Glass with care | 小心玻璃 |
| 26. Open here | 由此开启 |
| 27. Guard against damp | 勿使受潮 |
| 28. net weight | 净重 |
| 29. gross weight | 毛重 |
| 30. shipment | 装运 |
| 31. shipping instructions | 装运指示 |
| 32. shipping advice | 装船通知 |
| 33. partial shipment | 分批装运 |
| 34. transshipment | 转船装运 |
| 35. gross shipment | 总发货量 |
| 36. prompt shipment | 立即发货 |
| 37. date of shipment | 发货日期 |
| 38. port of shipment | 发运港 |
| 39. urge shipment | 催促装运 |
| 40. suspend shipment | 暂停发货 |
| 41. shipment by installment | 分批发运 |
| 42. shipping company | 装运公司 |
| 43. shipping container | 集装箱 |
| 44. shipping documents | 装运单据 |
| 45. shipping order | 装运单 |
| 46. shipping space | 船位,载位 |
| 47. tropical packing | 适合热带气候的包装 |
| 48. shipping marks | 发货、装船标记,唛头 |

## 三、保险、索赔、理赔

| | |
|---|---|
| 1. insurance | 保险 |
| 2. insurance arrangement | 保险安排,保险计划 |
| 3. insurance company | 保险公司 |
| 4. insurance agent | 保险代理人 |
| 5. insurance certificate | 保险凭证 |
| 6. insurance policy | 保险单 |
| 7. insurance premium | 保(险)费 |
| 8. cover insurance | 投保,洽办保险 |
| 9. excessive insurance | 附加险 |
| 10. marine policy | 海洋保险 |
| 11. All Risks | 一切险 |
| 12. War Risks | 战争险 |
| 13. bill of lading | 提货单 |
| 14. complaints | 投诉 |

| 15. claims | 理赔 |
| 16. adjustments | 调解 |
| 17. wrong dispatch | 错发货物 |
| 18. lodge a claim | 提出索赔 |
| 19. damaged goods | 受损的货物 |
| 20. accept a claim | 接受索赔 |
| 21. bill of exchange | 汇票 |
| 22. confirm a purchase | 确认购买 |
| 23. sales contract | 销售合同 |
| 24. weight memo | 重量单 |
| 25. commercial invoice | 商业发票 |
| 26. certificate of origin | 产地说明书 |

# Unit *9*

# Business Correspondence (II)

Unit Objectives

In this unit you should

➢ familiarize yourself with the format of business correspondence.

➢ master the basic words and useful expressions of business correspondence.

➢ have a good command of the translating skills of the negative sentences.

## ❓ Section 1   Theme Lead-in

**Read the following passage to gain a better understanding of this unit.**

As business English letters are the principle and indispensable means in the international business communication, it can be said that without them, much of the routine activities in the business world would not be possible and all international trade and business will fall apart. Business English correspondence is used to sell products or services, request material of information, answer customer enquiries, maintain good public relations, and serve a variety of other business functions. Generally business letters can obtain and transfer information, serve as the permanent records, and act as public relation materials.

First and foremost, business English letter functions as an effective way to convey and retain information. Despite oral communication can provide us with great convenience and efficiency by sending messages, some of these activities in transaction can not be handle over the phone. And few business people have time to visit every client personally, especially when they are doing foreign business, and long distance telephone calls can be time-consuming and expensive. More importantly, it is observed that people can only retain about twenty-five percent of what they hear. And the chance of message being forgotten and oral communication usually results in being misunderstood. As a result, letters remain the best form to secure that your message is accurately received, particularly when the receiver is geographically dispersed, and high and technical information are required in details.

In addition, business English letter also functions as a permanent record, a form that can be fully recognized by the courts. Letters of agreement are often drawn up between companies and independent suppliers or consultants. They are binding on both parties. For example, when there is any question about the amount of the order from the customer, the details of the offers and the counter-offers as well as the claims and replies, just checking the letters received or sent will be helpful to solve all the doubts. Either side that breaks the terms under the record will take political, economic or moral responsibilities. You can not do the same with a phone conversation unless you record every outgoing and incoming call.

Last but not the least, business English letter serves as a formal or informal public relation material. They can help build goodwill between you and your clients, creditors, suppliers and other public groups. Customers form their impression of the firm from the tone and quality of the letters it sends out. How you express yourself and what language style you adopt in your letters will leave an impression of you and your business in the reader's mind.

## Section 2   Translation Warming-up

**A: Translate the following sentences into Chinese, paying attention to the underlined parts.**

1. We regret our inability to accept your claim.

2. No one has nothing to offer to the company.

3. It is beyond my power to sign such a contract.

4. The demand for our products exceeds the supply.

5. The significance of this incident wasn't lost on us.

6. The damage was apparently attributable to faulty packing.

7. Your explanation for the delayed delivery of the goods is pretty thin.

8. We would appreciate your informing of us whether these requirements could be met.

9. If this event is dealt with improperly, we are going to cease our business relationship with you.

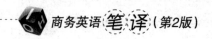
10. Sometimes a spontaneous comment will get away from me <u>before</u> I've had time to think about what I'm saying.

**B：Translate the following sentences into English，paying attention to the underlined parts.**

1. 收据<u>未</u>经签证，<u>不</u>得付款。

2. <u>不</u>怕<u>不</u>识货，就怕货比货。

3. 优者<u>未</u>必胜，劣者<u>未</u>必败。

4. 这个法宝是万万不可弃之<u>不</u>用的。

5. 事情发生后，人们可<u>不</u>能<u>不</u>信了。

6. 要保护这些机器<u>不</u>受海水和潮气侵袭。

7. 所有的损失都加在我方头上是<u>不</u>公平的。

8. 非常遗憾，因为我当天有另外一个约会而<u>不</u>能接受您的善意邀请。

9. 我方一接到贵方寄来的样品，就知道这些<u>正</u>是我方想要购买的手提包。

10. 国际贸易中存在的关税问题和其他人为障碍在国内贸易中<u>是不</u>存在的。

## Section 3　Topic Features and Translation Principles

### 一、商务英语信函的词汇使用特点

**1. 用词规范、正式**

商务英语信函经常以意义相同或相近的书面语代替基本词汇和口语词汇，充分体现规范正式、公事公办的特性。如以 inform 或 advise 代替 tell，以 duplicate 代替 copy，以 dispatch 代替 send，以 otherwise 代替 or；以介词短语代替简单的介词，如以 as for，in respect to，in connection with 和 with regarding to 等代替 about 等。

**2. 表意准确、专业性强**

商务信函用词表意准确、专业性强，主要表现在使用大量的专业术语、外来词、行话、缩略语以及一般词语在商务英语语境中的特殊用法。专业术语不胜枚举，如 trimming charges 平仓费，insurance policy 保险单，coverage 保险项目，establishment 开证，counter offer 还盘，pro forma invoice 形式发票，估价发票，premium 保险费，underwriter 保险人，L/C 信用证，CIF 到岸价格，FOB 离岸价格，C.B.D. 付现提货等。

外来词汇也很多，如拉丁语的 status quo（现状），意大利语的 delcredere（保付货价的），汉语中的 litchi（荔枝），tung oil（桐油），mango（芒果）等。

行话指的是长期的函电交往使人们在使用术语上形成共识，本来意义差异很大的词汇在特定的语境中所表达的内涵和外延却非常相似。如 offer，quotation 表示"报价，发盘"，pamphlet，brochure，booklet，sales literature 表示商家用于宣传介绍自己公司或产品的"说明材料"，shipment 和 consignment 表示"所发出的货物"，financial standing/reputation/condition/position 用于表示公司的"资信财务情况"等。

商务信函的准确性主要体现在数量词的大量运用：商务信函中的时间、地点、价格、数量、金额和规格等问题贯穿商贸活动始终，数字的表达应言之确凿，避免模棱两可。

 例句

例 1. We usually pack each piece of silk dress in a poly bag, a dozen to a box and 10 boxes to a wooden case.

我方通常把一件真丝裙装入一个聚乙烯袋内，一打装入一盒，十盒装入一个木箱。

例 2. Mr. Smith requests the pleasure of Ms. White at the banquet celebrating 20th anniversary at Reception Hall in Holiday Inn at 7:00 p.m. Friday February 10,2022.

史密斯先生很荣幸地邀请怀特小姐参加公司成立 20 周年庆典宴会，时间是 2022 年 2 月 10 日周五晚 7 时，地点在假日酒店大厅。

### 3. 用语朴素、淡于修饰

商贸信函的主要功能是传递信息，使收发信函双方发生贸易往来、达成交易，因此用语简单（simple）、明了（clear）、直接（direct），除了必须使用专业术语等手段准确传达自己的信息意图外，还要求信函语言明白易懂、朴实平易，避免使用过多的修饰词，很少使用文学文体中常用的修辞手法。

 例句

例 1. Having recently completed a full-time course in budgeting and cash-flow forecasting, I am writing to enquire about the possibility of employment in your company.

我最近刚完成一个全日制的有关预算和现金流转预测的课程培训，现写信咨询是否有在贵公司谋得一个职位的可能性。

例 2. I have been offered another post which I have accepted as the work hours will allow me to take educational courses in the evening.

我被提供并接受了另外一个职位，原因是这个工作的工作时间可以允许我上一些晚上的教育课程。

### 二、商务英语信函翻译的原则

商务信函朴素规范，表意准确且专业性和针对性强，没有华丽的辞藻，为了便于业务交往，商务信函大量使用礼貌用语。对于商贸术语的翻译，必须使用商贸类专业人士已经认可的规范译法。因此，作为译者应当尽可能地记住这些商贸信函中的英语专业术语及其英汉对译，这样才能更好地做到译文的准确性、规范性。

 例句

例 1. Mr. Smith cordially requests the honor of Mr. White's presence at our company's 10th anniversary.

史密斯先生诚挚地请求怀特先生赏光莅临我公司的 10 周年庆典。

例 2. Miss White regrets that owing to bad health she is unable to accept Mr. Smith's kind invitation to the dinner party.

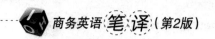

很遗憾由于身体状况欠佳，怀特小姐不能接受史密斯先生的善意邀请来参加此宴会。

### 三、商务英语信函翻译的注意事项

（1）商务信函大多以传递信息的功能为主，较少运用修辞手段，一般不存在语言与文化的差异，在翻译时无须作太多变动，多数情况下可按原句结构直译。

例句

I have pleasure in apprising you that, under the auspices of several highly respected and influential houses here, I have commenced business as a shipping and assurance broker and general agent.

我十分高兴地通知您，在本地几家有名望、有影响力的公司的支持下，我做起了运输与保险经纪以及总代理的生意。

（2）由于商务英语信函重在纪实，因此要求译文不求虚饰但求简洁、严谨、准确。确保术语、缩略语、具有商务术语性质的词语以及商务套语翻译的规范性和准确性，这就要求采用对应的汉语术语翻译原文中的商贸术语。

例句

例 1. We are deeply sorry for the inadequacy of the reserve.
因储备量不足，我方对此深表遗憾。

例 2. We wish to apologize for the late dispatch of order 3241.
我方想对 3241 订单货物的迟发道歉。

原文中的一般性叙述，在翻译时应当采用简明、易懂的汉语加以转译，保留原文的简洁流畅与易懂性。此外，还须确保事实细节（如日期、数量、金额等）的准确翻译，不得疏漏。

例 3. The market here for this product is active, and the best price we can offer is US $150 or over per long ton.
该产品在本地销售看好，我方出价可达每长吨 150 美元或以上。

（3）翻译时应注意保留原文的文体正式性和委婉礼貌性，对原文情态、礼貌程度、语气和态度应当仔细分析、整体把握并在译文中充分再现。试体会下面几个句子在语气、态度上的细微差别，并注意在译文中的体现。

例句

例 1. Would you please let me know whether you might soon have on your project staff a vacancy for which I could be considered?
请问，贵公司项目策划人员是否有可能很快出现职位空缺，您是否可以把我考虑在内？（礼貌客气）

例 2. If you grant me an interview, our discussion will show you, I believe, that I could become a useful member of your staff.

如果您给我一个面试的机会,我相信,我们的谈话可以让您了解到我会成为贵公司员工中有用的一员。(直率自信)

(4)汉语商务信函用语和行文都讲究郑重,常用文言词语,套语亦多。常用的信函词语包括"收悉、承蒙、乞谅、见告、为盼、赐复、如蒙、惠、贵"等。

例句

例1. We would like you to come and have a look at the exhibition. We guarantee that you would find it worthwhile.

敬请莅临展会。我们保证您会不虚此行。

例2. Thank a lot for considering my application and I am looking forward to receiving your notice for an interview soon.

承蒙您考虑我的申请,万分感谢。殷盼能早日接到您的面试通知。

# Section 4  Translating Strategies, Samples and Training

## ✓ Translating Strategies

否定句式(negative sentences)的翻译是商务信函翻译中常见的翻译句式之一。通常来说,一种语言以某种形式表达的概念,在另一种语言中也用同一种形式来表达,可是英汉语言中的否定概念,由于使用的词汇、语法手段以及语言逻辑方式有差异,往往在英汉翻译时需做正反处理。有时英语中的否定形式在译成汉语时需要转换成肯定形式,反之亦然。因此,在进行英汉对译时,要考虑到英汉的习惯表达,以及强调和修辞方面的特征,正确选择否定或肯定句式,以准确表达出原文的精神风貌。

英语中的否定句型大致可以归纳为以下几种:全部否定、部分否定、意义上的否定、双重否定、偏离式肯定。通常的翻译方法可以是:正说反译、反说正译、正反译均可。本节还特别提到双重否定句、偏离否定句和部分否定句的翻译,并强调在翻译过程中要结合上下文的线索,根据不同语言的不同思维方式和表达方式,仔细推敲,理解原作语言中变化多端的表达形式,熟悉并尊重译入语的表达习惯,从而进行合理的翻译。

## 一、正说反译

英语中有些动词、名词、介词、连词、形容词和副词等,虽属于肯定形式,汉译时却要靠否定词才能确切表达其意义。如 difficult 可以译成"不容易",Exactly 可以译成"一点不错"等。

英语中有些词组虽说形式上是肯定的,但表达的是否定的含义,在翻译中也要进行适当的正反翻译的处理。这样的常见词组有:but for(如果没有),short of(缺少,达不到),in the dark(一点也不知道),free from(没有,免于),safe from(免于),too…to do(过于/太……以至于不……),in vain(无效,徒然),but that(要不是,若非),rather than(而不是),instead of(代替,而不是),make light of(不把……当成一回事)等。

商务信函一般要求尽量避免或减少否定形式,因此,英语译成汉语时,应格外注意根据汉语的表达习惯,正确地选择肯定或否定的形式。

 **例句**

例 1. I wonder whether you could give me the opportunity to have an interview.
我不知道您能否给我一个面试的机会。（动词）

例 2. The failure might be the making of me. I wouldn't give up.
这次不成功将成为我成功的基础。我不会放弃的。（名词）

例 3. Your responsibility for the damage is above suspicion.
贵方应对损失负责,这是毋庸置疑的。（介词）

例 4. We won't accept an applicant unless we have had a thorough inspection of him.
如果不经过全面的调查,我们是不会接收一名申请者的。（连词）

例 5. I'm sorry to tell you that the manager's decision is final.
很遗憾地告诉你,经理的决定是不能更改了。（形容词）

例 6. "He is a qualified worker." We may safely draw a conclusion.
"他是一名合格的工人。"我们可以这样下结论,万无一失。（副词）

英语中有许多表达方式从结构上看貌似肯定,其实表达的是否定意义,而且往往是强烈的否定,汉译时必须要进行正说反译。

 **例句**

例 7. That applicant is anything but fit for this position.
那个申请者一点也不适合这个职位。

例 8. The goods you delivered are far from enough to meet all our customers' needs.
贵方发的货物远远不能满足我方所有客户的需要。

在汉译英中,汉语正面表达,可以或必须译为英语否定的,亦不乏其例。

 **例句**

例 9. 比尔这些年以来一直是全勤。
Bill has never missed a day's work for these years.
例 10. 货物的包装和运输问题仍应注意。
The packing and shipment of the goods can not be neglected.

## 二、反说正译

英语中有些貌似否定的含蓄表达方法,往往掩盖着实质上的肯定内涵,汉译时就需要通过变换语气的方法,把原文的否定式译为汉语的肯定式。同样这种情况也会涉及英语中有些动词、名词、形容词和副词,以及一些词组的翻译,翻译时恰当运用反说正译的方法可以使译文自然流畅。从反面表达,主要指译文中用否定词语 no,not 或带有 de-,dis-,im-,in-,un-,less 等词缀的词汇。

**例句**

例 1. Since your order covers so big a quantity we are unable to meet your requirements for the moment, but we will do our utmost to secure supply for you, and where the position improves we <u>will not fail</u> to let you know.

因为贵方订单数量很大,目前不能满足贵方要求,但是我方将尽最大努力为贵方取得货源,<u>一</u>旦情况好转,<u>一定</u>告知。(动词)

例 2. As a qualified interviewer, you cannot show your strong <u>dislike</u> for an interviewee even though you don't like him at all. (名词)

作为一名合格的面试者,即使你一点也不喜欢一名被试者,你也不能表现出<u>厌恶情绪</u>。

例 3. The effects of this event is <u>not immediate</u>.

这一事件的影响显现得<u>缓慢</u>。(形容词)

例 4. The inspector must have gone through the goods <u>carelessly</u> and then let them off.

检查人员肯定只是<u>马马虎虎</u>地看了一下货物就算过了。(副词)

例 5. You <u>cannot</u> stress the importance of proper packing too seriously.

合理包装的重要性怎么强调也<u>不为过</u>。(词组)

例 6. We <u>won't</u> keep you waiting <u>long</u> for the results of the interview.

我们<u>很快</u>就会通知你面试的结果。(句子)

同样,汉语中的一些含有否定形式的句子,英译时也可以或必须转换成英语的肯定形式。

 **例句**

例 7. 令我方失望的是贵方未能按合同规定的日期发货。

To our disappointment, you <u>failed</u> to deliver the goods on time as has been stated in the contract.

例 8. 这些细节问题没有引起我方装船检查人员的注意。

These details <u>escaped</u> out our lading inspectors.

## 三、正反译均可

在实际英汉翻译当中,有些表达方式既可以用肯定,也可以用否定形式来翻译,就要根据上下文,看哪一种翻译更符合上下文的意思。

 **例句**

例 1. I'm <u>new</u> to the job.

对于这份工作我是生手。/我<u>不熟悉</u>这工作。

例 2. David is <u>free</u> with his money.

大卫花钱<u>大手大脚</u>。/大卫花钱从<u>不吝啬</u>。

例 3. Susan realized that she was <u>in trouble</u>.

苏珊意识到自己遇到了麻烦。／苏珊感到自己的境遇不妙。

例 4. The airport is no distance at all from our company.

机场和我们公司近在咫尺。／机场离我们公司一点也不远。

## 四、双重否定句的翻译

英汉两种语言里都有一些双重否定的表达方式。否定之否定即为肯定，然而在翻译时却不能机械地套用公式，双重否定理应理解为肯定，但表达起来形式就不尽相同了，通常有两种形式：一是转化成译文的双重否定形式，二是转化成译文的肯定形式。

（1）有些英语的双重否定翻译时转换成汉语的双重否定。

 **例句**

例 1. It is not fair not to assume your responsibilities for that accident.

贵方不对该事故负责是不公平的。

例 2. Since we have spent so much money, it seems impossible not to carry on this project.

既然我们已经花了这么多钱，这项工程看来不进行下去是不行的。

（2）有些英语双重否定的句子只适合转换成汉语肯定的形式。

例 3. Jack was nothing if not a qualified worker.

杰克是个地道的合格工人。

例 4. There is no man who has no shortcomings.

凡人都有缺点。

（3）英语中的双重否定有时由一个否定词和另外一个含有否定含义的词（或称为"暗否定词"）构成，转换方式和上面的相同。

 **例句**

例 5. There is no rule but has an exception.

任何规则都有例外。

例 6. I don't doubt that you have the ability to accomplish the task successfully.

我肯定你一定能成功地完成任务。

（4）汉语中的双重否定转换成英语时，要么保留双重否定的形式，要么直接转译成英语的肯定形式。

 **例句**

例 7. 中国有句俗语："不是冤家不聚头。"

There is a popular saying in China, "Opponents always meet."

例 8. 我不得不提醒您采取一些有效的措施来解决这个问题。

I must remind you to take some effective measures to solve this problem.

**五、偏离否定句的翻译**

偏离否定,又称转译否定,是英语中特有的语言现象,即形式上的否定点与意义上的否定点发生偏差,"声东击西",因此汉译时必须"纠偏",以符合汉语表达的习惯。

 **例句**

例 1. We neither believe nor reject anything because any other person has rejected or believed it.

我们不会因为别人反对或相信什么就跟着反对或相信什么。

例 2. One's ability is not great because his reference said so.

人的能力强弱不在于他的推荐人怎么说。

在某些英语句子中,从形式上看是否定主句的谓语动词,而实际意义上否定的却是宾语从句中的谓语动词,汉译时就必须把否定语气从主句转译到从句当中。英语中具有这一特点的动词有很多,如:think,believe,suppose,imagine,reckon,fancy,seem,trust,figure,fear 等。

例 3. I didn't think there should be so many people applying for this position.

我觉得不会有那么多人申请这个职位。

例 4. I don't imagine you will reject my application because I am disabled.

我觉得您不会由于我是残疾人而拒绝我的申请。

英语中 no 作形容词修饰名词或代词,构成名词性短语在句中作主语或宾语时,汉译时则往往把否定意义移至谓语上,而且语气比较强烈。

例 5. No words can describe my thankfulness to you.

任何词语都无法描述我对您的感谢之情。

汉语英译时则应"反其道而行之",按英语表达习惯将否定语气进行合理的转译。

例 6. 我认为任何人都不会反对我的提议。

I don't think any one will object to my proposal.

**六、部分否定句的翻译**

英语中的部分否定句最容易使中国读者误入迷津。这主要表现在英语中含有总括意义的代词、形容词、副词等与否定词连用时,只否定一部分。

 **例句**

例 1. All that glitters is not gold.

闪闪发光物未必尽是黄金。

例 2. None of us are afraid of difficulties,but all of us are not good at conquering difficulties.

我们都不害怕困难,但并非都善于克服困难。

在翻译部分否定的句子时,要根据上下文进行逻辑上的分析,以进行正确的翻译。有些句子,如不根据上下文,至少有两种译法。

例 3. The manager didn't mention her mistake on purpose.

经理故意不提她的失误。/经理不是故意提到她的失误的。

例 4. We didn't write to have the refund on the goods.

我们没有写信索要货物的退款。/我们写信不是为了索要货物的退款。

## Translating Samples

## 一、推荐信

 案例

To Whom It May Concern,

I highly recommend Mary Smith for summer employment in your company. As a freshman and sophomore, Mary worked for me as an assistant in our company. She performed various clerical duties, including word processing, photocopying and proofreading, filing, delivering mails and errands to clients' offices.

My staff and I found her extremely tactful in dealing with clients and flexible in changing priorities almost daily. We appreciate her word processing speed and accuracy in customizing our technical forms and documents. In addition, she was punctual and had no absence during the two summers with us—quite a record, considering the schedule of today's busy youth.

Regrettably, Mary will not be able to continue employment with us this coming summer because our company has been transferred to another city.

If you could provide a position for her in your company, I'm sure you will be satisfied with her excellent performance.

Yours truly,

×××

**译文：**

敬启者:

我极力推荐玛丽·史密斯在暑假期间在贵公司工作。玛丽在大一和大二时曾在我的公司担任助理,负责多项业务,包括文字处理、复印与校对资料、将资料归档、递送邮件给客户和其他差事等。

事务所的职员和我都觉得玛丽在处理客户事务时很得体机智,而且几乎每天灵活地安排处理事务的优先顺序。我们都很欣赏她文字处理的速度与定制专业表格与文件时的准确性。除此之外,她很守时,在两个暑假内从没请过假,想想现在年轻人的日程多满就知道这是相当不简单的记录了。

遗憾的是,由于我公司迁到了另一个城市,玛丽这个暑假将不能再到我们公司工作了。如果贵公司能为她提供一个暑期工作的职位,我保证您将会对她的出色表现而满意。

谨启

## 二、求职信

 案例

To Whom It May Concern,

　　I am writing this letter to apply for the position of a marketing executive.

　　As you will see from the enclosed resume, my formal educational qualifications appear to meet your requirements. Since my graduation, I have had 6 years' experience in the field of which your company operates. During this period I have accumulated a comprehensive knowledge and experience of marketing.

　　I am willing to travel and work a reasonable amount of overtime.

　　I believe that, if appointed, I could quickly pick up the routines of the post in question and become productive.

　　If you think that a person with my qualifications might become a useful member of the company's staff, I should be glad to attend an interview to hear about the exact duties of the post in question.

　　I'm looking forward to your reply soon.

Yours sincerely,

×××

**译文：**

敬启者：

　　我现写信是为了申请贵公司销售主管的职位。

　　可以在随附的简历里看到，我的正规教育资格似乎正符合您的要求。自毕业以来，我已在贵公司经营的领域有了 6 年的工作经验，在此期间，我积累了有关市场营销全面的知识和丰富的经验。

　　我愿意出差，并愿意进行合理的加班。

　　我相信，一旦我被雇佣并任命，我会很快步入正轨，并很快就能有成果产出。

　　如果您认为具备我这样资格的人可以成为贵公司一名有用的职员，我很高兴能参加面试，以听取有关该职位职责的一些具体事宜。

　　盼复。

谨上

## 三、简历

 案例

肖燕飞

北京交通大学计算机科学学院

北京 100044

个人信息：

性别：女　　　　　　　　出生日期：1999 年 5 月 2 日

籍贯：上海　　　　　　　　婚姻状况：未婚

身体状况：良好

电子邮件：fyxiao@ bjtu.edu.cn　　　电话：13622335566

预谋职业：北京某外企中的一名程序设计师。

资格条件：四年广泛操作电脑的经验，已经完成学校课程的教育准备。

专业经历：2018 年至今，在北京奇迹电脑公司担任程序设计员。操作流程图、收集商业
管理信息、更新操作方法、研发一个计算机处理的工资系统。

教育背景：2018 年 9 至今北京交通大学理科学士。课程包括计算机科学、系统设计与
分析、PASCAL 语言、操作系统、COBOL 语言、DBASE 语言、FORTRAN 语言、
系统分类管理。

2012 年 9 月—2018 年 6 月，上海中学。

英语水平：大学英语四级和六级考试证书，能用英语流利地交流、阅读、书写。

爱好：　　围棋、古筝、绘画、游泳。

推荐信：　如需要可以提供。

**译文：**

Xiao Yanfei

**Computer Science Department of Beijing Jiaotong University**

Beijing, 100044

**Personal Information**

Sex：Female　　　　　　　　Date of Birth：May 2,1999

Native Place：Shanghai　　　Marital Status：Single

Health：Excellent

E-mail：yfxiao@ bjtu.edu.cn　　　Phone：13622335566

**Position Sought：**　　To work as a computer programmer in a foreign enterprise in Beijing.

**Qualifications：**　　Four years' work experience operating computers extensively, coupled with educational preparation.

**Professional Experience：**　Computer Programmer, Beijing Wonder Computer Company, from 2018 to date. Operate flow-charts, collect business information of management, update methods of operation, develop a computerized payroll system.

**Educational Background：**　Sep. 2018-present, Beijing Jiaotong University. Bachelor of Science in computer science. Courses included：Computer Science, Systems Design and Analysis, PASCAL Programming, Operating Systems, COBOL Programming, DBASE Programming, FORTRAN Programming, Systems Management.

Sep. 2012—July, 2018, Shanghai Middle School.

**English Proficiency：**　Certificates of College English Test Band 4 and 6, fluent in speaking, reading and writing.

| | |
|---|---|
| **Hobbies**: | Weiqi, zither, painting, swimming. |
| **References**: | Will be supplied upon request. |

## 四、辞职信

 **案例**

例 1. I wish to give notice of my intention to leave the service of the company.

Please consider December 31 next as my last day of employment.

**译文**:

我想表明我想离开本公司的意图。

请注意: 12 月 31 日将是我最后一天来公司上班。

例 2. 由于我加薪的请求没有得到满足, 我已决定从本公司辞职。

请注意: 11 月 30 日将是我的最后一个工作日。

**译文**:

As my request for an increase in salary has not been granted, I have decided to resign from the company's service.

Please consider November 30 next as my last working day.

## 五、邀请函

 **案例**

**正式邀请函**

Robert Bush

**Moonlight Piano Corporation**

Request the pleasure of the company of

Mr. Philip Lee

at the banquet celebrating Moonlight's 30th anniversary

to be held at

The Banquet Hall

Holiday Inn

19 Xueyuan Road

Beijing

at 7:00 p.m. on Friday November 23, 2021

Suggested dress code: formal

Robert Bush

The President

**Moonlight Piano Corporation**

19 Xueyuan Road

Beijing

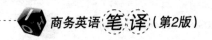

RSVP

Yours faithfully,

×××

译文:

罗伯特·布什

**月光钢琴有限公司**

有幸邀请

菲利浦·李先生

参加为庆祝月光成立30周年纪念日而举行的宴会

于北京市学院路19号假日酒店宴会大厅

2021年11月23日,周五晚7:00

着装建议:正式

罗伯特·布什

月光钢琴有限公司董事长

北京市学院路19号

敬请赐复

## Translating Training

**A: Translate the following sentences about business correspondence into Chinese.**

1. As exporters dealing exclusively in Chinese Art & Craft Goods, we express our desire to trade with you in this line.

2. We have the pleasure to inform you that on January 1, we established ourselves as commission merchants for the Japanese goods at the above address.

3. We would like to handle one or two good lines from your country which could be distributed throughout China at competitive prices, and which would be conductive to establishing a steady supply and lasting market.

4. Enclosed please find our monthly statement up to and including March 31, and, the amount of ¥320,000 remaining unpaid last month.

5. We shall gladly join with you in the purchase of 100 bales of wool, to be shipped in moieties by two different vessels, to sail about a month apart.

6. We regret to note that you claim that the quality is inferior to the original sample sent, and request that we credit you with $8 per kilogram.

7. We should be obliged for any information as to the standing of the firm, and you may rest assured that anything thus communicated will go no further.

8. You will observe that the prices quoted are very reasonable and as they are likely to rise very soon following the bullish trend in the world market, we would advise you to place your order as soon as possible.

9. Would you kindly let us know whether you will take them back, or allow us to sell them at

a discount of 50 per cent?

10. We think the letter of credit opened by us will be with you through the informing bank at the latest by the end of this week.

**B：Translate the following sentences about business correspondence into English.**

1. 从中国国际贸易促进会获悉,贵方有意采购电器用品。

2. 为安排装船,信用证不得迟于 9 月 1 日到达我方。

3. 贵方 3 月 4 日来函收悉,得知我方发错货物,深表遗憾,我方会尽力做一些补偿。

4. 按照贵方 7 月 1 日来函要求,现随函附寄 300 美元支票一张。

5. 若贵方想安排交货日程,请告知我方有关装船安排。

6. 因交货长期延误,我方遇到许多麻烦,因此我方坚持要求立即交货,否则将不得不按合同规定取消订货。

7. 我们很想知道贵方是否容许我方将交货时间延期 20 天,如果贵方容许我方延期 20 天,请速传真回复。

8. 谢谢贵方 10 月 11 日寄给我方样品,现我方乐意订货,详情请见所附订单。

9. 贵方应按合同规定期限将货物装上"白熊"轮,否则空舱费概由贵方承担。

10. 鉴于供货数量有限,若我方报价能满足贵公司要求,则请早日订购。

**C：Translate the following business letters into Chinese.**

1. To Whom It May Concern,

It is my great pleasure to recommend Song Ge to you as the bilingual secretary of your company, as she was one of my best students.

Miss Song began attending my English classes in Beijing Foreign Studies University in 2019. Though it has been over two years since we had the last classes, the deep impression she made on me has not faded in the least. She is a very intelligent, honest, responsible, creative, insightful, articulate and adaptive person. Her high academic achievements speak for themselves: she consistently scored in the top 3% in class and passed Band 8 for English majors with excellent grades in the first year of her university life.

I am certain that Miss Song would make great contributions to your company, and I strongly recommend her for the position. Please do not hesitate to inquire further if I can be of help to you.

Sincerely,

×××

2.                                        **Resume**

| | |
|---|---|
| **Name**： | Catherine Nelson |
| **Nationality**： | American |
| **Date of Birth**： | June 3, 1992 |
| **Marital Status**： | Married |
| **Address**： | 23 Washington Avenue, Boston |
| **Education**： | |
| 2007—2010 | The Third Middle School, Washington D.C. |

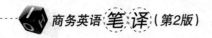

| 2010—2014 | A-level chemistry, mathematics, French and so on |
| | The Harvard University |
| | Received B.A. in Business Administration, June 2014 |
| **Languages:** | English(mother tongue) |
| | French(spoken and written well) |

**Work Experience:**

| 2014—2015 | Assistant Manager in Apple Company |
| | Reason for leaving: a more challenging job offered by Microsoft, a multinational computer company |
| 2015—2018 | Sales Manager in Microsoft Company, New York |
| | Reason for leaving: moved to China |
| 2018—present | Sales Manage in IBM, a large computer company in Beijing |
| | Reason for leaving: being homesick |
| **Hobbies:** | Swimming, tennis and painting |
| **References:** | |
| Mr. Zhang Ming | Top Manager, IBM Computer Company, Beijing 100080 |

3. Dear Mr. Peter Thompson,

Allow me to convey my sincere congratulations on your promotion to General Manager. I am delighted that many years' service you have given to your company should have been recognized and appreciated.

We wish you great accomplishments in your new post and look forward to closer cooperation with you in the future development of trade between our two companies. Once again, please accept my sincerest apologies.

Sincerely,

×××

4. Dear Mr. Brown,

I was very concerned when I received your letter of yesterday complaining that the central heating system in your new house had not been completed by the date promised.

On referring to our earlier correspondence, I found that I had mistaken the date for completion. The fault is entirely mine and I deeply regret that it should have occurred.

I realize the inconvenience our oversight must be causing you and will do everything possible to avoid any further delay. I have already given instructions for the work to have priority and the engineers working on the job to be placed on overtime. These arrangements should see the installation completed by next weekend.

Yours faithfully,

×××

5. Dear Mr. Anderson,

I would like to show my gratitude to you for your generous offer to help us out of the recession. The recession almost reduced us to bankruptcy. But we struggled through it with your bold cooperation and now our business is flourishing. I sincerely hope the relationship between our two companies will become more and more prosperous and productive.

I once again want to thank you for your assistance during the difficult period.

Yours faithfully,

×××

**D：Translate the following business letters into English.**

1. 求职信

敬启者：

贵公司在广告招聘一名程序设计师。我在编程领域所受的教育和积累的经验证明我可以请求您考虑我来担任这个职务。

从我的简历中可以看到,我在编程领域有贵公司所要求的 3 年经验,因此,我相信,一旦我被录用任命,我就能在短时间内掌握这一职位所要求的职责,并很快就会有成果。

我在思达卓公司任职 3 年内从没有因为个人原因而缺勤。

至于"期望的工资值",我愿意接受根据公司正常薪级表计算出来的工资。

只要接到录用通知,我随时可以来上班。

当然,面试可以使您判断我是否有足够的资格来胜任这一职务。我很高兴能在您方便的时候进行面试。

谨上

2. 辞职信

因为我已经接受了另外一个高工资的职务,我希望把我的意愿通知给您：从明天起一个月后,即 2022 年 1 月 1 日,就会终止我在本公司的雇佣关系。

3. 邀请函

尊敬的卡尔·米勒先生：

为了答谢新老客户对我们的一贯支持,我们将在 27 层空中酒廊举办商务客户答谢会,敬请期待您的光临。

时间：2021 年 12 月 3 日,星期六,上午 10：00

地点：海淀区中关村大街 6 号

联系人：刘明

电话：8266××××,1391103××××

传真：8266××××

4. 感谢信

敬爱的部长先生：

我现写信是为了感谢您在我和我们代表团一行访问贵国时所给予我们的盛情款待。我还要感谢您和我进行的会谈,充分的信息使我受益匪浅。

在整个访问过程中,包括我在内的整个代表团都为贵国商业代表对与中国合作表示出来的热情所感染。真诚地希望我们两国之间能有更多类似的交流,这样我们也能继续对话,从而尽可能扩大两国的双边经济与贸易关系,并能把两国的商业人士联合起来。

诚请您能早日来中国访问,这样我方可尽地主之谊,报答您对我们的盛情款待,也正是您的盛情款待使我们在您那美丽国度短暂的停留变得终生难忘。

顺便带去我个人的问候！

谨上

5. 贺信

布莱克经理：

我谨代表我们思达贸易公司对贵公司成立 25 周年纪念日表示真心的祝贺。我和我的同事们都希望贵公司的生意越来越红火。

谨上

## Section 5　Extensive Expression

### 一、推荐信、求职信、简历

| | |
|---|---|
| 1. reference | 证明书(人)，推荐书(人) |
| 2. a strong sense of responsibility | 强烈的责任感 |
| 3. recommend | 推荐 |
| 4. a pleasant personality | 性格好 |
| 5. outstanding performance | 出色表现 |
| 6. fulfill one's duty | 完成任务 |
| 7. academic records | 学业积累 |
| 8. job hunting | 求职 |
| 9. recruitment | 招聘 |
| 10. resume | 简历 |
| 11. applicant | 申请者 |
| 12. application | 申请 |
| 13. candidate | 候选人 |
| 14. interview | 面试 |
| 15. interviewer | 面试者 |
| 16. interviewee | 被面试者 |
| 17. vacancy | 职位空缺 |
| 18. opening | 空职 |
| 19. qualification | 资格 |
| 20. bachelor | 学士 |
| 21. master | 硕士 |
| 22. doctor | 博士 |
| 23. M.S. | 理学硕士 |
| 24. M.A. | 文学硕士 |
| 25. M.A.,Journalism | 新闻硕士 |
| 26. B.A.,Engineering | 工程学学士 |
| 27. dismiss/fire | 解雇 |

| 28. | employ/hire | 雇佣 |
| 29. | alias | 别名 |
| 30. | present/current address | 现住址 |
| 31. | permanent address | 永久住址 |
| 32. | date of birth | 出生日期 |
| 33. | native place | 籍贯 |
| 34. | nationality | 民族;国籍 |
| 35. | marital status | 婚姻状况 |
| 36. | single/married | 未婚/已婚 |
| 37. | health condition | 健康状况 |
| 38. | date of availability | 可到职时间 |
| 39. | contact number | 联系号码 |
| 40. | reference | 推荐人 |
| 41. | diploma | 文凭 |
| 42. | competent | 胜任的 |
| 43. | educational background | 教育背景 |
| 44. | secure a position | 寻求职务 |
| 45. | interpersonal skills | 人际沟通能力 |
| 46. | expected salary | 预期工资 |
| 47. | part-time job | 兼职 |
| 48. | temporary job | 临时工 |
| 49. | practical experience | 实际经验 |
| 50. | working experience | 工作经验 |

## 二、工作职务、邀请函、感谢信、致歉信

| 1. | welfare | 福利 |
| 2. | capability/aptitude | 能力 |
| 3. | administrative manager | 行政经理 |
| 4. | assistant manager | 副经理 |
| 5. | computer engineer | 计算机工程师 |
| 6. | management consultant | 管理顾问 |
| 7. | marketing executive | 销售主管 |
| 8. | programmer | 程序设计师 |
| 9. | regional manager | 地区经理 |
| 10. | sales supervisor | 销售主管 |
| 11. | administrative assistant | 行政助理 |
| 12. | civil engineer | 土木工程师 |
| 13. | engineering technician | 工程技术员 |
| 14. | legal assistant | 法务助理 |

| | | |
|---|---|---|
| 15. | marketing representative | 销售代理 |
| 16. | personnel clerk | 人事部职员 |
| 17. | project staff | 项目人员 |
| 18. | bonus | 奖金 |
| 19. | promote, promotion | 提升 |
| 20. | professional ethics | 职业道德 |
| 21. | work milieu | 工作环境 |
| 22. | paid holiday | 带薪休假 |
| 23. | probation | 试用, 见习 |
| 24. | probationary period | 试用期 |
| 25. | starting salary | 起薪 |
| 26. | commencing salary | 起薪 |
| 27. | pay rise | 涨工资 |
| 28. | pension | 养老金 |
| 29. | overtime | 加班, 超时 |
| 30. | subtle discrimination | 轻微的歧视 |
| 31. | farewell party | 惜别会 |
| 32. | anniversary | 周年纪念 |

# Unit *10*

# Business Contracts and Agreements

Unit Objectives

In this unit you should

➢ familiarize yourself with the format of business contract and agreement.

➢ have a good command of the basic words and useful expressions of business contract and agreement in this unit.

➢ enable yourself to acquire the translating skills of the passive sentences.

## Section 1　Theme Lead-in

**Read the following passage to gain a better understanding of this unit.**

A contract is an agreement which sets forth binding obligations of the relevant parties. It is enforceable by law, and any party that fails to fulfill his contractual obligations may be sued and forced to make compensation, though most contracts do not give rise to disputes. Contract is becoming more and more important in the business. Without contract, trade couldn't be performed successfully.

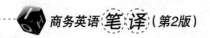

The contract is based on agreement, which is the result of business negotiations. A contract including both the rights and duties of the contracting parties has long been the only legal document between the parties. A contract is entered into by two or more parties with the serious intention of creating a legal obligation or obligations, which may or may not have elements in writing. Contracts can also be formed orally. Therefore, there are two types of business negotiations: oral and written. The former refers to direct discussions conducted at trade fairs or by sending trade groups abroad or by inviting foreign customers. Business discussions through international trunk calls are also included in this category. Written negotiations often begin with inquiries made by the buyers to get information about the goods to be ordered such as quantity, specifications, prices, time of shipment and other terms. Once it is signed, it should not be easily changed, so it is proper to obtain legal advice as to the best set of contractual terms appropriate to the product and type of business.

Using a contract in business dealings helps ensure an agreement is acted on, insofar as a broken contract could result in a lawsuit or out of court settlement and the payment of damages caused by the breach. The remedy at law for breach of contract is usually "damages" or monetary compensation. In equity, the remedy can be specific performance of the contract or an injunction. Both remedies award the damaged party the "benefit of the bargain" or expectation damages, which are greater than mere reliance damages, as in promissory estoppel.

As a means of economic ordering, contract relies on the notion of consensual exchange and has been extensively discussed in broader economic, sociological, and anthropological terms. In American English, the term extends beyond the legal meaning to encompass a broader category of agreements.

## Section 2　Translation Warming-up

**A：Translate the following sentences about contracts and agreements into Chinese.**

1. Hereafter called "the Purchaser".

2. The vendor shall deliver the goods to the vendee by June 15.

3. Both parties shall act in accordance with the provisions of the agreement.

4. Either party reserves the right to terminate this agreement upon negotiation.

5. The execution of the contract depends on the procurements of necessary permits in Hong Kong and Nigeria.

6. All the activities of both parties shall comply with the contractual stipulations.

7. The Purchaser is desirous of importing the said goods for sale in the said territory.

8. This Contract hereby comes into effect from the date of execution by the Purchaser and the Builder.

9. The Seller is desirous of exporting the undermentioned products to the territory stipulated below.

10. The undersigned hereby agrees that the new products whereto this trade name is

appropriate are made in China.

**B：Translate the following sentences about contracts and agreements into English.**

1. 本合同有效期至 2023 年 12 月 31 日。

2. 我们相信你方见到我们的汇票时即照付。

3. 交货期改为 8 月并将美元折合成人民币。

4. 我公司的条件是：3 个月内，即不得晚于 5 月 1 日，支付现金。

5. 买卖双方同意按下述条款购买出售下列商品并签订本合同。

6. 货物负责人应有权按当时的条件和手续，从暂存货栈提取其货物。

7. 争议各方可以事先承认委员会或理事会的建议对该方有约束力。

8. 随函附 3000 美元支票一张，以支付截至目前所欠你方的全部佣金。

9. 如果上述货物对船舶和（或）船上其他货物造成任何损害，托运人应负全责。

10. 于生效日期届满六年后，受托人须尽全力于其认为实际可行之情况下尽速以现金代价出售当时信托资产所包括之所有原先股份或其他证券。

## Section 3　Topic Features and Translation Principles

### 一、商务合同和协议

商务合同和协议是一种特殊的应用文体，重在记实，用词行文的一大特点就是准确与严谨。翻译商务合同貌似简单，实则不然。商务合同和协议属于法律性公文，所以翻译时，要符合法律公文的特点，要做到译文结构严谨、逻辑严密、言简意赅。其中，商务合同包含买卖合同、用工合同、租赁合同等。

### 二、商务合同和协议的翻译原则

作为具有法律效力的商务合同或协议，应注意以下原则：

#### 1. 用词需要准确明晰、庄严朴实

商务合同和协议需要将合同双方的意愿用清晰的语言表达出来，注意语言的明晰性，用词的准确性，注意同近义词的差别。合同属于法律文本，规定合同双方当事人的权利和义务以及其他相关事宜，对双方都具有法律约束力。那么就要求译者使用准确规范的措辞，措辞要具体完整，具有专业性、单义性和法律性。其表现主要包括合同中长句与大写字母的运用、shall 等法律词语的运用以及商务术语。

经贸术语：L/C 信用证，collection 托收，more or less 公差或溢短装，commence 开始，fixed assets 固定资产，registered capital 注册资本。

法律术语：claim 索赔，arbitration award 仲裁裁决，force majeure 不可抗力，infringement 侵犯，in the presence of 见证人，breach the contract 违约。

 例句

例 1. 采取欺诈或者胁迫的手段订立的合同无效。

Contracts concluded by means of fraud or duress shall be void.

例 2. 卖方应保证货物达到质量标准，没有瑕疵。

The seller shall guarantee that the goods meet the quality standards and without blemish.

例 3. 当事人双方都违反合同的，应当各自承担相应的责任。

If both parties breach the contract, each shall be commensurately liable for the breach of contract that is its responsibility.

例 4. 由于不可抗力因素造成迟交或不交货物，卖方可免除责任，但应尽快通知买方。

In case of Force Majeure, the Sellers shall not be responsible for late delivery or non-delivery of the goods but shall notify the Buyers without delay.

例 5. 未经披露方事先同意，接收方不得向除自己员工以外的人披露保密信息。

The receiving Party shall not disclose the confidential information to anyone other than its own employees without a prior consent from the disclosing Party.

### 2. 用词正式，多古体词，惯用副词

为了体现商务合同和协议的法律性和严肃性，因此英文合同的用词较正式、多古体词。hereafter 在（此）下文，herebefore 在（此）上文，hereby 根据本……，特此，herein 在本……，hereinbefore 在（包括）此上文，hereinafter 在（包括）此下文，hereof 对此，hereto/hereunto 关于，hereunder 在下文，hereupon 就此，herewith 于此（一起）；thereafter 在（所指）以下，thereby 因此，therefrom 自（所指），therein 关于（所指），thereinbefore 在（包括）及上文，thereinafter 在（包括）及下文，thereof 由此，thereon 关于那一点，thereto（参见）那一点，thereunder 在（所指）以下，thereupon 所以，therewith（所指）于此；whereas 根据/鉴于，whereby 根据/按照，wherein 在（所指）中，whereof 关于那（一项），whereon 在（所指）上。

 **例句**

例 1. 下列签署人兹保证所供应之货物在美国国内制造。

The undersigned hereby certify that the goods to be supplied are made in USA.

例 2. 对于因履行本合同所发生的一切争议，本合同双方应友好协商解决。

All disputes arising form the performance of this Contract shall, through amicable negotiations, be settled by the Parties hereto.

例 3. 本合同所称对外贸易经营者，是指依照本法规定从事对外贸易经营活动的法人和其他组织。

Foreign trade dealers as mentioned in this Contract shall, in accordance with provisions hereof, cover such legal entities and other organizations as are engaged in foreign trade dealings.

例 4. 本协议及其附件包含本协议双方间完整的协议和磋商，取代以前所有与本协议标的有关的协议和磋商。

This agreement with Exhibits embodies the entire agreement and understanding between the parties hereto and supersedes all prior agreements and understandings in relation to the subject matter hereof.

例 5. 如果买方在规定的时间内未付清货款，买方的保证金将不予退还，而且买方应承担卖方由此引起的一切损失。

The deposit by the Buyers shall not be refunded if the Buyers fail to make full payment within the time herein specified and the Buyers shall be liable for all losses incurred therefrom to the Sellers.

### 3. 格式化结构和表达方式

作为应用文体,商务合同和协议多使用格式化的套用句式或结构。在翻译合同和协议时,译文应表述客观,不带有任何感情色彩的词汇,也不适用文学中的拟人、夸张和比喻等手法,内容表达严谨,通常以长句为主,常用句法为定语从句。

able and willing 能够并愿意,any and all 任何及所有,alteration/modification or substitution 更改或修正,amendments and revisions 修改,approve and accept 接受,by and between 双方,claim and demand 要求,complete and final understanding 全部和最终的理解,compensation or damages 补偿或赔偿,custom fees and duties 关税,covenants and agreements 契约和协议,due and payable 到期应付的,furnish and provide 提供,in full force and effect 完全有效的,losses and damages 损失和损坏,made and signed 由……签,null and void 无效、失效,protect and save 保护及挽救,terms and conditions 条款,rights and interests 权益。

 例句

例 1. 本协议特由中国公司(以下简称甲方)与公司(以下简称乙方)于……日期订立。

This agreement is hereby made and entered into on ( Date ) , by and between Co. China ( hereinafter referred to as Party A ) and Co. ( hereinafter referred to as Party B ) .

例 2. 承租人也同意立即以现金方式补偿出租人所支付的对设备征收的所有动产税费。

Lessee also agrees to promptly reimburse Lessor, in cash, forany and all personal property taxes levied against equipment and pain by Lessor.

例 3. 承租人应保证赔偿出租人全部的责任、索赔或要求,不论是基于设备的位置、条件或使用与否。

Lessee shall indemnify Lessor of and from all liability, claim and demand whatsoever arising form the location, condition, or use of equipment whether in operation or not.

例 4. 本协议各方同意,一方对于有关生产及装配许可证产品或部件所做的改进、修整、更新发明或设计均应立即全部通知另一方。

The parties to this Agreement agree that either Party hereto shall, immediately and fully, notify the other Party of any such matters comprising an improvement, modification, further invention or design as the Party in question may discover, make or develop with respect to manufacture and assembly of the Licensed Products or components thereof.

例 5. 承租人应由此同意保护并使出租人免于任何因火灾、洪水、爆炸、偷盗造成的任一和全部损失或对设备造成的损害。

Lessee shall and does hereby agree to protect and save Lessor harmless against any and all losses or damages to equipment by fire, flood, explosion or theft.

### 4. 合理补充公文语及惯用语

为了使译文结构严谨、逻辑严密、言简意赅，且符合英文商务合同的表达习惯，在英译时，酌情使用英语惯用的一套公文语副词，会使译文更地道、流畅。如：in the event of 如果，in case 如果，in witness whereof 作为协议事项的证据，in consideration of 考虑到，以……为约因，now these presents witness 兹特立约为据，provided that 前提是，in accordance with/pursuant to 根据，依据，按照……的规定，without prejudice to 在不影响……前提下，for the purpose of... 就……而言，subject to 在……条件下。

 **例句**

例 1. 如果本合同提前终止，则合同附件也随之终止。

In case the Contract terminates prematurely, the Contract Appendices shall likewise terminate.

例 2. 本协议书上面所签订的日期由双方根据各自的法律签订并执行，特立此据。

In Witness Whereof, the parties hereto have caused the agreement to be executed on the day and year first before written in accordance with their respective laws.

例 3. 各方在平等互利的基础上，经友好协商，一致同意依照相关法律和本合同的规定签订这份销售合同。

After friendly consultation conducted in accordance with the principles of equality and mutual benefit, the Parties have agreed to enter into a sales contract in accordance with Applicable Laws and the provisions of this Contract.

例 4. 合同当事人可以选择处理合同争议所适用的法律。当事人没有选择的，适用与合同有最密切联系的国家的法律。

The parties to a contract may choose the proper law applicable to the settlement of contract disputes. In the absence of such a choice by the parties, the law of the country that has the closest connection with the contract shall apply.

例 5. 若因任何交货延误导致的代理方损失，代理方可凭代理方所在地行政当局登记的损失清单向制造方索赔，但须出具证明。

In the event of any loss caused by the delay in the delivery, the Representative can claim a compensation from the Manufacturer with a certificate and detailed list registered by the administration authorities of the Representative's site.

## Section 4  Translating Strategies, Samples and Training

### Translating Strategies

#### 被动句的翻译

所谓被动句（the passive sentences）的翻译，即把原文中的主动语态译成被动语态。无论是口语表达，还是书面用语，英语中多用被动语态，在处理汉英翻译的过程中，可以将汉语中的主动语态翻译成英语中的被动语态,更符合英语的表达习惯,易于理解。此外,被动结构比主动结构更少主观性,更适合商务合同以及科技论著型文章的翻译。被动结构更能突出主要特征,说明对象,引人注目。

被动句的翻译主要是指主动句中处于宾语的受事者被提到主语位置上,被动句强调被动者或受事者的被动地位和被动状态。凡是在不必说出主动者,不愿说出主动者,无从说出主动者或者为了便于连贯上下文等场合,往往使用被动语态。

 例句

例 1. 本合同一式两份,在见证人出席下双方签字。

The contract is made in duplicate and signed by both parties in the presence of witness.

例 2. 卸货条件为港口习惯快速装卸,按此办法不发生滞期费或速遣费问题。

Discharging is based on C.Q.D terms, it shall be made at Customary Quick Dispatch, where neither demurrage nor dispatch money is called for.

例 3. 有关本合同买卖双方之间所引起的任何纠纷、争议或歧见,可付诸仲裁。

Any disputes, controversies or differences which may arise between the parties in connection with this contract may be referred to arbitration.

例 4. 货物的质量和价格必须使进出口双方都能接受。

The quality and prices of the commodities to be exchanged between the ex-importers in the two countries shall be acceptable to both sides.

例 5. 合同签订时先预付货款总额的三分之一,装船后凭跟单汇票再付三分之一,剩余的三分之一在货物抵达时凭光票一次性付清。

One third of the total amount shall be paid with the order when the Contract is signed, one third by documentary bill when shipment is effected, and the balance by clean bills when the goods have arrived.

此外,值得注意的是,英译汉时汉语译文可以采用主动语态,但并不一定要有主语,而汉译英时汉语原文中的无主句译成英语后必须添加主语。商务合同中经常用代词 it 作句子的形式主语,常用句型为 it is + done that...结构,其翻译方法通常是采用被动译为主动并将施事者译出或直接译出从句,不译被动态。通过用 it 作形式主语,避免了合同的主观性,表现出合同的客观公正性。

 例句

例 1. 经双方考虑,同意按下列条款签订本合同。

It is mutually considered that the two parties agree to enter this contract under the terms and conditions set forth as follows.

例 2. 双方同意,销售报告应由甲方财务主任签署。

It is mutually agreed that the sales report shall be signed by chief financial officer of Party A.

例 3. 必须强调,买方应于收到本合同之日起 3 天内签字并退还合同的副本。

It is essentially stressed that the Buyer is requested to sign and return the duplicate of this Contract within 3 days from the date of receipt.

例 4. 卖方对由保险公司、船舶公司和其他转运单位或邮政部门造成的损失不承担责任。

It is understood that the Seller shall not be liable for any discrepancy of the goods shipped due to causes for which the Insurance Company, Shipping Company, other Transportation Organizations and/or Post Office are liable.

例 5. 双方同意制造厂出具品质及数量或重量检验证明书作为买方向付款银行议付货款单据之一。

It is mutually agreed that the certificates of quality and quantity or weight issued by the Manufacturer shall be part of the document to be presented to the paying bank for negotiation of payments.

另一点是有些英语被动句在翻译成汉语时仍以被动语态出现，但避开用"被"字，根据具体的上下文可用受、为、由、为……所、需、使、经等表示被动概念的词语代替。

 例句

例 1. 保险应由卖方支付。

The insurance shall be paid by Seller.

例 2. 由甲方按发票价格的110%投保共同海损险和战争险。

To be covered by Party A for 110% of the invoice value, covering W.A. and War Risk.

例 3. 技术转让协议的期限由合资公司与乙方签订并经审批机关批准。

The term for the technology transfer agreement is signed by the Joint Venture Company and Party B and it shall be approved by the approval authority.

例 4. 货物需经独立的检验员检验，其出具的品质及数量检验证明书应为最后确认标准。

Goods are to be inspected by an independent inspector whose certificate of the inspection of quality and quantity is to be final.

例 5. 因本合同产生的或与本合同有关的任何争议，都应交由中华人民共和国管辖权的法院处理。

Any dispute arising out of or in connection with this Contract shall be submitted to the competent court in the People's Republic of China.

Translating Samples

一、外贸合同

编号：

日期：

签约地点：

卖方:

地址:　　　　　　　　　邮政编码:

电话:　　　　　　　　　传真:

买方:

地址:　　　　　　　　　邮政编码:

电话:　　　　　　　　　传真:

买卖双方同意按下列条款由卖方出售,买方购进下列货物:

1. 货号:

2. 品名及规格:

3. 数量:

4. 单价:

5. 总值:数量及总值均有_____%的增减,由卖方决定。

6. 生产国和制造厂家:

7. 包装:

8. 唛头:

9. 装运期限:

10. 装运口岸:

11. 目的口岸:

12. 保险:由卖方按发票全额110%投保至_____为止的_____险。

13. 付款条件:

买方须于_____年_____月_____日将保兑的,不可撤销的,可转让、可分割的即期信用证开到卖方。信用证议付有效期延至上列装运期后15天在中国到期,该信用证中必须注明允许分运及转运。

14. 单据:

15. 装运条件:

16. 品质与数量、重量的异议与索赔:

17. 人力不可抗拒因素:

由于水灾、火灾、地震、干旱、战争或协议一方无法预见、控制、避免和克服的其他事件导致不能或暂时不能全部或部分履行本协议,该方不负责任。但是,受不可抗力事件影响的一方须尽快将发生的事件通知另一方,并在不可抗力事件发生15天内将有关机构出具的不可抗力事件的证明寄交对方。

18. 仲裁:

在履行协议过程中,如产生争议,双方应友好协商解决。若通过友好协商未能达成协议,则提交中国国际贸易促进委员会对外贸易仲裁委员会,根据该会仲裁程序暂行规定进行仲裁。该委员会决定是终局的,对双方均有约束力。仲裁费用,除另有规定外,由败诉一方负担。

19. 备注:

20. 卖方:　　　　　　　　　买方:

签字:　　　　　　　　　签字:

**译文：**

No：

Date：

Signed at：

Sellers：

Address： Postal Code：

Tel： Fax：

Buyers：

Address： Postal Code：

Tel： Fax：

The seller agrees to sell and the buyer agrees to buy the undermentioned goods on the terms and conditions stated below.

1. Article No.：

2. Description & Specification：

3. Quantity：

4. Unit Price：

5. Total Amount：

With _____% more or less both in quantity and amount allowed at the sellers option.

6. Country of Origin and Manufacturer：

7. Packing：

8. Shipping Marks：

9. Time of Shipment：

10. Port of Loading：

11. Port of Destination：

12. Insurance：To be effected by buyers for 110% of full invoice value covering _____ up to _____ only.

13. Payment：

By confirmed, irrevocable, transferable and divisible L/C to be available by sight draft to reach the sellers before ____/____/_____ and to remain valid for negotiation in China until 15 days after the aforesaid time of shipment. The L/C must specify that transhipment and partial shipments are allowed.

14. Documents：

15. Terms of Shipment：

16. Quality/Quantity Discrepancy and Claim：

17. Force Majeure：

Either party shall not be held responsible for failure or delay to perform all or any part of this agreement due to flood, fire, earthquake, drought, war or any other events which could not be predicted, controlled, avoided or overcome by the relative party. However, the party affected by the event of Force Majeure shall inform the other party of its occurrence in writing as soon as possible

154

and thereafter send a certificate of the event issued by the relevant authorities to the other party within 15 days after its occurrence.

18. Arbitration

All disputes arising from the execution of this agreement shall be settled through friendly consultations. In case no settlement can be reached, the case in dispute shall then be submitted to the Foreign Trade Arbitration Commission of the China Council for the Promotion of International Trade for Arbitration in accordance with its Provisional Rules of Procedure. The decision made by this commission shall be regarded as final and binding upon both parties. Arbitration fees shall be borne by the losing party, unless otherwise awarded.

19. Remark：

20. Sellers：                                    Buyers：

　　Signature：                                 Signature：

## 二、聘用合同

_____（聘方）聘请_____（受聘方）为_____（职务）。双方本着友好合作的精神,同意签订并遵守本合同。合同条款如下：

1. 聘期为,自_____年____月____日起,至_____年____月____日止。

2. 受聘方的工作任务经双方协商确定如下：

3. 聘方每月(日、年)支付给受聘方薪金￥_____并提供如下待遇(住宿费、膳食费、医疗费等)：

4. 双方均不得无故解除合同。

5. 聘方如中途终止合同,则除按照待遇条件承担受聘方的有关费用外,还须作出如下补偿：

6. 如受聘方中途提出辞职,聘方自同意之日起即停发工资,受聘方不再享有各种待遇。

7. 本合同自受聘方到职之日起生效,聘期届满即自行失效。如一方要求延长聘期,必须在本合同期满之前向对方提出,经双方协商确认后,再另行签订延长聘期合同。

8. 受聘方同意本合同的各项条款。

9. 本合同用中、英文两种文字写成,两种文本具有同等效力。

聘方：

受聘方：

_____年____月____日

**译文**：

_____( the engaging party ) has engaged _____( the engaged party ) as _____ ( position ). The two parties in the spirit of friendship and cooperation have entered into an agreement to sign and to comply with the following terms：

1. The duration of service is _____, i. e. from ____/____/_____ to ____/____/_____

2. By mutual consultations the work of the engaged party is decided as follows：

3. The engaging party pays the engaged party a salary of ￥_____ by month ( day, year) and provide the engaged party：( acco mmodation , board, medical care, etc. )

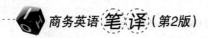

4. Neither party shall cancel the contract without sufficient causes or reasons.

5. If the engaging party finds it imperative to terminate the contract, in addition to bearing the corresponding expenses for wages, it shall pay the engaged party _____ as compensation allowance：

6. If the engaged party submits his resignation in the course of his service, the engaging party shall stop paying the engaged party the salary from the day when his resignation is approved by the engaging party, and the engaged party shall no longer enjoy the salary and benefits stipulated.

7. The present contract shall come into effect on the first day of the term of service herein stipulated and cease immediately to be effective at its expiration. If either party wishes to renew the contract, the other party shall be notified before it expires. Upon agreement by both parties through consultation a new contract can be signed.

8. The engaged party agrees to all the articles in this contract.

9. The present contract is done in Chinese and English, both versions being equally valid.

____/____/_____（for example：November 6,2021）

The engaging party：

The engaged party：

## 三、建筑合同

Party A：                          Party B：

Contract No

Date：

Signed at：

Witnesses that the Party A for considerations hereinafter named, contracts and agrees with the Party B that Party A will, within _____ days, next following the date hereof, build and finish a Library Building for Party B. (the building hereinafter is referred to as the said building.) The said building is of the following dimensions, with reinforced concrete, brick, stones and other materials, as are described in plans and specifications annexed.

In consideration of the foregoing, Party B shall, for itself and its legal representatives, promise to pay Party A the sum of _____ RMB yuan. And the remaining sum will be paid upon the completion of the work.

It is further agreed that in order to be entitled to the said payments (the first one excepted, which is otherwise secured), Party A or its legal representatives shall, according to the architect's appraisement, have expended, in labor and material, the value of the payments already received by Party A, on the building, at the time of payment.

For failure to accomplish the faithful performance of the agreement aforesaid, the party so failing agrees to forfeit and pay to the other _____ RMB yuan as fixed and settled damages, within one month form the time so failing.

In witness where of we have hereunto set our hands and seals the day and year first above written.

Signed, sealed and delivered.

in the presence of

Party A:                                    Party B:

**译文：**

甲方：                                    乙方：

合同编号：

日期：

签约地点：

特约定：

甲方基于下文所列各种因素，特与乙方达成了协议并一致同意：由甲方在订约日期之翌日起_____天之内为乙方建造并完成_____（涉约建筑）。涉约建筑之规模及所需的钢筋、水泥、砖块、石子和其他建筑材料之数量，均在作为合同附件的设计图和施工细则中予以说明。

基于上述情况，乙方及其法定代表人郑重承诺向甲方支付人民币_____元整。剩余款项将在竣工后支付。

订约双方并同意由甲方或其法定代表人在领取各项付款时，为证明有权领用上述各次付款（第一次付款除外，因其另有保证），必须由建筑师作出评定，证明已经收到的付款之价值已经消耗在劳务及材料费用之中。

上述协议如未能忠实执行，则违约一方同意其应享有权利自动丧失，且在违约之日后一个月之内，向对方或其法定代表人赔偿人民币_____元整，作为商定之损失赔偿费。

为示信守，各方谨于上文起首载明之日期签名、盖章。

本合同当下列人员之面交付。

甲方：                                    乙方：

### 📖 Translating Training

**A：Translate the following sentences about contracts & agreements into Chinese.**

1. Any increase or decrease in the freight after the date of sale shall be for the buyer's account.

2. The Seller hereby confirms having sold to the Buyer the following goods on the terms and conditions as specified below.

3. In witness whereof, the parties hereto have hereunder set their respective hands and seals.

4. The undersigned Sellers and Buyers have agreed to close the following transactions in accordance with the terms and conditions stipulated below.

5. The production design, technology of manufacturing, means of testing, materials prescription, standard of quality and training of personnel shall be stipulated in Chapter 5 in this contract.

6. The packing of the goods shall be preventive from dampness, rust, moisture, erosion and shock, and shall be suitable for ocean transportation.

7. The Appendix hereto shall, through the contract period, be deemed to be construed as part of this contract.

8. According to the contract, both parties are entitled to take protective measures to guard against hostile takeover.

9. What you should pay attention to is that claim must be made within the term of validity stipulated in the contract.

10. We have drawn a draft at sight on you against the documents for the amount of invoice through the Bank of Asia.

11. If any party results in the damage of another party, the party breaking the agreement shall be liable for compensation and bear legal liability.

12. Contracts shall be concluded according to the principle of equality and mutual benefit and the principle of achieving agreement through consultation.

13. The Contractor shall not assign the Contract or any part thereof, or any benefit or interest there in or there under without the prior written consent of the Employer.

14. The contract shall be valid for 20 years from the effective date of the contract, on the expiry of the valid term of the contract; the contract shall automatically become null and void.

15. A proposal for concluding a contract addressed to one or more specific persons constitutes an offer if it is definite and indicates the intention of the offer or to be bound in case of acceptance.

**B：Translate the following sentences about contracts & agreements into English.**

1. 双方同意组成一个有限责任合资经营公司（以下简称 JVC），在主管工商行政管理局登记注册。

2. 卖方应于本合同规定的装船期前 40 天，以电报形式通知买方以下内容：合同号、品名、数量、价值、件数、毛重、尺码、港口、装运日期，以便买方洽订舱位。

3. 假如劳动成本、材料价格、设备租金等比预期价格增加 10% 以上（含 10%），合同金额应作自动调整。

4. 甲方应于合同签订日后 30 天内委派技术员对乙方的工作人员进行培训，费用由乙方负责。

5. 在合理时期内若无人认领货物或货物变质、腐烂、失去价值，承运人可按其留置权自行予以变卖、抛弃或处置该货物而不负担任何责任，全部风险和费用由货方承担。

6. 本租赁合同生效日起，承租人应向出租人支付相当于两个月租金（4,000 美元）的押金，作为对忠实履行本租约的担保金，本押金将于 2022 年 5 月 11 日租约到期时，在承租人交还租房而设备完好的前提下，归还承租人（不计息）；或者，在租约提前终止时，按本租约规定办理。

7. 由于资金被许多业务占用，他们迫不得已要求较宽容的付款条件。

8. 在国际合同中，有两个具有更深意义的条款，这就是支付条件和交货条件。

9. 有了书面合同，更容易证明双方之间达成的条款，并消除就相关言论而产生的争议。

10. 当事人因不可抗力不能履行合同的全部或者部分义务的，免除其全部或者部分责任。

11. 就国际贸易合同的共同特征而言,最典型的可以说是内容的合法性,条款的完整性以及语言的准确性。

12. 口头合同具有法律效力,尽管它们常会受到误解,并且由于经常相互说法不一而难以在法庭得到证明。

13. 本协议及其附件包含本协议双方间完整协议和磋商,取代以前所有与本协议标的有关的协议和磋商。

14. 重要的是,合同的商定需要格外仔细,让买卖双方能够从条款中获益,并且清楚明白地了解他们需要履行的责任。

15. 因自然灾害或其他卖方无法控制的事故发生而致货物的全部或一部分未能交货,未交货部分的合同应予终止。

**C: Translate the following contracts & agreements into English.**

外贸合同

编号:

日期:

签约地点:

卖方:

地址:

电话:

邮政编码:

传真:

买卖双方同意按下列条款由卖方出售,买方购进下列货物:

1. 货号:

2. 品名及规格:

3. 数量:

4. 单价:

5. 总金额:

6. 生产国和制造厂家:

7. 包装:

8. 装运期限:

9. 装运口岸:

10. 目的口岸:

11. 保险:由卖方按发票全额110%投保至……为止的……险。

12. 付款条件:

买方须于_____年____月____日将保兑的,不可撤销的,可转让、可分割的即期信用证开到卖方。信用证议付有效期延至上列装运期后15天在中国到期,该信用证中必须注明允许分运及转运。

13. 单据:

14. 装运条件:

15. 品质和数量、重量的异议与索赔：

16. 人力不可抗拒因素：

由于水灾、火灾、地震、干旱、战争或协议一方无法预见、控制、避免和克服的其他事件导致不能或暂时不能全部或部分履行本协议，该方不负责任。但是，受不可抗力事件影响的一方须尽快将发生的事件通知另一方，并在不可抗力事件发生 15 天内将有关机构出具的不可抗力事件的证明寄交对方。

17. 仲裁：

18. 备注：

卖方：                          买方：

签字：                          签字：

**D：Translate the following contracts & agreements into Chinese.**

Contract

Contract No._____          Date _____

Messrs. _____（the Buyers）

Messrs. _____（the Sellers）

Have reached an agreement, whereby it is agreed that the Buyer undertakes to buy and the Seller undertakes to sell the following goods on terms and conditions as stipulated here below：

Name of Commodity：

Specification：

Quantity：

Unit Price：

Total Amount：

Packing：

Shipment：

Destination：

Insurance：

Terms of Payment：

Remarks：

Buyer's Signature                Seller's Signature

Date                            Date

## Section 5　Extensive Expression

### 一、常用词汇

1. acceptance                    承诺

2. agree                         约定

3. award                         裁定

| | |
|---|---|
| 4. beneficiary | 收益方 |
| 5. bid | 标书 |
| 6. commitment | 承诺 |
| 7. compensation | 赔偿 |
| 8. conciliation | 和解 |
| 9. controversy | 纠纷 |
| 10. covenant | 立约 |
| 11. construe | 解释 |
| 12. creditor | 债权人 |
| 13. debtor | 债务人 |
| 14. default | 违约 |
| 15. delay | 延误 |
| 16. demurrage | 滞期 |
| 17. dispute | 争议 |
| 18. enclose | 附上 |
| 19. grace | 宽限期 |
| 20. exemption | 免征税款 |
| 21. indemnities | 赔偿 |
| 22. inspection | 检验 |
| 23. integration | 最终性条款 |
| 24. investment | 投资 |
| 25. mediation | 调解 |
| 26. protest | 拒付书(金融) |
| 27. raise | 筹集(资金) |
| 28. reimbursement | 偿付 |
| 29. rectify | 弥补,纠正 |
| 30. remedy | 救济 |
| 31. remuneration | 报酬 |
| 32. require | 要求 |
| 33. royalties | 版税 |
| 34. rescind | 解除 |
| 35. sanction | 批准,认可 |
| 36. specifications | 规格 |
| 37. stipulate | 规定 |
| 38. standstill | 停滞 |
| 39. violate | 违反 |
| 40. withdrawal | 回避 |

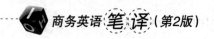

## 二、常用短语

| | |
|---|---|
| 1. arbitration agreement | 仲裁协议 |
| 2. arbitration commission | 仲裁委员会 |
| 3. acceleration of maturity | 提前到期 |
| 4. accept bills of exchange | 承兑汇票 |
| 5. award of contract | 授予合同 |
| 6. bear the legal liability and responsibility | 承担法律责任 |
| 7. breach of contract | 违约 |
| 8. capital gain | 资本利润 |
| 9. contract object | 标的 |
| 10. come into force | 生效 |
| 11. documentary letters of credit | 跟单信用证 |
| 12. documentary proof | 证明文件 |
| 13. draw up | 草拟 |
| 14. equality and mutual benefit | 平等互利 |
| 15. exemplary damage | 惩罚性赔偿 |
| 16. exemption of tax | 免税 |
| 17. force majeure | 不可抗力 |
| 18. in duplicate | 一式两份 |
| 19. interest rate | 利率 |
| 20. irrevocable credit | 不可撤销信用证 |
| 21. issuing bank | 开证行 |
| 22. jointly sign | 会签 |
| 23. legal entity | 法人 |
| 24. loan term | 借款期限 |
| 25. merger clauses | 合并条款 |
| 26. refund of tax | 退税 |
| 27. termination of agreement | 解除合同 |
| 28. terms and conditions | 条件 |
| 29. valuable considerations | 等价回报 |
| 30. wind up a business | 停业 |

# Unit *11*

# International Business Credit

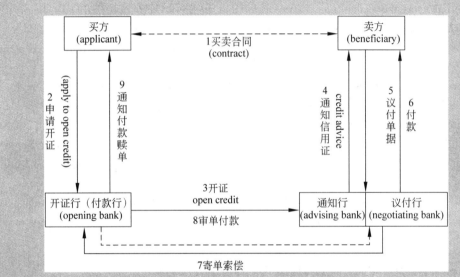

Unit Objectives

In this unit you should

➢ familiarize yourself with the format of business credits.

➢ enable yourself to acquire the basic words and useful expressions of the business credits in this unit.

➢ have a good command of the translating skills of simile, metaphor, metonymy, synecdoche, synaesthesia, personification, hyperbole, parallelism, euphemism, allegory, irony and pun.

## ❷ Section 1 Theme Lead-in

**Read the following passage to gain a better understanding of this unit.**

The letter of credit is the most widely used instrument of international banking. It has had a long and successful history as a means of facilitating international trade, particularly during times of economic and political uncertainty.

The letter of credit is the bank instrument that assures the person selling merchandise of payment if he makes the agreed upon shipment. On the other hand, it also assures the buyer and that he is not required to pay until the seller ships the goods. It is thus a catalyst that provides the buyer and the seller with mutual protection in dealing with each other.

An international trading transaction begins when a buyer and a seller sign a contract that records all the elements of transaction.

In the contract, the buyer and the seller must arrange payment. The buyer will want possession before paying, and the seller will want payment before making delivery. Since each party often has an incomplete knowledge of the other, there is a certain caution to their dealings. At this point, the letter of credit can be extremely useful. The buyer requests his bank to issue a letter of credit in favor of the seller. Assuming that the credit risk is acceptable to the bank, it issue its letter of credit. The bank has thus substituted its credit for that of the buyer, which might also be good but probably is not as well known. The letter of credit also protects the buyer, for he knows that he will not be called upon for payment by his bank until the evidence shows that the shipment has actually been effected.

The documentary requirements are designated by the buyer in his bank application for the letter of credit. The bank follows these in preparing its letter of credit.

A typical letter of credit may call for the following documents: an invoice, a bill of lading, marine insurance, a packing list, a weight list, an inspection certificate, and a certificate of origin. (a consular statement of the country of origin). The customary letter of credit calls for a "full set on board ocean bills of lading to order of shipper, blank endorsed".

Not all of these documents are required in every letter of credit transaction. Sometimes, other documents must be used. For example, food shipments coming into the United States require clearance by the Food and Drug Administration.

## Section 2　Translation Warming-up

**A：Please match the Chinese translation in column B with the English expressions in column A.**

| A | B |
|---|---|
| 1. under the new import license | A. 即期的或远期的 |
| 2. effect payment in pound | B. 即期信用证 |
| 3. against the sales confirmation or contract | C. 6 月 18 日到期 |
| 4. the documents required | D. 装船前开立信用证 |
| 5. expiring on 18th June | E. 有效期将延长至 5 月 5 日 |
| 6. open the credit before shipment | F. 请在交货前开出发票 |
| 7. the validity will be extended to 5th May | G. 按照新的进口许可证规定 |
| 8. open the invoice before the date of delivery | H. 用英镑支付 |
| 9. at sight or after sight | I. 凭销售确认书或合同 |
| 10. letter of credit at sight | J. 限制性条款 |

**B：Fill the following sentences' blanks with the same meaning as the former Chinese ones.**

1. 本信用证仅凭提示如下单证及即期汇票一式两份在中国任何银行办理议付。

This credit is available with any bank in China by negotiation against presentation of the documents detailed herein _____.

2. 对本信用证予以加保并在此保证，凡向本银行提示符合本信用证诸条款的汇票时予以议付或承兑。

At the request of the correspondent, we confirm their credit and also affirm to you _____.

3. 根据本信用证开具的汇票和单据，完全符合本信用证条款并及时提交，本银行保证向贵方履行付款责任。

The drawee who pays an endorsable check is bound _____, but not the signature of the endorsers.

4. 我行特在此向依本信用证条款出具汇票的出票人、背书人及善意(正当)持票人承诺本汇票在提示时将予以兑付。

We hereby agree with you that _____ will be duly honored on presentation and on delivery of the documents specified to the Drawee Bank.

5. 保兑的不可撤销的信用证须在合约签订之后十五天内开立，而且该信用证须在货物付运月之后至少十五天内继续有效，以便议付有关票据。

A confirmed irrevocable letter of credit shall be established within 15 days after the conclusion of the contract and such a letter of credit _____.

## Section 3　Topic Features and Translation Principles

### 一、信用证

信用证是由银行发行的证书，授权持证者可从开证行(Opening Bank)，其支行或其他有关银行或机构提取所述款项。在国际贸易中，往往存在买卖双方互不信任的矛盾，出口人担心先将货运单据交给进口方却收不到货款，进口人担心先将货款支付给出口方却收不到代表货物所有权的单据，于是就出现了银行保证付款的信用证(Letter of Credit, L/C)结算方式，其性质属于银行信用，从根本上解决了进出口双方互不信任的矛盾，同时也方便了进出口方向银行融通资金，加快其资金周转。

采用信用证的支付方式已成为国际贸易结算中的一种最重要的支付方式。信用证支付方式中所涉及的最基本的当事人有：开证申请人(进口人)、开证行(进口地银行)和受益人(出口人)。通常的当事人有六个：开证申请人(Applicant)、开证行(Opening Bank 或 Issuing Bank)、通知银行(Advising Bank 或 Informing Bank)、受益人(Beneficiary)、议付银行(Negotiating Bank)和付款银行(Paying Bank 或 Drawee Bank)。

### 二、信用证的主要内容

1. 对信用证本身的说明，如其种类、性质、有效期及到期地点。
2. 对货物的要求，根据合同进行描述。

3. 对运输的要求。

4. 对单据的要求。

5. 特殊要求。

6. 开证行对受益人及汇票持有人保证付款的责任文句。

7. 国外来证大多数均加注："除另有规定外,本证根据国际商会《跟单信用证统一惯例》即国际商会 500 号出版物(《UPC600》)办理。"

## 三、信用证的种类

### 1. 不可撤销信用证与可撤销信用证

不可撤销信用证指信用证已经开出,在有效期内未经受益人及有关当事人同意,开证行不能片面修改或撤销的信用证;可撤销信用证指信用证的开证行有权在信用证开出后不征求受益人的同意随时撤销或修改信用证。

### 2. 保兑信用证与不保兑信用证

不可撤销的保兑信用证指根据开证行的授权和要求,另一银行保证对符合信用证条款规定的单据履行付款责任;不可撤销的不保兑信用证指开证行的不可撤销跟单信用证被一家通知行予以通知,该通知行除了合理谨慎地核验所通知信用证的表面真实性以外,对受益人不承担任何责任。

### 3. 付款、承兑、议付信用证

即期付款信用证指信用证规定的受益人开立即期汇票或不需汇票仅凭单据即可向指定银行提示请求付款的信用证;延期付款信用证指不需汇票,受益人仅凭单据审核相符,确定银行承担延期付款责任起,延长一段时间,至到期日付款的信用证。承兑信用证指开证行或付款行在收到符合信用证条款的单据及远期汇票后给予承兑,凭汇票到期时再行付款的信用证。议付信用证可以分为公开议付信用证和限制议付信用证。公开议付信用证即任何银行均可按信用证的条款自由议付的信用证。限制议付信用证是指开证行指定某一银行或开证行本行进行议付的信用证。

### 4. 可转让信用证

可转让信用证指信用证的受益人可以请求授权付款,承担延期付款的责任,承兑或议付的银行,可以要求信用证特别授权的转让行,将信用证全部或部分转让给一个或数个受益人使用的信用证。

### 5. 对背信用证和对开信用证

对背信用证指一个信用证的受益人以这个信用证为保证要求一家银行开立以该银行为开证行,以这个受益人为申请人的一份新的信用证;对开信用证指以交易双方互为开证申请人和受益人、金额大致相等的信用证。

### 6. 预支信用证和循环信用证

预支信用证指允许出口人在装货交单前可以支取全部或部分货款的信用证;循环信用证指该信用证的部分金额或全部金额被使用后,能够重新恢复原金额再被使用,如此循环使用,直到达到总金额为止的信用证。

此外还有备用信用证和商业信用证、即期信用证与远期信用证。

## 四、信用证的翻译原则

信用证是一项约定,具有法律文书的语言特点,用词严谨、正规、严肃、专业。在国际贸易中,信用证主要用英文起草,信用证开立主要有信开、电开和 SWIFT 三种方式。在信用证的翻译中,译者要遵循准确严谨、规范通顺的翻译原则。

由于信用证具有格式化、规范化、严肃庄重、专业性强等特点,在信用证翻译中要注意以下几个方面。

### 1. 省略句式的使用和翻译

 例句

例 1. Latest shipment (is) Sept. 25,2020. (省略系动词"be")

最后装运期限为 2020 年 9 月 25 日。

例 2. Each document (is) to show B/L number and date and to be dated not earlier than 5 days from B/L date.("be to + 动词结构"表示将来概念时省去"be")

每个文件都显示提单号码和日期,文件日期不得早于提单日期 5 天。

例 3. 允许分批运输。

Partial shipment (is) allowed.(被动语态结构省去助动词"be")

例 4. 受益人用信用证号码发电传副本给进口人,提示装运细节。

Copy of beneficiaries' telex to the buyer quoting L/C number mentioning details of shipment.(分词短语作定语,独立成句)

### 2. 被动结构的使用和翻译

为把论述对象置于主语位置,削弱句子的主观色彩,信用证中广泛使用被动结构,以适用严肃庄重的文体。译者翻译时,注意被动语态和主动语态的适当转换。

 例句

例 1. The advising bank is requested to notify the beneficiary without adding their confirmation.

开证行请求通知行通知受益人,没有加具他们的保兑。

例 2. At the request of the correspondent,we confirm their credit and also affirm to you that drafts dawn in conformity with the terms of this credit will be paid by us.

根据通汇银行的要求,本银行确认此信用证并借此向贵方保证,凡出具符合信用证所列条款的汇票,届时付款。

例 3. 本银行(通知行)受通汇行(开证行)的委托,对本信用证加以保兑,并在此保证,凡提交贵公司(受益人)依信用证条款签发的汇票,届时由本银行兑付。

At the request of the correspondent (the Issuing Bank),we (the Advising Bank) have been requested to add our drawn by you(Beneficiary) in accordance with the terms of the credit will be duly honored by us.

### 3. 条件句的使用和翻译

信用证中关于条件的表达非常丰富,从语气上讲,开证行站在自己的角度,通过限制性词句,要求受益人或第二方该如何运作。以下词语经常出现在信用证的条件句表述中：in case of, only if, only after, provided, unless, if, in view of, on condition that, providing that。

 **例句**

例 1. In case of transfer, document No. (M) is no longer required, provided that the bank of China, Qingdao certifies it has transferred the credit.

如果要转移信用,无需提供 M 号文件,只需提供证明,证明青岛的中国银行已经转移了信用。

例 2. Transshipment is allowed on the condition that the entire voyage is covered by thorough B/L.

允许转运的情况下,整个航程都涵盖了周密的提单。

例 3. 如未开出信用证,将被视为违约行为,需按照卖方建议对此违约行为进行补救或采取其他补救措施。

Failure to open such Letter of Credit shall be considered a breach of contract subject to seller's advice on remedies or other action regarding such breach of contract.

### 4. 介词与书面术语的使用和翻译

信用证中大量使用介词短语来代替简单介词,如 in favor of, in compliance with, as per, in view of 等；大量使用 here, there 的复合词,如 therein, thereafter, hereinafter, thereby, thereof, hereof, hereto, hereunder 等,此外还有一些信用证专门术语。译者翻译时要格外注意。

 **例句**

例 1. This credit bears our confirmation and we hereby affirm to negotiate or to accept on presentation to us, drafts drawn and presented in conformity with the terms of this credit.

本信用证予以加保并在此保证,凡向本银行提示符合本信用证诸条款的汇票时予以议付或承兑。

例 2. We (the Issuing Bank) thereby affirm with the drawers, endorsers and bona-fide holders of drafts drawn under and in compliance with the terms of the credit that such drafts shall be duly honored on due presentation and delivery of documents as specified.

本银行(开证银行)向出票人、背书人及正当持票人保证,凡依本信用证所列条款开具的汇票,于提交时承担付款责任。

例 3. 我方兹开立不可撤销信用证,本证受益人开给申请人的 30 天一式两份汇票付款,不计利息,承兑交单。

We thereby establish this Irrevocable Credit which is available against the beneficiary's drafts drawn in duplicate on 30 days on-sight free of interest for 100% of the invoice value. Document against acceptance.

## Section 4　Translating Strategies, Samples and Training

### Translating Strategies

英语中的修辞与汉语的修辞相比,分类细、种类多。下面将英语的修辞简单介绍如下:

### 一、明喻(**Simile**)

明喻是将具有共性的不同事物作对比。这种共性存在于人们的心里,而不是事物的自然属性。标志词常用 like,as,seem,as if,as though,similar to,such as 等。

 **例句**

例 1. He was like a cock who thought the sun had risen to hear him crow.

他就像一只公鸡,以为太阳升起是为了听他打鸣似的。

例 2. Einstein only had a blanket on,as if he had just walked out of a fairy tale.

爱因斯坦只披着一条毯子,好像刚刚从童话中走出来。

### 二、隐喻,暗喻(**Metaphor**)

隐喻是简缩了的明喻,是将某一事物的名称用于另一事物,通过比较形成。

 **例句**

例 1. Hope is a good breakfast,but it is a bad supper.

希望是美好的早餐,却是糟糕的晚餐。

例 2. Some books are to be tasted,others swallowed,and some few to be chewed and digested.

一些书用来"浅尝",一些书用来"吞食",较少的一些书是用来"咀嚼和消化"的。

### 三、借喻,转喻(**Metonymy**)

借喻不直接说出所要说的事物,而使用另一个与之相关的事物名称。

 **例句**

以容器代替内容,如:

例 1. The room(people in the room)sat silent. 全屋人安静地坐着。

以资料、工具代替事物的名称,如:

例 2. Lend me your ears(listen to me),please. 请听我说。

以作者代替作品,如:

例 3. a complete Shakespeare(works of Shakespeare)莎士比亚全集

以具体事物代替抽象概念,如:

例 4. I had the muscle(strength),and they made money out of it.

我有力气,他们就用我的力气赚钱。

## 四、提喻（Synecdoche）

提喻用部分代替全体，或用全体代替部分，或用特殊代替一般。

 **例句**

例 1. There are about 100 hands（workers）working in his factory.
他的厂里约有100名工人。
例 2. He is the Newton（an expert in physics）of this century.
他是本世纪的牛顿。

## 五、通感，联觉，移觉（Synaesthesia）

这种修辞法是以视、听、触、嗅、味等感觉直接描写事物的。

 **例句**

例 1. The birds sat upon a tree and poured forth their lily like voice.
鸟儿落在树上，倾泻出百合花似的声音。
例 2. Taste the music of Mozart.
品味莫扎特的音乐。

## 六、拟人（Personification）

拟人是把生命赋予无生命的事物。

 **例句**

例 1. The night gently lays her hand at our fevered heads.
黑夜轻轻地抚摸着我们发烫的额头。
例 2. I was very happy and could hear the birds singing in the woods.
我当时如此高兴，能听到树林里鸟儿的歌唱。

## 七、夸张（Hyperbole）

夸张是以言过其实的说法表达强调的目的。它可以加强语势，增加表达效果。

 **例句**

例 1. I love you. You are the whole world to me, and the moon and the stars.
我爱你，你就是我的整个世界，我的月亮、我的星星。
例 2. When she heard the bad news, a river of tears poured out.
当她听到这个坏消息时，泪水流成了河。

## 八、排比，平行（Parallelism）

这种修辞法是把两个或两个以上的结构大体相同或相似，意思相关，语气一致的短语、句子排列成串,形成一个整体。

 **例句**

例 1. No one can be perfectly free till all are free; no one can be perfectly moral till all are moral; no one can be perfectly happy till all are happy.

没有人是完全自由的,除非所有人都获得自由;没有人是完全道德的,除非所有人都拥有了道德;没有人是完全幸福的,除非所有人都获得幸福。

例 2. In the days when all these things are to be answered for, I summon you and yours, to the last of your bad race, to answer for them. In the days when all these things are to be answered for, I summon your brother, the worst of your bad race, to answer for them separately.

当所有这一切需要偿还时,我要你和你的全家,直到你的种族中最后一个人,为之付出代价。当所有这一切需要偿还时,我要叫你的弟弟,你的种族中最坏的一个人,单独为之付出代价。

## 九、委婉,婉辞法(**Euphemism**)

婉辞法指用委婉、文雅的方法表达粗恶、避讳的话。

 **例句**

例 1. He is out visiting the necessary.
他出去方便一下。

例 2. Deng Xiaoping passed away in 1997.
邓小平于 1997 年去世了。

## 十、讽喻、比方(**Allegory**)

这是一种源于希腊文的修辞法,意为"换个方式的说法"。它是一种形象的描述,具有双重性,表层含义与真正的意思是两回事。

 **例句**

例 1. Make the hay while the sun shines.
趁热打铁。

例 2. It's time to turn sword into plough.
铸剑为犁,罢兵从耕。

## 十一、反语(**Irony**)

反语指用相反意义的词来表达意思的作文方式。如在指责过失、错误时,用赞同过失的说法;而在表扬时,则用近乎责难的说法。

**例句**

例 1. It would be a fine thing indeed not knowing what time it was in the morning.

不知道早上几点了,的确是件好事情。

例 2. "Of course,you only carry large notes,no small change on you." the waiter said to the beggar.

"当然了,您身上只带大额钞票,不带小额钞票。"侍者对那个乞丐说。

## 十二、双关(**Pun**)

双关就是用一个词在句子中的双重含义,借题发挥,作出多种解释,通过旁敲侧击达到意想不到的滑稽效果。它主要以相似的词形、词意和谐音的方式出现。

 **例句**

例 1. An ambassador is an honest man who lies abroad for the good of his country.

大使是为了自己的国家在国外撒谎的诚实的人。

例 2. If we don't hang together,we shall hang separately.

如果我们不团结一致,我们将各自上吊。

### Translating Samples

## 一、申请信用证

Opening an L/C

Dear sirs,

We open an irrevocable Letter of Credit No.325 in favor of :ABC Company,New York for account of :China National Import & Export Corporation,Qingdao to the extent of :$75,000 (U.S. Dollars Seventy-Five Thousand only),and 5% more or less is allowed.

This credit is available by beneficiary's draft(s),drawn on us,in duplicate,without recourse, on sight,for 100% of the invoice value,and accompanied by the following shipping documents:

A full set of clean "on board" "freight prepaid" Ocean Bills of Lading,made out to order and unendorsed,marked: "Notify China National Foreign Trade Transportation Corporation,at the port of destination."

Invoice in quintuplicate copies,indicating the Contract numbers.

Weight Memo/Packing Lists in duplicate,indicating gross and net weight of each package.

Certificates of Quality,Quantity/Weight in 3 copies issued by the manufacturers.

Please advise the beneficiary of the terms of credit.

We thank you for your assistance in the matter.

Yours sincerely,

×××

**译文:**

兹开立第325号不可撤销的信用证,受益人纽约ABC公司,开证人中国进出口公司青岛分公司,最高金额 75,000 美元,溢交或短交货物金额以 5% 为限。

本信用证凭受益人开具以我行为付款人按发票金额 100% 计算无追索权的即期汇票用款,该汇票一式两份,并须附有下列装运单据:

全套情节无疵,"货已装船""运费议付",空白抬头,空白背书的海运提单,并须注明"通知目的港中国对外贸易运输公司"。

发票一式五份,注明合同号码。

重量单/装箱单一式两份,载明每箱毛重和净重。

制造商出具的品质,数量/重量证明书一式三份。

请将本证通知受益人为荷。

感谢贵方的协助。

## 二、备用信用证

 案例

例 1

### Standby Letter of Credit

To：The Bank of China, Branch _____

At the request of _____ (herein referred to as Applicant) and according to the Contract Form on Opening a Bank Guarantee No. _____, we hereby issue an irrevocable standby letter of credit No. _____ in your favor for the duty/tax amount plus interest on its deferments, which the Applicant should pay in U.S. dollars equivalent to RMB _____ (in figures) _____ (in words).

If, under this standby letter of credit, Customs claims an indemnity from you, we shall pay you the above-mentioned duty/tax amount plus interest on the deferment, if any, against your attested telex stating that the Applicant has not fulfilled its obligation to turn in duty/tax plus interest on its deferment.

Within 7 business days after receipt of your arrested claim telex, we shall remit the amount to you as instructed.

For figuring out the amount of your claim, you shall apply the buying rate for US dollars as quoted by your bank on the date of claim.

This standby letter of credit remains valid until the 30th after the expiry of your letter of guarantee on duty/tax payment, therefore, any claim you may have must be served to our bank by that deadline.

This standby letter of credit is subject to the Uniform Customs and Practice for Documentary Credit (1993 Revision). ICC Publication No.500.

_____ Bank

(seal)

(authorized signature)

Date：_____

**译文：**

致中国银行＿＿＿＿＿＿＿＿＿分行

应＿＿＿＿＿＿＿＿申请人的要求，根据＿＿＿＿＿＿＿＿ 海关＿＿＿＿＿＿＿＿号《银行保证台账开设联系单》，我行兹开设以你行为受益人的＿＿＿＿＿＿＿＿号不可撤销的备用信用证，担保金额为与申请人应缴纳的税款（小写金额）＿＿＿＿＿＿＿＿元，大写金额＿＿＿＿＿＿＿＿及缓税利息合计等值的美元。

在本备用信用证下，如果海关向你提出索赔，我行将凭你行提交的声明申请人未履行缴税责任的加押索赔电向你行支付上述税款及缓税利息。

当收到加押索赔电后，我行将在 7 个银行工作日内，根据你行指示汇付索赔金额。

在你行计算索赔金额时，汇率将适用你行索赔当日中国银行公布的美元买入价。

本备用信用证的效期至你行税款保付保函失效后 30 天止，任何索赔，务必在该日期前送达我行。

本备用信用证适用于《跟单信用证统一惯例》（1993 年版），国际商会第 500 号出版物。

＿＿＿＿＿＿＿＿ 银行（盖章）

有权签字人：＿＿＿＿＿＿＿＿

年 月 日

**例 2**

### 备用信用证

开证行：中国银行纽约支行

纽约公园大道 307 号，邮编 10172

受益人：＿＿＿＿＿＿＿＿（银行名称和地址）

应＿＿＿＿＿＿＿＿（申请人姓名）的要求，我行兹开立以＿＿＿＿＿＿＿＿（收益银行名称和地址）为受益人的 ＿＿＿＿＿＿＿＿号不可撤销的备用信用证。担保金额为 80,000,000 美元，大写金额为捌仟万美元。本信用证依据受益人汇票连同以下文件在中国银行纽约支行见票即付。

受益人签署的提取以下款项的声明即为并包括＿＿＿＿＿＿＿＿（公司名称和地址）未支付之债务及信用融通包括但不限于由＿＿＿＿＿＿（收益银行名称和地址）提供的信用证承兑款项。

特别提示：

与信用融通相关的费用和利息均可以包括在任何提款中。

有效期：壹年零壹天。

我行由此与贵行确定：所有符合本信用证条款的汇票均予以见票承兑。

本备用信用证使用于《跟单信用证统一惯例》（1993 年版），国际商会第 500 号出版物。

＿＿＿＿＿＿＿＿ 银行（盖章）

有权签字人：＿＿＿＿＿＿＿＿

年 月 日

**译文：**

Issuing Bank：Bank of China New York branch

307 Park Avenue, New York NY 10172.

Beneficiary: Bank Name and Address

At the request of (name and applicant), we hereby issue this irrevocable Standby Letter of Credit numbered _____ in favor of (Beneficiary Bank Name and Address) up to the aggregate amount of USD 80,000,000—US Dollars eighty million only, with us by payment against beneficiary draft(s) drawn on sight at the Bank of China New York branch accompanied by the following document.

The Beneficiary's signed statement certifying that the amount drawn hereunder represents and covers unpaid indebtedness owing from (company name & address) in connection with credit accommodation including but not limited to letters of credit acceptance loans extended by _____(beneficiary bank name and address).

Special instruction:

Fees and interests incurred in relation to credit accommodations may be included in any drawings.

Expiry date: one year and one day.

We hereby affirm to you that all drafts drawn under and in compliance with the terms of this credit shall be duly honored upon presentation.

This credit is subject to the Uniform Customs and Practice for Documentary Credit (1993 Revision) ICCP Publication No. 500.

_____ Bank

(seal)

(authorized signature)

Date: _____

### 📖 Translating Training

**A: Translate the following sentences about business credit into Chinese.**

1. How long can you arrange for a credit under the new import license?

2. Please open the L/C 10 to 15 days before the date of delivery.

3. We had to pay too much for such a letter of credit arrangement.

4. We open a letter of credit in pounds with a bank inUK.

5. When do they have to open the letter of credit?

6. In the same way as other forms of sales promotion, long-term credit is a key selling tool which should be priced/valued.

7. All parties concerned actually deal in documents, instead of goods in a documentary letter of credit operations.

8. As a typical letter of credit, it may call for the following documents: an invoice, a bill of lading, marine insurance, a packing list, a weight list, an inspection certificate and a certificate of origin.

9. This documentary credit is subject to the Uniform Customs and Practice for Documentary Credits International Chamber of Commerce（Publication No.500）.

10. A seller should always have a clear understanding of your risks in concluding a contract of sale and requirements in relation to the worthless of the buyer, the political, economic and legal situation in the buyer's country and the buyer's liquidity. This helps you to decide what kind of documentary letter of credit you may require—revocable letter of credit, unconfirmed irrevocable letter of credit or confirmed irrevocable letter of credit.

**B：Translate the following sentences about business credit into English.**

1. 请按下述意见修改第 635 号信用证。

2. 你们拒绝修改信用证就等于取消订单。

3. 你还要缴纳银行开立信用证的手续费。

4. 我们进口货物的成本会因为开具信用证而增加。

5. 卖方需要对信用证进行修改。

6. 本信用证项下签发的汇票并符合信用证所列条款,则其出票人、背书人及正当持票人于 2022 年 3 月 15 日以前向议付银行提示议付,开证银行保证于提交单据时付清票款。

7. 如果买方未能向卖方提供如上规定的信用证,卖方有权选择转售合约规定为买方的货物,或推迟付运和(或)随时撤销任何订单,损失和风险由买方承担。

8. 凡依本信用证条款开具并提示汇票,本银行保证对其出票人、背书人和正当持票人于交单时承兑付款。

9. 本信用证待＿＿＿＿＿＿＿＿银行开具对开信用证后生效,对开信用证以＿＿＿＿＿＿为受益人,金额为＿＿＿＿＿＿＿＿,货物由＿＿＿＿＿＿＿运至＿＿＿＿＿＿。本信用证的生效将由＿＿＿＿＿＿＿＿银行用电传通知受益人。

10. 凭原受益人提示于＿＿＿＿＿年 ＿＿＿月 ＿＿＿日＿＿＿＿＿＿＿＿银行(原信用证的开证银行)开立的第＿＿＿＿＿＿＿＿号原信用证规定的单据之后,才兑付备用信用证下的汇票。

## Section 5　Extensive Expression

### 一、常用词汇

| | |
|---|---|
| 1. Form of Credit | 信用证形式 |
| 2. Terms of Validity | 信用证有效期 |
| 3. Expiry Date | 效期 |
| 4. Date of Issue | 开证日期 |
| 5. L/C amount | 信用证金额 |
| 6. L/C number | 信用证号码 |
| 7. to open by airmail | 信开 |
| 8. to open by cable | 电开 |

| | |
|---|---|
| 9. to open by brief cable | 简电开证 |
| 10. to amend L/C | 修改信用证 |
| 11. revocable L/C | 可撤销信用证 |
| 12. irrevocable L/C | 不可撤销信用证 |
| 13. confirmed L/C | 保兑信用证 |
| 14. unconfirmed L/C | 不保兑信用证 |
| 15. sight L/C | 即期信用证 |
| 16. usance L/C | 远期信用证 |
| 17. transmissible L/C | 可转让信用证 |
| 18. unassignable L/C | 不可转让信用证 |
| 19. divisible L/C | 可分割信用证 |
| 20. undivisible L/C | 不可分割信用证 |
| 21. revolving L/C | 循环信用证 |
| 22. reciprocal L/C | 对开信用证 |
| 23. documentary L/C | 跟单信用证 |
| 24. clean L/C | 光票信用证 |
| 25. deferred payment L/C | 延付信用证 |
| 26. anticipatory L/C | 预支信用证 |
| 27. back to back L/C | 对背信用证 |
| 28. With recourse L/C | 有追索权信用证 |
| 29. fixed L/C or fixed amount L/C | 有固定金额的信用证 |
| 30. L/C with T/T reimbursement clause | 带电汇条款信用证 |

## 二、常用句型

| | |
|---|---|
| 1. for account of Messrs | 付(某人)账 |
| 2. at the request of Messrs | 应(某人)请求 |
| 3. on behalf of Messrs | 代表某人 |
| 4. by order of for account of Messrs | 奉(某人)之命并付其账户 |
| 5. at the request of and for account of Messrs | 应(某人)的要求并付其账户 |
| 6. in accordance with instructions received from principal applicants | |
| | 根据已收到的委托开证人的指示 |
| 7. in one's favor | 以(某人)为受益人 |
| 8. to drawn on/upon; to value on; to issued on | 以(某人)为付款人 |
| 9. advised through…bank | 通过……银行通知 |
| 10. advised by airmail/cable through… bank | 通过……银行航空信／电报通知 |
| 11. up to an aggregate amount of Hong Kong Dollars… | 累计金额最高为港币…… |

| | |
|---|---|
| 12. to the extent of HKD... | 总金额为港币…… |
| 13. for the amount of USD... | 金额为美元…… |
| 14. for an amount not exceeding total of JPY... | 金额的总数不得超过……日元的限度 |
| 15. accompanied against to documents hereinafter | 随附下列单据 |
| 16. drafts are to be accompanied by... | 汇票要随附…… |
| 17. available by drafts at sight | 凭即期汇票付款 |
| 18. draft(s) to be drawn at 30 days sight | 开立 30 天的期票 |

# Unit 12

# The Memorandum

Unit Objectives

In this unit you should

➤ familiarize yourself with characteristics of the memorandum.

➤ enable yourself to acquire the basic words and useful expressions of the memorandum in this unit.

➤ have a good command of the translating skills of division and combination.

## ❷ Section 1   Theme Lead-in

**Read the following passage to gain a better understanding of this unit.**

Memo is the short form for memorandum which is a simple and efficient message that is used to remind of or draw someone's attention to certain matters. It is one of the common forms of written communication within a company. This internal communication can be from superior to subordinate down the chain of command, for example, from Managing Director to Accounting Manager, or the other way round; it can also go between equals, for example, from one section chief to another. Generally speaking, there are five kinds of memos: instruction memo, request memo, announcement

memo, transmittal memo and authorization memo.

As memos are meant for internal communication, the language can be made more relaxed than in business letters. However, that is no excuse for the sentences to be chatty or impolite. As far as formality is concerned, a memo is something between a business letter and a note. In the way of the tone of memos, a major consideration should be over the status of the sender and the recipient in the organization. We should take determined effort to respond positively to the need for producing a practical and visible plan that can bring about absentee reduction and efficiency promotion.

**Steps for Writing Memos**

(1) Outline the memo.

(2) Draft the memo.

(3) Check the memo to make sure that it includes all the necessary parts.

(4) Improve and edit the memo.

(5) The body of the minutes should contain a separate paragraph for each topic.

(6) The last paragraph of the minutes should state the time of adjournment and, if appropriate, the time set for the next meeting.

(7) The minutes should be signed by the person preparing them. If someone rather than the chair prepares the minutes, they should be read and approved by the chair before being distributed.

(8) The minutes should be in time and brief.

(9) Do not use too many abbreviations.

**Tips for Writing Memos**

(1) The memo heading has four basic items: to, from, date and subject.

(2) All lines of the memo begin at the left margin.

(3) The text begins two spaces after the subject line.

(4) Memos do not begin with a salutation.

(5) Select a phrase for the subject line that will immediately tell the reader that main point of the memo.

(6) State the purpose of your memo in the first sentence.

(7) Close with the request for the action you want if appropriate and a date by which it should be carried out.

(8) No closing remark such as 'Sincerely' or 'Best regards' is necessary.

### Section 2　Translation Warming-up

**A: Translate the following sentences about memorandum into Chinese.**

1. I am pleased that the Board has agreed to contract for this excellent coverage.

2. As you know, construction of the new office is scheduled to begin this fall.

3. This company pursues a merit policy. It gives top priority to human resource development.

4. When construction is completed, we'll have a nice office with bright lightning and an assigned space for each staff member.

5. We believe that this policy will ensure the economic vitality of our company while giving our employees and their families the best protection possible.

6. The projection is that these rates will climb gradually in the coming months, so agents may wish to stress to customers the advantages of making their purchases now.

7. Statistics are in for housing sales in March and the market looks be strengthening. We sold 240 units, increase from last month and 50% higher than the figures for March the last year.

8. The inspired and aligned work force became the chief source of competitive advantage, despite the company's ever-increasing size and the general tendency for organizations to lose employee commitment over time.

9. At the staff meeting on September 10, we will present a more complete report on sales, but the preliminary data suggests that the market is still stronger for starter homes under RMB 1,500,000 and weakest for homes at price levels above RMB 2,500,000.

10. It has long abolished the no-dismissal, no-demotion and fixed-wage system. Instead, it employs all staff on a contractual basis and through open competition; eight of ten department heads were recruited in this way. In addition, it also emphasizes the training of managers.

**B：Translate the following sentences about memorandum into English.**

1. 我们的新产品质量上乘,比其他厂家的同类产品有明显优势。

2. 我公司已不再生产纯棉衬衫,因为其零售价格只能吸引高档消费者。

3. 一旦我们就行动计划达成一致意见,我们将安排一次高级管理人员会议。

4. 除了涉及货物进出口的有形贸易,还涉及国家之间服务交换的无形贸易。

5. 这是目前我所见到的对工厂运行所作的最全面的分析。我特别请你们留意他们的建议。

6. 为避免今后给客户带来不便和烦恼,同时也为了减少开支,我们正在寻求改进包装的方法。

7. 怀特先生已经完成了我们在海源工厂的能源审计报告,现将该报告复印件随本备忘录下发。

8. 在市场经济大潮中,即使在最有利的情况下,公司要想改产较为适销的产品,也难免要冒一点损失利润的风险。

9. 请仔细阅读该报告,并尽快告知你们认为我方应该采取什么措施来提高生产效率。如能在我们见面之前将你们的建议交给我方过目,则十分有益。

## Section 3　Topic Features and Translation Principles

### 一、备忘录

备忘录是一种录以备忘的公文,在机关或公司内部使用最多。主要用来通报消息(会议安排、情况报告、责任确认、问题处理)回复来函、评估成绩等内部公务。它是对公司事务的书面记载,之后复印报送有关部门和有关人员。其目的在于公布某项公司重大事件,或提出某项重大建议,或向有关部门征询决策意见。备忘录有正式和非正式之分,通常使用客观的语气和报道的风格。备忘录的格式没有统一规定，只有惯例，一般采用醒目的格式。备忘录根据内容不同可分为三类：

### 1. 信息式备忘录（Information Memo）

用来通告某项举措、变动、动态等，主要是提供阅读，不需要作出反应，其阅读对象通常是具体的个人。

### 2. 建议式备忘录（Persuasive Memo）

旨在解决问题或提出决策，常以给出建议收尾。

### 3. 征询式备忘录（Enquiry Memo）

通常对公司的生存和发展方面提出具体问题和质疑，并写明征收答复的期限。

## 二、备忘录的格式

收件人姓名、职务；

发件人姓名、职务；

保密级别（分为三类 top secret，secret，confidential，不用保密就空着）；

文件编号：发件人方文件编号和收件人方文件编号；

发件日期；

备忘录标题线；

正文；

签名、职务；

誊写备忘录的人和打字员姓名首字母缩写；

附件数目；

抄送：如果送给收件人以外的人要注明。

## 三、备忘录的翻译原则

备忘录的特点是：主题明确、话题单一、语言简洁、语气随意。公司的备忘录语言和语篇特点是：格式标准化、用语书面化、语法正规化。译者在翻译公司备忘录时要注意：

### 1. 在形式上使用省略句式和礼节性套语

（1）省略句式

To：（呈交：）

From：（发自：）

Subject 或 Re：（关于：）

Date：（日期）

CC 或 Copies to：（抄送：）

Message（正文）

Signature（签名）

（2）礼节性套语

例 1. I have the honor to inform you that...

我很荣幸地通知您……

例 2. I would like to remind you that( our office is in want of a new English typewriter).

提醒您一下,(我们办公室急需一部英文打字机)。

例 3. Please feel free to contact me (if you need further information).

(如果需要更多信息)请随时与我联系。

例 4. I highly appreciate your consideration to( these proposals).

我期待你能考虑一下(这些建议)。

### 2. 在句型上多用复合句或较为书面化的介词短语引导状语

例 1. 人民生活状况改善的原因有两点。首先,我们一直在贯彻执行改革开放政策。其次,国民经济正在迅速发展,而且出生率已经得到控制。

There are two reasons for the improvement in people's living conditions. In the first place, we have been carrying out the reform and opening-up policy. Secondly, there has been a rapid expansion of our national economy. Furthermore, the birth rate has been put under control.

例 2. 人们希望建立更多的医院、购物中心、娱乐中心、电影院和其他公用设施来满足人民日益增长的需求。

It is desirable to build more hospitals, shopping centers, recreation centers, cinemas and other public facilities to meet the growing needs of people.

例 3. 我对解决这个问题的建议如下。首先,迫在眉睫的是建立自然保护区。其次,有些濒临灭绝的珍稀野生动物应该收捕、人工喂养并繁殖。最后,对于捕猎珍稀野生动物的人必须严惩。

My suggestions to deal with the problem are as follows. In the first place, it is urgent to create nature reserves. Secondly, certain rare wild animals that are going to be extinct should be collected, fed and reproduced artificially. Finally, those who hunt them must be punished severely.

例 4. 就拿汽车为例。汽车不仅污染城市空气,而且使城市拥挤不堪。此外,汽车也会造成许多交通事故。汽车所产生的噪声使居住在街道两旁的居民日夜不得安宁。

Let's take cars for example. They not only pollute the air in cities, but make them crowded. Furthermore, they cause a lot of traffic accidents. The noise made by cars disturbs the residents living on both sides of streets all day and night.

### 3. 在时态上,多用现在时态或将来时态;在语态上多用被动语态

例 1. This is further to your memo dated June 6, 2021, in which you proposed that employees adopt the "punch in" system.

回复你 2021 年 6 月 6 日关于员工实行打卡考勤制度的备忘录。

例 2. 如果你有什么问题,请和我的助手简·西蒙兹联系,她将在 12 月 6 日星期二前去拜访你。谢谢你的帮助。

If you have any queries, please contact my assistant, Jane Simmonds, who will be visiting you on Tuesday, December 6. Thank you for your help.

例 3. 常言道:"事物总是一分为二的。"如今人们从科技发明中得到越来越多的好处。

另一方面,科技进步也给我们带来了许多麻烦。现在许多国家的人民饱受公害之苦。

As a popular saying goes, Everything has two sides. Now people are benefiting more and more from scientific and technological inventions. On the other hand, the progress of science and technology is bringing us a lot of trouble. People in many countries are suffering from public hazards.

例 4. 人们普遍认为,在发达国家人口增长的主要原因与其说是出生率的上升,不如说是由于医疗保健的改善使死亡率下降了。

It is generally believed that the chief reason for the increase in population in developed countries is not so much the rise in birth rates as the decline in death rates as a result of the improvement in medical care.

# Section 4   Translating Strategies, Samples and Training

## Translating Strategies

拆译(division)与合译(combination)：这是两种相对应的翻译方法。拆句法是把一个长而复杂的句子拆译成若干较短而简单的句子,通常用于英译汉;合译法是把若干个短句合并成一个长句,一般用于汉译英。汉语强调意合,结构较松散,因此简单句较多;英语强调形合,结构较严密,因此长句较多。所以汉译英时要根据需要注意利用连词、分词、介词、不定式、定语从句、独立结构等把汉语短句连成长句;英译汉时常常要在原句的关系代词、关系副词、主谓连接处、并列或转折连接处、后续成分与主体的连接处,以及意群结束处将长句切断,译成汉语分句。这样就可以基本保留英语语序,顺译全句,顺应现代汉语长短句相替、单复句相间的句法修辞原则。

## 一、拆译

### 1. 简单句的拆译

 例句

例 1. Illogically, she should have expected some kind of miracle solution.

她竟希望会有某种奇迹般的解决办法,这是不合情理的事。(副词的拆译)

例 2. Not having been discovered, many laws of nature actually exist in nature.

虽然自然界的许多规律尚未发现,但它们确实存在于自然界中。(分词短语的拆译)

例 3. His failure to observe the safety regulations resulted in an accident to the machinery.

他没有遵守安全规则,结果造成机器故障。(名词短语的拆译)

例 4. The secret letter had been all of time just out of reach.

密信一直就在那儿,可就是没有人能够得手。(介词短语的拆译)

例 5. That question is too hard for me to answer.

那个问题太难了,我回答不了。(不定式的拆译)

**2. 并列复合句的拆译**

 **例句**

例 1. The recruitment of Chinese labor was not universally accepted in the racially conscious 19th century America and some white workers were unsettled by their appearance in large numbers.

在种族意识十分强烈的 19 世纪的美国,招募中国劳工的做法并非普遍为人所接受。由于工地上出现大批中国劳工,某些白人工人感到心绪不安。(在分句连接处拆译)

例 2. While the men worked to strengthen the dam, the rain continued to fall; and the river, which was already well above its normal level, rose higher and higher.

人们在奋力加固堤坝,雨还在不停地下。河面已远远超过正常水位,而且越升越高。(在分句连接处拆译)

例 3. She might have some difficulties in handling the class, for she was not yet experienced in teaching, although her students loved her very much.

她在掌控课堂方面还有一些困难。尽管学生很爱她,她却缺乏教学经验。(在分句连接处拆译)

例 4. However, travelers will find they can also use the new currency in some places outside the official euro zones; several large UK-based retail chains will accept the new notes and coin, including Marks & Spencer, Virgin, Selfridges and Dixons.

然而,游客们也会发现,在法定的欧元区之外的一些地方,这种新货币也可以流通使用。一些总部设在英国的大型零售连锁企业也会接受顾客使用新的欧元纸币和硬币来付账,其中包括玛莎百货、维珍公司、谢尔弗里奇公司和狄克森公司。(在分句连接处拆译)

**3. 主从复合句的拆译**

 **例句**

例 1. We climbed to the top of the hill so that we might get a better view.

我们爬到了山顶,这样我们就可以看到更好的风景。(状语从句的拆译)

例 2. His delegation agreed with the executive director that the fund should continue working for a better understanding of the interrelationship between economic, social and demographic factors.

他的代表团同意执行主任的意见,认为该基金会应继续努力,以求更好地了解经济、社会和人口这三方面的相互关系。(定语从句的拆译)

例 3. It has been rightly stated that this situation is a threat to international security.

这个局势对国际安全是个威胁,这样的说法是完全正确的。(主语从句的拆译)

例 4. We wish to inform you that we specialize in the export of Chinese textiles and shall be glad to enter into business relations with you on the basis of equality and mutual benefit.

我们希望您能了解，我们公司专门办理中国纺织品出口业务，我们愿意在平等互利的基础上同贵公司建立业务关系。（宾语从句的拆译）

## 二、合译

 例句

例 1. 美国军费开支世界第一，1999 年美国军费高达 2879 亿美元，约为欧盟、日本、俄罗斯以及中国总和的 1.5 倍。

The United States ranks first in military spending in the world, with the 1999 figure totalling U.S. $287.9 billion, about 150 percent of the combined military expenditures of the European Union, Japan, Russia and China.（用介词短语合并）

例 2. 中国是个大国，百分之八十的人口从事农业，但耕地只占土地面积的十分之一，其余为山脉、森林、城镇和其他用地。

China is a large country with four-fifths of the population engaged in agriculture, but only one tenth of the land is farmland, the rest being mountains, forests and places for urban and other uses.（用介词短语和连词合译）

例 3. 他攒了 5 年的钱买了一架照相机。然后，他带着相机走遍全国，拍摄了许多祖国名胜古迹的照片。

With the money he had saved for 5 years, he bought a camera, with which he then traveled around the country, taking numerous pictures of the scenic spots and places of historic interest of our homeland.（用非限制定语从句合译）

例 4. 现在每年都有几百万人到长城游览。在旺季，几处最著名的景点总是让成群结队的游客挤得水泄不通。

Now, millions of people journey to the Great Wall each year, making its most popular sites besieged by hordes of tourists during busy seasons.（将两个简单句译为复合句）

例 5. 中国是一个发展中的沿海大国。中国高度重视海洋的开发和保护，把发展海洋事业作为国家发展战略。

As a major developing country with a long coastline, China attaches great importance to marine development and protection, and takes it as the state's developing strategy.（将两个简单句译为复合句）

例 6. 我国人口众多，人均资源有限，资金不足。发展精加工、高附加值的产品出口，是今后扩大出口的关键。

Considering the large population, limited per capita resources and shortage of funds in China, we should increase export of finely processed products and of those with high added value, which is central to further expansion of exports in the future.（将两个简单句译为复合句）

**Translating Samples**

## 案例

例 1

Memo

To：Jane Larson

From：William Black

Subject：Scheduling the film

Date：March 16,2022

We'd better rearrange the showing schedule for next week's film.

As you know,we are going to show the film,The Smiths,next week in the projection room, which holds only fifty people comfortably without overcrowding. It is not big enough for the whole staff to see the film at the same time. So I suggest we show the film in different times. For example,we can arrange 40 people to see the film there on Tuesday at 3：00 p. m. , and the remaining 40 on Thursday at the same time.

If there's any problem about this arrangement,please let me know.

William Black

C. Stan Clark

译文：

备 忘 录

收件人：卡尔·福勒

发件人：威廉·布莱克

主题：电影日程安排

日期：2022 年 3 月 16 日

我们最好能够重新安排下周电影的播放时间。

你知道我们打算下周在放映厅播放《史密斯夫妇》这部电影,但放映厅只能同时容纳 50 人。我们的员工不能同时看电影。所以我建议将放映时间选在不同时段。比如,40 人在周二下午 3 点在那里看这部影片,剩下的 40 人在周四同一时间、同一地点观看。

如果对此安排有什么问题请通知我。

威廉·布莱克

抄送:斯坦·克拉克

例 2

Memo

To：All full-time employees

From：HR Manager,Li Ming

Subject：Computer course

Date：May 9th,2022

An investigation conducted by the HR Department last month reveals the fact that a high rate of computer illiteracy contributes to a severe inefficiency of our company. As a result, it has been decided that all full-time employees are to attend a computer course—which will take place every Monday night from 7pm to 9pm in the company meeting room A and B—for the duration of two months. Employees are able to sign up for the basic or advanced levels of the course according to their present computer skills. Please register for the course at the company reception desk before May 15th. Further suggestions will be appreciated so that the program can be more fruitful.

译文：

**备 忘 录**

收文人：所有全职员工

发文人：人力资源经理，李明

主题：计算机课程

日期：2022 年 5 月 9 日

　　人力资源部上个月进行的一项调查显示，公司的许多人不会使用电脑，导致了工作效率的低下。因此，我们决定为所有的全职员工开办一个为期两个月的计算机课程，于每周一晚上 7 点到 9 点在公司的 A 会议室和 B 会议室举行。每个员工都可以根据自己目前的计算机水平选择初级或高级课程。请于 5 月 15 日之前到公司接待处报名。欢迎提出更好的意见和建议，以便使我们这个项目更加富有成果。

　　例 3

**备 忘 录**

致：北京风帆外贸进出口公司所有部门

自：北京风帆外贸进出口公司办公室

主题：新作息时间

日期：2021 年 9 月 15 日

从 10 月 1 日起开始执行以下新的作息时间表。请遵照执行。

| 时间 | 事项 |
| --- | --- |
| 7:50—8:20 | 早餐 |
| 8:20—8:30 | 办公室清洁 |
| 8:30—9:00 | 例会 |
| 9:00—12:00 | 处理日常办公事务 |
| 12:00—13:00 | 午餐 |
| 13:00—16:00 | 市场研发 |
| 16:00—16:30 | 报告 |
| 16:30 | 下班 |

译文：

**Memo**

To：All departments of Beijing Fengfan Foreign Trade I/E Corp.

From：Office of Beijing Fengfan Foreign Trade I/E Corp.

Subject：New timetable

Date：Sept.25,2021

A new timetable listed below is to come into effect from Oct.1. 2021. Please follow it.

| Time | Item |
| --- | --- |
| 7:50—8:20 | breakfast |
| 8:20—8:30 | office cleaning |
| 8:30—9:00 | regular meeting |
| 9:00—12:00 | handling routine matters in office |
| 12:00—13:00 | lunch |
| 13:00—16:00 | R$D of the market |
| 16:00—16:30 | report |
| 16:30 | off duty |

**例 4**

### 备 忘 录

致：人事部所有员工

自：张亮,人事部秘书

主题：为李明举行欢送会

日期：2021 年 12 月 15 日

　　我们的同事李明下个月将要退休,我部门决定为他举行一个欢送会。我们的总经理和经理也将出席。

　　如果有人愿意出节目,请尽快告诉我。

　　欢迎所有人事部的同事参加。欢送会将在我们部门的会议室举行,时间定在 1 月 21 日,下周五晚 7 点钟。另外,如果大家还有什么关于欢送会的建议,欢迎提出。

**译文：**

### Memo

To：All employees of Personal Department.

From：Zhang Liang,secretary of Personal Department

Subject：Farewell Party for Li Ming

Date：Dec.15,2021

　　Our colleague,Li Ming,is going to retire next month. Our department has decided to hold a farewell party for him. Our general manager will be present,too.

　　If anyone is willing to give performances,please let me know as soon as possible.

　　All the colleagues of Personal Department are invited to attend the party which is scheduled on January 21,next Friday and will begin at 7 o'clock in the evening at the meeting room of our department. Besides,all suggestions on the party are welcome.

### Translating Training

**A：Translate the following sentences and memos into Chinese.**

1. I apologize for the inconvenience,but I am sure that you will agree that the long-term

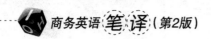

benefits of the new facilities will greatly outweigh any temporary problems.

2. In the face of globalization, financial liberalization and WTO accession, the government has no other choice but make a thou decision: pushing the commercial banks onto the international financial market to secure a place for them through improved competition.

3. During construction we will not be able to use our parking lot, so beginning on November 5, however, those of you who drive to work will have to mark other arrangements for parking your personal vehicles.

4. A female finds her first job or changes her job in three ways: recommendation by friends or relatives, the labor market, and others such as classified advertisements, want ads, government allocation upon graduation, worker recruitment or succession to retired relatives.

5.

Memo

To: Every Employees

From: Wang Wei

Subject: Fitness Center

Date: June 15, 2021

The board of directors approved the idea for a newFitness Center at its meeting yesterday.

Work on the Fitness Center will begin right now and should be completed within 90 days. An employee representative from each division will be appointed to determine the type of equipment and programs that will be made available.

We are happy to be able to provide a facility that will contribute to the physical fitness of all our employees. Your representative on the task force will contract you soon for your suggestions about activities and equipment.

Wang Wei

Administration Office, Manager

6.

Memo

To: All Staff in Personnel Department

From: Zhang Qiang, Administrative Officer

Subject: Opening Instructions for New Copying Machines

Date: March 15, 2022

A new photocopier has been installed in the general office. All staffin Personnel Department are welcome to use it.

To ensure the copier's survival, we must keep the following procedures in mind.

1. Use the machine for no longer than 30 minutes a time.

2. After use, allow the machine to cool for at least 5 minutes.

3. Make sure the switch is turned off after using.

Please speak to me if you have any questions about the machine.

7.

Memo

To：All members of staff，Northern Branch

From：K.L.J.

Subject：Personal Computers

Date：Dec. 5，2021

The board urgently requires feedback on our experience with PCs in Northern Branch.

I need to know，for my report：

1. What you personally use your PC for and your reasons for doing this. If you are doing work that was formerly done by other staff，please justify this.

2. What software you use. Please name the programs.

3. How many hours per day you spend actually using it.

4. How your PC has not come up to your expectations.

5. What unanticipated uses you have found for your PC that others may want to share.

Please FAX this information directly to me by 5p.m. on Wednesday，7 December.

If you have any queries，please contact my assistant，Jane Simmonds，who will be visiting you on Tuesday，6 December. Thank you for your help.

8.

Memo

To：David Green，Chief of Operations

From：Tony Party，Supervisor

Subject：Comments on the "Punch-in" System

Date：March 22，2022

This is further to your memo dated March. 20，2021，in which you proposed that employees adopt the "punch-in" system.

I fully agree with you that we must increase productivity. As far as your proposal that if the "punch-in" system is adopted，we would have a tighter control over the employees is concerned. However，I don't think so. I personally think that，to accomplish this，we should give the employees more incentives to work faster. I feel that if we (the supervisors) could meet with you，we could discuss different possibilities to create such incentiveness.

Your consideration of this suggestion would be appreciated.

Tony Party

**B：Translate the following memos into English.**

1. 备忘录

致：人事部所有员工

自：张强，行政干部

主题：新复印机的使用说明

日期：2021 年 3 月 15 日

在总办公室安装了一台新的复印机。欢迎所有员工来使用。

为保证复印机的寿命,我们必须记住以下操作程序。

(1) 每次使用不得超过 30 分钟。

(2) 使用后,让机器冷却不得低于 5 分钟。

(3) 使用后,务必关机。

如有疑问,请来问我。

2. 谅解备忘录

中国职业技术教育项目

鉴定过程(2016 年 10 月—12 月)

新加坡项目筹备研讨会

2017 年 1 月 10 日—19 日

内容目录

Ⅰ. 背景

Ⅱ. 审核程序

Ⅲ. 参观各省后的发现

Ⅳ. 新加坡的项目筹备研讨会

Ⅴ. 项目理念

Ⅵ. 后续工作

附件目录

1. 参加会议的名单以及参观考察广东、辽宁和山东的名单

2. 代表团参观的学校或者相关学院

3. 代表团参观的企业

4. 筹备这次研讨会的新加坡政府机构和政府官员名单

5. 新加坡世界银行研讨会的议程

6. 参加研讨会的名单

7. 研讨会评估结果

# Section 5  Extensive Expression

## 一、公司各种会议列表

| | |
|---|---|
| 1. assembly | 大会 |
| 2. convention | 会议 |
| 3. party | 晚会,社交性宴会 |
| 4. pink tea | 正式茶会 |
| 5. tea party | 茶会 |
| 6. dinner party | 晚餐会 |

| 7. garden party | 游园会 |
| 8. ball | 舞会 |
| 9. reading party | 读书会 |
| 10. fishing party | 钓鱼会 |
| 11. sketching party | 观剧会 |
| 12. birthday party | 生日宴会 |
| 13. Christmas party | 圣诞晚会 |
| 14. luncheon party | 午餐会 |
| 15. fancy ball | 化装舞会 |
| 16. commemorative party | 纪念宴会 |
| 17. banquet | 酒宴 |
| 18. charity dinner | 慈善餐会 |
| 19. buffet party | 立食宴会 |
| 20. cocktail party | 鸡尾酒会 |
| 21. welcome meeting | 欢迎会 |
| 22. farewell party | 惜别会 |
| 23. year-end dinner party | 年终餐会 |
| 24. new year's banquet | 新年宴会 |

## 二、召开会议常见术语

| 1. rostrum | 讲台 |
| 2. public gallery | 旁听席 |
| 3. notice board | 布告牌 |
| 4. to convene | 召开 |
| 5. convocation | 会议 |
| 6. standing orders | 议事程序 |
| 7. rules of procedure | 议事规则 |
| 8. constitution/statutes | 章程 |
| 9. procedure | 程序 |
| 10. agenda | 议程 |
| 11. timetable/schedule | 日程表,时刻表 |
| 12. item on the agenda | 议程项目 |
| 13. other business | 其他事项 |
| 14. to place on the agenda | 列入议程 |
| 15. working paper | 工作文件 |
| 16. opening | 开幕 |
| 17. the sitting is open | 会议开幕 |
| 18. appointment | 任命 |

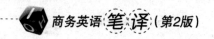

### 三、出席会议代表术语

| | |
|---|---|
| 1. member | 成员 |
| 2. membership | 成员资格 |
| 3. member as of right | 法定代表 |
| 4. life member | 终身成员 |
| 5. full-fledged member | 全权代表 |
| 6. head of delegation | 代表团团长 |
| 7. permanent delegate | 常驻代表 |
| 8. representative | 代表 |
| 9. alternate/substitute | 副代表 |
| 10. observer | 观察员 |
| 11. technical adviser | 技术顾问 |
| 12. auditor | 审计员 |
| 13. office | 职务 |
| 14. holder of an office | 职称 |
| 15. honorary president | 名誉主席 |
| 16. chairman | 主席 |
| 17. presidency/chairmanship | 主席团 |
| 18. interim chairman | 临时主席 |
| 19. vice-president/vice-chairman | 副主席 |
| 20. rapporteur | 文书,秘书 |
| 21. secretary general | 秘书长 |
| 22. executive secretary | 执行秘书 |
| 23. director general | 局长,处长 |
| 24. deputy director general | 副局长,副处长 |

# Unit *13*

# Business Reports

Unit Objectives

In this unit you should

➢ familiarize yourself with the format of business report.

➢ enable yourself to acquire the basic words and useful expressions of business report in this unit.

➢ have a good command of the translating skills of the subject.

## ❷ Section 1   Theme Lead-in

**Read the following passage to gain a better understanding of this unit.**

Business reports are crucial in business. Business people, by means of business reports, can gain and give valuable information, which is the basis of business decision being made. A written business report is a document that conveys information to a reader who will use the information (perhaps along with other information) to make a decision.

Most business reports are written because readers want and expect them. Business reports

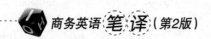
usually go up the chain of command and are used to help managers make decisions. Managers expect business reports to contain helpful, accurate information and to present that information in a suitable—often prescribed—style and format.

Business reports are assigned and written to enable managers to make decisions when they cannot directly observe the materials, personnel, and other factors involved in running an organization. Managers must rely on the observations and business reports of others when they.

(1) are too far removed from a particular operation to observe it directly;

(2) do not have time to supervise an operation directly;

(3) do not have the technical expertise to make accurate observations.

Business reports go from a person who is in a position to make direct accurate and reliable observations to a person who will make decisions about the observations. This means that business reports usually go up chain of command from lower-raking individuals to those of higher rank. Some business reports, however, are exchange among of equal rank. As a rule, business reports are distributed down the chain of command only as a means of disseminating information.

According to their functions, business reports are generally divided into three major categories: investigation reports, feasibility reports and routine reports. In general, investigation reports are to summit the result of some investigations, and feasibility reports are to evaluate the feasibility of a program or strategy-to-be, while routine reports are to summarize the progress of a specific assignment during the past period.

## Section 2　Translation Warming-up

**A: Please match the Chinese translation in column B with the English expressions in column A.**

| A | B |
|---|---|
| 1. professional attitude will need to be encouraged through training | A. 加快生产速度 |
| 2. additional staff should be recruited | B. 产品的需求极大 |
| 3. the future looks hopeful for the company | C. 推行此项制度 |
| 4. selecting a certain number of higher potential customers for further development | D. 被起诉违反版权法 |
| 5. analyzing data in the Human Resources files | E. 广告销售利润下降 |
| 6. production be stepped up | F. 招聘新员工 |
| 7. demand for products is high | G. 培训鼓励员工形成职业化的工作态度 |
| 8. prosecuted for infringement of copyright laws | H. 公司的前景将会很有希望 |
| 9. the scheme will be introduced | I. 发展一些潜力较大的客户 |
| 10. fall in profit from advertising sales | J. 分析人力资源档案资料 |

**B：Fill the following sentences' blanks with the same meaning as the former Chinese ones.**

1. 市场对价格波动异常敏感。

The market is _____.

2. 我们需要提高员工与外国顾客交流的能力。

We need to _____ to communicate with foreign customers.

3. 我们认为导致这次事故的原因很可能是电力方面的问题。

We feel that the most likely _____.

4. 由于许多员工对他们的事业发展不满意,公司员工正在流失到竞争对手那里。

The company is losing staff to its competitors _____.

5. 除此之外还有几个方案,但是比较而言,它们的优势并不明显,因此这个方案是我们的最佳选择。

There are several alternatives to this plan,but _____,so this plan is our best choice.

## Section 3　Topic Features and Translation Principles

### 一、商务报告

商务报告是商务英语写作中的一个重要组成部分,它通常是公司决策和行动的基础,也是员工与员工之间,员工与上级之间传递信息、交流沟通的途径之一。一份商务报告可以是为某一具体目的所作的研究,也可以是所做工作的结果或就某个问题所提出的建议,或是对已发生的事件的叙述等。商务报告与其他商务文书不尽相同,它主要有以下几个特点:格式不同;需要搜集一定的资料;对所搜集的资料要进行分析;就资料或数据分析结果进行客观、公正的评论;根据实际情况提出合理的建议。

从功能上划分,商务报告一般可以分为三类:调查报告、可行性报告和日常事务报告。调查报告一般是由上级部门或上级领导下指令而写的报告。此类报告应建立在实地考察或调查研究的基础上,用以提供客观的事实、数据和分析等。调查报告是为未来的战略或决策提供信息。此类报告也可以为提出某种要求或未解决问题而写。可行性报告就是从许多的可选方案中选出最佳方案的报告。这类报告是在对项目的充分研究及对该项目将来可能的利弊全面考虑的基础上写就的。可行性报告应对所提方案、意见给予充分的论证。日常事务报告是定期或不定期地向上级管理部门报告销售或生产等情况的报告。

### 二、商务报告的翻译原则

商务报告是公司决策和行动的基础,译文的质量直接影响决策及执行工作。因此,在翻译商务报告时,要特别注意以下几点:

(1) 商务报告译文最重要的是要忠实原文。翻译时务必紧跟原文语义和作者思想,不可随意更改和发挥,强加入译者的个人行为和观点。

(2) 商务报告是一种商务格式文本,文本的规范性能够反映出写作者对于报告正式程度的要求。因此翻译中应尽最大可能保留作者原文中的文本形式。通常商务报告包含以下四部分:介绍部分(introduction);标题(title)(在报告的顶部,通常加了下划线);受调查的范围（terms of reference）；调查行为（proceedings）。

（3）在译文语言的把握上，应该遵循准确通顺、术语规范和语气贴切这三个基本原则。

### 1. 准确通顺

商务报告翻译的准确通顺不仅反映在译文的正确与否，还体现在准确传递原文的逻辑关系。特别是商务报告作为相对正式的商务文本形式，句子一般较长，结构复杂，所以在组织译文句子方面，要注意句子之间的连贯和必要的调整，使译文意思清晰明了，易于被读者接受和理解。请看下面的例句：

 **例句**

It is our aim to stimulate plastic raw material sales in the sports shoe market, and to seek potential customers within the sports shoe market who might be interested in using Krypton's newly developed APC raw material in the manufacture of their products.

本报告的目的是刺激塑胶原料在运动鞋市场中的销售量，并在运动鞋市场中寻找有望使用 Kryton 新开发的 APC 原料进行生产的潜在客户。

本句译文中，通过主语的转换、语序的调整使意思表达更清晰，句式更通顺，更符合中国读者的语言习惯。

### 2. 术语规范

如果想将术语翻译准确，必须掌握相关领域的商务背景。由于商务报告涉及众多行业领域，而各个行业领域中有许多术语，这些术语体现非常明显的行业知识。在翻译到自己不熟悉的商务术语、公司名称或人名时，不能想当然地去译，要询问知情者，或保留原文，以免产生误会。如：force majeure（不可抗力），target market（目标市场），segmentation（市场细分），counter-offer（还盘），balance sheet（资产负债表）等。

### 3. 语气贴切

为了体现报告内容的客观公正和语气上的委婉客气，中文往往选择一些严谨的措辞，而英文常常用被动语态或情态动词来达到同样的目的。以第三人称写报告可以使作者置身其外，并且有助于强调调查的结果。请看下面这段报告中正式而又客观的语气：

 **例句**

Here is shown the total broadcast audience in this district：the percent of households with either radio or television set turned on throughout the average weekday in survey period. The chart below shows the combined audience：the percent of households with either radio or television set or both turned on. This is the maximum potential exposure of any message appearing simultaneously on all eighteen radio stations and four commercial television stations.

这里显示本地区广播电视听众总数。在调查期间，工作日平均每天收听收音机或收看电视的家庭比例。图表显示联合听众，即要么收听收音机，要么收看电视，或两者同时收听收看的家庭比例。这是所有通过 18 家广播电台和 4 个商业电视频道传送的信息的最大收听（视）率。

在这里,正式的语气是通过使用第三人称,表明事实,引用数据和不表达个人对报告所传达信息的观点、情感和态度等来实现的。

# Section 4　Translating Strategies, Samples and Training

## ✓ Translating Strategies

英语是主语突出的语言(subject-prominent language),而汉语则是主题突出的语言(topic-prominent language)。因此,任何英语句子都必须有主语,由于英语中每个句子都要求有主语,从汉语的思维角度看,英语中的某个句子不可能有主语时,英语中便使用 it 来充当主语,使得主语那个位置不至于空缺。英语中使用无生命主语的现象也很多,而在以人为本的汉语中则很少使用无生命的名词充当主语。另外,由于汉语中很少使用无生命的名词充当主语,那么在碰到英语中使用名词充当主语的情况时,就有必要对英语中的表达进行调整,如果直译就会引起文字不顺。下面分别针对英译汉和汉译英的过程中可能遇到的主语如何翻译的问题用实例进行说明。

### 一、英译汉中的主语如何翻译

英语句子在大多数情况下都有主语(只在祈使句、人物对话或个人简历中有时可以省略),汉语句子的主语在许多情况下都可以省略,因此汉语有大量无主句。汉译英时,有时可以省去主语,译为无主句。许多情况下翻译主语时需要变换角度,力求译文自然通顺。

(1) 英文中的被动语态往往被翻译成汉语中的无主句。

 例句

例 1. The installation should be commenced as soon as all the remaining problems have been cleared up.

待剩下的问题都解决之后就应立即开始安装。

例 2. Mechanical energy can be changed into electrical energy by means of a generator.

利用发电机可以把机械能转变成电能。

(2) 由 that,what,whether 引导的主语从句,一般位于句子的后面,代词 it 作形式主语放在句首。It 有时可以省略不译,但表示强调时应译出。

 例句

例 1. It is recommended that this year's shareholders' dividend be halved to 4%.

建议今年将股东的分红减半到 4%。

例 2. It was felt from the above evaluation that A country is a distinct advantage in establishing a factory.

从以上的评价可以看出,在 A 国建厂有明显的优势。

(3) 主语从句直接放在句首时,翻译时可按原句语序。

**例句**

例 1. That theory must go hand in hand with practice is a principle we should always keep in mind.

理论必须与实际紧密结合是我们应该谨记在心的。

例 2. The jubilant crowd surged through the streets like the sea waves.

欢乐的人群从街道上汹涌而过,宛如大海的波涛。

## 二、汉译英中的主语如何翻译

汉译英时,在大多数情况下都应把主语译出,否则英语句子不能成立;此外,在确立英语主语时应抓住核心意义。

### 1. 汉语句中的形容词性成分作为译文主语

 **例句**

例 1. 中国的人均农业土地面积比不上世界上其他许多国家。

China compares unfavorably with many other countries in terms of per capita agricultural land.

例 2. 成功者与失败者的区别就在于成功者坚持不懈,失败者半途而废。

A successful person differs from an unsuccessful one in that the former perseveres whereas the latter gives up halfway.

### 2. 汉语句中的名词性成分作为译文主语

 **例句**

例 1. 一个企业的前途怎样,在很大程度上要看它的经营管理人员,尤其是市场管理人员的素质。

The quality of managing executives, especially those with marketing responsibilities, goes a long way in determining the future of a corporation.

例 2. 改革开放以来,中国发生了巨大的变化。

Great changes have taken place in China since the introduction of the reform and opening policy.

### 3. 汉语句中的副词性成分作为译文主语

 **例句**

例 1. 通过进一步研究,科学家们推测存在着一种迄今尚未为人所知的粒子。

Further research by scientists pointed to the possible existence of a previously unknown particle.

例 2. 在历史上,由于长江不断改道,在武汉地区形成了众多的湖泊。

The constant changes of the course of Changjiang River in history helped form a great many lakes in the areas around Wuhan.

### 4. 汉语句中的动词性成分作为译文主语

 **例句**

例 1. 中国近年来在国际化方面的巨大跨越,不仅使中国与国际全面接轨,独创的成就和独特的文化,更令世界为之折服。

The enormous progress China achieved in globalization has aligned the country with the practice of the world community, meanwhile amazed the global village with its own unparalleled achievements and unique culture.

例 2. 孩子们看电视过多会大大地损害视力。

Too much exposure to TV programs will do great harm to the eyesight of children.

### 5. 添加主语

 **例句**

例 1. 希望一切顺利,并速签合同。

We hope this will go smoothly and you are able to conclude the contract soon.

例 2. 在这个紧要关头,我们尤其不该为了已经无法挽回的事情相互埋怨。

The last thing we should do at this crucial moment is no blaming one another for what is beyond remedy.

### 6. 汉语中表示原因的状语往往翻译成英文中的主语

 **例句**

例 1. 由于市区缺乏合适的土地,大部分公共房屋必须在郊区兴建。

Shortage of suitable land in the urban areas has made it necessary to build most new public housing in the suburbs.

例 2. 由于华人移民的餐饮业在唐人街日益昌盛,进中华酒楼、吃中式菜肴早已成为不少欧美人士和全球旅游者的时尚。

The boom of Chinese restaurants in the China Towns has led to the popularity of Chinese cuisines among European and American people and global tourists to China.

### 7. 汉语中表时间或地点的状语往往可翻译成英文中的主语

但在这里需要用到英语中的一种特殊结构,英语中的动词 see, find, witness 都可以用于这种结构,即"时间名词/地点名词+saw/found/witnessed+名词",表示在某个时间或者地点里发生或者见证了某种事情。

 **例句**

例 1. 五年中产量持续增长。

The five years witnessed a continuing rise in the production.

例 2. 本世纪头二十年是我国的重要战略机遇期，我国进入了全面建成小康社会、加快推进社会主义现代化建设的发展阶段。

The first 20 years of this century should prove a strategically crucial period of opportunities for the country's strategic planning. It will be a period in which China is embarked on her building a comfortable community for her people, and in which the socialist modernization construction will rev up.

**8. 汉语中的"所……的"结构，往往翻译成英语中由代词 what, how 等引导的主语从句**

 **例句**

例 1. 我们（所）最为关心的是如何生产出更多更好的汽车。

What we are most interested in is how we can produce more and better cars.

例 2. 我们所有人所关心的是高级工是如何提高产量的。

How the advanced worker managed to raise production is of interest to us all.

 **Translating Samples**

## 一、调查报告（Investigation Report）

 **案例**

### Report on Increasing the Company's Business

**Introduction**：

The purpose of this report is to identify ways to increase our business on the basis of the comparison of our company's vacuum cleaners with BBF's.

**Findings**：

Although BBF vacuum cleaners are average in price, the people in the survey considered our vacuum cleaners cheaper. They also commented highly on the standard of services we provide. However, the quality and reliability of BBF vacuum cleaners were rated much higher than ours. Moreover, BBF vacuum cleaners were considered more attractive in appearance, and above all, people were impressed by the availability of BBF vacuum cleaners.

**Conclusions**：

BBF vacuum cleaners have achieved a great success due to the higher quality and reliability, attractive appearance and availability of their vacuum cleaners. Their strengths, however, are our weaknesses.

**Recommendations**：

1. Methods should be worked out to make our vacuum cleaners stronger and less prone to mechanical failure.

2. New designs should be created for next model.

3. It's suggested that we examine ways of increasing the availability of vacuum cleaners, particularly in the northern region.

译文:

### 关于提高公司业务量的报告

**引言:**

本报告旨在通过将我公司生产的拖拉机与 BBF 公司生产的拖拉机进行对比,从而找到提高我公司业务量的方法。

**调查结果:**

尽管 BBF 公司的拖拉机价格适中,但被调查者仍认为我公司生产的拖拉机更便宜。被调查者对我公司的服务水平也给予了高度评价。BBF 公司的拖拉机的可靠性方面的得分比我们高出很多。另外,BBF 公司的拖拉机在外观上也更吸引人。总的来说,顾客能更方便地购买到 BBF 公司的拖拉机。

**结论:**

BBF 公司的拖拉机在质量、可靠性、吸引人的外观和购买的方便程度上都取得了相当大的成功。而他们的优势恰恰是我们的弱点。

**建议:**

1. 应该采取措施加强我们的产品质量,减少机械问题的发生。

2. 要为新型产品注入新的设计。

3. 建议增加销售渠道,特别是在北部地区。

## 二、可行性报告 (Feasibility Report)

 案例

### Report on the Reinvestment of This Year's Profit

**Introduction**

I was asked by the board to prepare a report based on the examination of the feasibility of the company's reinvestment of this year's profits.

**Options**

The options of the company's reinvestment of this year are as follows:

1. The purchase of new administrative software.

2. The provision of language training courses.

**Evaluations**

1. The purchase of new administrative software.

The currently-used administrative software was just purchase last year, and is sufficient for our present administrative management. Therefore the purchase of the new administrative software would not be necessary.

2. The provision of language training courses.

The company intends to increase exports, particularly in Japan and Spain. Consequently, language training courses would be a marvelous solution for those staff members who handle business partners and customers abroad. Moreover, training courses would make the staff more motivated at work, for staff would understand that the company is investing in them. Thus language training would be an alternative.

**Conclusions**

1. Buying new administrative software is unnecessary now.

2. Providing language training courses are beneficial both to the company's operation and employees' development.

**Recommendation**

It is felt that the better option for both the company and employees would be to invest in language training course. It is suggested that the company should organize courses in Japanese and Spanish. Those employees who deal with foreign partners should be given priority but other interested employees should also be permitted to attend.

译文:

### 关于本年度利润再投资的报告

**引言**

董事会要求我对公司本年度利润再投资准备一份可行性报告。

**可考虑的再投资项目**

本年度列入再投资考虑范围的项目有:

1. 购买新的行政管理软件;

2. 提供外语培训课程。

**评估**

1. 购买新的行政管理软件

现在使用的行政管理软件是去年刚刚购买的,对于现在的行政管理工作已经足够用了。因此,不需要购买新的行政管理软件。

2. 提供外语培训课程

公司有意增加出口,尤其是增加对日本和西班牙的出口业务。因此,举办外语培训班对在海外有业务伙伴和客户的员工来说是十分有益的。而且,培训课程也有助于提高士气,因为员工会意识到公司愿意为他们投资。因此,提供外语培训课程是可取的。

**结论**

1. 目前并没有购买新的行政管理软件的必要。

2. 提供外语培训课程对公司的运作和员工的发展都有好处。

**建议**

综上所述,对公司和员工都有利的方案是投资于提供外语培训课程。建议公司组织日语和西班牙语的培训课程。与业务伙伴有关的员工应优先考虑,其他感兴趣的员工也应允许参加。

## 三、日常事务报告（Routine Report）

 案例

### Report on the Drops in the Sales

**Introduction**

The first quarterly sales this year was falling, 25% less than that of the same period last year. The sales of the first quarter last year were $12 million while those of the first quarter this year were $8.5 million.

**Sales Figures**

Our most important markets are in the northeast, northwest and north regions. The sales in these regions account for three fourth of the whole sales. The following is their first quarter sales：

| Region | Target Sales | Actual Sales |
| --- | --- | --- |
| The Northeast | 2.8 mil. | 1.2 mil. |
| The Northwest | 3.2 mil. | 1.5 mil. |
| The North | 3.5 mil. | 2.3 mil. |

**Causes of Drop**

We ascribe the drops to the following factors：

1. The long rainy weather. This should be taken into consideration on the drops on sales.

2. The pressing market competition. It was very difficult to keep sales at the same level as those of last year, as there are too many competitors' products. Take the northeast region for example, there are at least 10 other major brands of central cooling systems.

**Conclusion**

The market is slow but competition is pressing. Even if the sales dropped this year, it is no doubt that our products still have a good market share, as we have established so many clients and distributors. We might get over the fierce competition as long as we could offer strong support and better after sales service. However, in order to deal with the rainy season, we should develop a wider range of products to adjust to it.

**Recommendation**

1. A promotion campaign is needed.

2. After-sales team should be strengthened.

3. New products should be researched and developed.

译文：

### 关于销售量下滑的报告

#### 引言

本年度第一季度的销售下降，与去年同期相比，下跌了25%。去年第一季度的销售额为1200万美元，今年只有850万美元。

### 销售数据

我们主要的市场在东北、西北和北部。这三个地区的销售额占总销售额的3/4。第一季度三个地区的销售额如下：

| 地区 | 销售目标 | 实际销售 |
| --- | --- | --- |
| 东北 | 280万 | 120万 |
| 西北 | 320万 | 150万 |
| 北部 | 350万 | 230万 |

### 下降原因

我们认为下降的原因如下：

1. 很长的雨天。这点应被考虑为销售下滑的原因。

2. 激烈的市场竞争。由于中央制冷系统的市场同类产品竞争激烈，销售要与去年保持同一水平有一定困难。以东北地区为例，同类的其他厂家产品就至少有10种。

### 结论

市场疲软但竞争仍然激烈。尽管我们今年的销售下滑，但由于我们已有了一些稳固的客户和分销商，因此仍占有相当大的市场份额。如果我们能够提供更好的支持和售后服务，那么我们还是可以在激烈的竞争中胜出。然而，由于很长的雨季，我们也应及时地调整产品方向以适应此趋势。

### 建议

1. 开展促销活动。

2. 加强售后服务部门的建设。

3. 研发新产品。

## 📖 Translating Training

**A：Translate the following sentences about business report into Chinese.**

1. He stayed abreast of what was going on in the market place by reading emails sent to him by custermers.

2. The surface of the internal glass is still smooth, while the external covering appears to have been badly scratched.

3. It is recommended that the above measures should be taken at once and the measures will bring about immediately savings for the company.

4. Over the past 3 years, we have spent around $30 million to modernize the equipment used in this division to supply the world's major corporations with a variety of components.

5. Management should make changed efforts to decrease travel costs.

6. This report evaluates the feasibility of establishing a new firm in east of China.

7. This report assesses the feasibility of establishing an interflow of commodities center in New York.

8. The following report summarizes the prospect we've made and the setback we've

experienced in the past half of year.

9. In order to attract foreign investment, governments and local bodies in that country often offer special conditions such as attractive subsidies to those companies wishing to set up in their country.

10. This report shows that with only a small investment in new equipment and a slight increase in personnel and associated expenses, KFC could increase its profit by about 15% simply by opening for breakfast.

**B：Translate the following sentences about business report into English.**

1. 建议我们继续和 Haier 公司保持联系，在设备升级完成后重新签订供货合同。

2. 为了解决这一问题，我们采取了很多措施，如削减成本和增加公司各部门的产量。

3. 如果存在较大的问题，而且目标没有完成，那么就需要改变公司的组织或者管理结构。

4. 他们对该财产进行了调查。

5. 经过全面比较，我建议我们的业务扩展到欧洲西北部。

6. 市场调查的结果不令人满意，因此必须立即采取有效的措施。

7. 尽管面临着两个问题，我们将尽最大努力去解决它们。我希望我们公司明年前景更美好。

8. 在经济形势方面，我国经济增长迅速，拥有有利于商业发展的环境和强劲的消费者购买力。

9. 从上面的表格能明显看出，尽管 P&G 公司产品的单价最便宜，但它们的折扣和运费并不令人满意。

10. 遵照董事长的要求，本报告根据全体员工提交的问卷结果，对于削减行政部门开支的方式进行了分析。

## Section 5　Extensive Expression

### 一、常用专业词汇

| | | |
|---|---|---|
| 1. status report | 现状报告 |
| 2. annual report | 年度报告 |
| 3. progress report | 进度报告 |
| 4. troubleshooting report | 以解决问题为目的的报告 |
| 5. justification report | 论证报告 |
| 6. investigative report | 调查报告 |
| 7. statistical report | 统计报告 |
| 8. primary research | 基于第一手材料的研究 |
| 9. secondary research | 基于第二手材料的研究 |
| 10. preliminary parts | 正文前面的部分 |
| 11. supplementary parts | 正文后的补充部分 |

| | |
|---|---|
| 12. bibliography or references | 文献目录,参考书目 |
| 13. easy-to-follow | 容易理解的 |
| 14. back and forth | 来回地 |
| 15. top management | 最高管理层 |
| 16. territory management | 推销区管理 |
| 17. customer installation | 客户基地 |
| 18. computer-generated | 电脑生成的 |
| 19. questionnaire | 问卷调查 |
| 20. feedback | 反馈信息 |
| 21. respondent | 参加问卷调查者 |
| 22. quarterly | 每季度的(地),每年四次的(地) |
| 23. biannual | 一年两次的 |
| 24. alternative | 可选方案 |
| 25. evaluation | 评价,评估 |
| 26. criteria（pl.） | 标准 |
| 27. goal/target sales figure | 目标销售额 |
| 28. account for | 占……比例 |
| 29. favorable measure | 优惠措施 |
| 30. attribute…to… | 把……归因于…… |
| 31. feasibilit | 可行性 |
| 32. market share | 市场份额 |
| 33. flextime working | 弹性工作时间 |
| 34. the second quarter | 第二季度 |
| 35. sales force | 营销队伍 |
| 36. public bid | 公开招标 |
| 37. pro-business environment | 有利于商业发展的环境 |
| 38. encounter | 面临 |
| 39. managerial structure | 管理结构 |
| 40. upgrade | 升级 |

## 二、集团合作表达

| | |
|---|---|
| 1. 经济稳定 | economic stabilization |
| 2. 互联互通蓝图 | Connectivity Blueprint |
| 3. 降低利率 | cut interest rate |
| 4. 金融危机 | financial crisis |
| 5. 世界多极化 | multipolar world |
| 6. 经济全球化 | economic globalization |
| 7. 文化多样化 | cultural diversity |
| 8. 国际通行规则 | international norms |

| | |
|---|---|
| 9. 资源配置 | resource allocation |
| 10. 互利共赢 | mutual benefit |
| 11. 友好国家 | friendly countries |
| 12. 人道主义救援 | humanitarian rescue |
| 13. 民事设施 | civilian facilities |
| 14. 提升政治互信 | boost political mutual trust |
| 15. 次区域共同体 | subregional community |
| 16. 长治久安 | a long period of stability |
| 17. 求真务实 | pragmatic |
| 18. 审时度势 | size up the trend of events |
| 19. 招商引资 | attract investment |
| 20. 超前消费 | premature consumption |
| 21. 紧缩政策 | deflation policy |
| 22. 过热的经济 | overheated economy |
| 23. 市场干预 | market intervention |
| 24. 源远流长 | have a long history |
| 25. 保持货币稳定 | maintain monetary stability |
| 26. 风险控制机制 | risk-control mechanism |
| 27. 区域经济合作 | regional economic cooperation |
| 28. 优势互补 | complement each other's advantages |
| 29. 誉满全球、举世闻名 | world-renowned |
| 30. 不进则退 | no progress simply means regression |

# Unit 14

# The Annual Report of Listed Companies

Unit Objectives

In this unit you should

➤ familiarize yourself with the basic concepts of the annual report of listed companies.

➤ enable yourself to acquire the basic words and useful expressions of the annual report of listed companies in this unit.

➤ have a good command of the translating skills of the numeral.

## Section 1　Theme Lead-in

**Read the following passage to gain a better understanding of this unit.**

When people buy stock, most do so through one of the securities exchanges or market places for stocks and bonds. These marketplaces are commonly called "stock exchange" where people can find their own buyer or seller. Since there is a common meeting place for these transactions, people interested in buying and selling go there (or send their representatives). The result is a very systematic market process, where transactions are handled in an orderly manner and the operations are both supervised and regulated by law.

### The New York Stock Exchange and the American Stock Exchange

With a handful of exceptions the stocks of most large publicly owned corporations are traded on either the New York Stock Exchange or the American Stock Exchange. There is most status in being listed on the New York Stock Exchange only because the minimum requirements for the total value of outstanding shares and the number of stockholders are somewhat tougher. From the perspective of a stock buyer the only difference of consequence is the higher trading volume on the NYSE, which makes it a bit easier to buy or sell large quantities of stocks without affecting the price very much.

### Commodity Futures

A commodity future contract is an agreement between a buyer and a seller to trade a special amount of commodity at a date in the future. Organized futures market for everything from coffee to lumber to platinum have been around for a long time. That is because businesses producing these commodities, along with businesses that use them as raw materials, need futures markets to hedge against the risk of price changes.

By law, commodity futures may only be bought and sold through organized, government-regulated exchanges. The exchange is a go-between, linking like-minded buyers and sellers. Once a contract to deliver this much frozen orange juice concentrate at that many cents per pound is made, the exchange takes the responsibility to enforce the agreement. Technically, commodity futures agreements are with the exchange, not the other party. So there is never any worry that it will be necessary to take the other party to court.

### Foreign Exchange

The foreign exchange market is the mechanism through which foreign currencies are traded. It is not an actual marketplace but a system of telephone and telex communications between banks, customers and middlemen. This market is enormous and growing. In part, that's because a torrent of foreign currency is needed to finance the trillion dollars' worth of goods and services that flow between countries each year. In part, it's because corporate managers have become sophisticated in searching for the highest, safest yields on their working capital.

##  Section 2　Translation Warming-up

A: Please match the Chinese translation in column B with the English expressions in column A.

| | |
|---|---|
| 1. the reform of the exchange rate | A. 汇率改革 |
| 2. appreciating in real terms by 18.5 percent against the US dollar | B. 股票交易市场 |
| 3. the fairly high proportion of non-performing loans | C. 自由货币兑换 |
| 4. the exchange rate of a country's currency | D. 纳斯达克 |

5. markets for the trading stocks

6. be freely convertible in the current account

7. the National Association of Securities Dealers Automated Quotation

8. market makers who concentrate on trading special stocks

9. achieve their desired growth successfully

10. strengthen financial assistance for small enterprises

E. 主要从事特殊股票买卖的经纪人

F. 市值的预期增长

G. 加强金融机构对小企业的支持

H. 对美元升值了 18.5%

I. 银行不良贷款的比例较高

J. 国家的汇率制度

**B：Fill the following sentences' blanks with the same meaning as the former Chinese ones.**

1. 股价下跌本身并不创造高价值，股票打折并不一定是好事。

A price decline does not in itself make a good value and _____.

2. 6 万美元中的 2,600 美元用于补偿你三年或十年间其他股票的资本收益。

The other $2,600 of the $60,000 is carried forward to _____ three or ten years hence.

3. 1973 年至 1974 年持续了 694 天的熊市，明显长于目前已经长达 421 天的熊市。

The 694-day bear market of 1973-1974 _____.

4. 流入发展中国家的大量资本主要是由国际环境造成的，而并非取决于地方经济的表现。

The volume of capital flowing into developing countries _____.

5. 如果你最终损失了 7 万美元的资本，那么其中每年只有 2,500 美元用于补偿你的工资和利息收入。

If you end up with a $70,000 capital loss, only $2,500 of it can be used annually _____.

## Section 3  Topic Features and Translation Principles

### 一、上市公司年报

上市公司的年度报告简称年报，实质上是一种每年定期刊行的财务报表，是该公司管理层根据有关规定就公司经营的主要方面，如：董事会情况、公司资产、负债、营收与支出等，向股东以及其他利益相关人做出的定期汇报和信息披露。年报中会列出公司的盈余、净利和其他股东感兴趣的信息。年报是投资者了解公司运营和收益情况并制定投资决策的重要依据，也是展示公司形象的宣传渠道。

在我国，上市公司的管理层必须依据中国证监会发布的《公开发行证券的公司信息披露内容与格式准则第 2 号〈年度报告的内容与格式〉》及其他有关文件全权负责编制年报的全文和披露公司的信息。该准则第二款还规定，已发行境内上市外资股及其衍生证券并在证券交易所上市的公司，应当同时编制年报的外文文本。

## 二、上市公司年报的主要内容及特点

### 1. 年报内容

一篇完整的上市公司年报通常长达 40~60 页,主要由以下几个部分组成:

（1）重要提示;

（2）公司概况;

（3）会计数据和业务数据摘要;

（4）股本变动和股东情况;

（5）董事、监事、高级管理人员和员工情况;

（6）公司治理结构;

（7）股东大会情况;

（8）董事会报告;

（9）监事会报告;

（10）重要事项;

（11）财务报告;

（12）备查文件目录。

其中(5)、(9)、(12)等项为中国内地关于信息披露的特别事项,在美英及中国香港地区上市的公司年报中不要求这类信息的披露。

### 2. 公司年报的行文特点

（1）内容完整:年报的全部内容围绕公司经营的各个方面展开,主要内容一项不能少。

（2）结构程式化:年报的行文结构相对固定,具有程式化的特点。

（3）以理服人:惯用小标题,行文中存在着明晰的论证结构,大量使用自利性归因手法。

（4）客观、准确、高效:注重纪实性,用语精确,段落短小精悍。

（5）高度专业化:内容涉及公司管理、经营和股票交易等专业方面。

（6）数据的广泛运用:每一个观点都有充分的数据支持。

### 3. 公司年报的语言特点

（1）各类行业术语丰富,广泛使用会计术语。

（2）用词正式、准确,常使用文言文词汇。

（3）大量引用数字和图表。

（4）套语和固定短语较多。

（5）句型具有较高的重复比例,大量使用原因状语从句、比较句、排比句和并列句。

## 三、上市公司年报的翻译原则

### 1. 遵循准确与精确原则

年报中的各类术语、数字、图表等要向读者准确传达有关的重要信息,因此这些术语、数字、图表的翻译要做到准确和精确。如下表列出的是某集团截至 2020 年 12 月 31 日 12 个月和截至 2021 年 12 月 31 日 12 个月的现金流量以及各个时期末的现金和现金等价物。

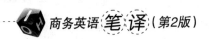
| | 截至 12 月 31 日 | |
| --- | --- | --- |
| | 2021 年 | 2020 年 |
| | 人民币百万元 | 人民币百万元 |
| 经营活动产生的现金流量净额 | 205,885 | 163,692 |
| 用于投资活动的现金流量净额 | (91,576) | (125,687) |
| 用于融资活动的现金流量净额 | (42,839) | (38,246) |
| 外币折算差额 | (485) | 246 |
| 期末现金和现金等价物 | 80,509 | 12,678 |

译文：

| | Years ended December 31 | |
| --- | --- | --- |
| | 2021 年 | 2020 年 |
| | RMB million | RMB million |
| Net cash from operating activities | 205,885 | 163,692 |
| Net cash used for investing activities | (91,576) | (125,687) |
| Net cash for financing activities | (42,839) | (38,246) |
| Currency translation differences | (485) | 246 |
| Cash and cash equivalents as at the end of year | 80,509 | 12,678 |

**2. 遵循译文文体正式原则**

要使用正确的会计术语、行业术语和文体正式的词汇，句型结构不能过于简单。

 **案例**

贵公司董事须负责编制真实与公平之财务表。在编制该等公平与真实的财务表时，董事必须选取并采用合适的会计政策。本核数师之责任乃根据我所审核工作的结果，对该等财务报表形成独立意见，并按照1981年百慕大公司法第90条将此意见向全体股东报告，不作其他用途。本核数师不会就本报告之内容向其他任何人士负责或承担任何责任。

译文：

The company's directors are responsible for the preparation of financial statements which give a true and fair view. In preparing financial statements which give a true and fair view, it is fundamental that appropriate accounting policies are selected and applied consistently. It is our responsibility to form an independent opinion, based on our audit, on those financial statements and to report our opinion solely to you, as a body, in accordance with Section 90 of the Bermuda Companies Act of 1981, and for no other purpose. We do not assume responsibility towards, or accept liability to, any other person for the contents of this report.

**3. 遵循名从主人原则**

年报中的公司名、人名、地名、组织名等必须翻译准确，采用主人自己的译名和业内已经广为人知的、约定俗成的名称。

**案例**

公司每位执行董事与高级管理人员年度薪酬在人民币 20 万～500 万元,具体分配金额由董事会薪酬委员会根据公司主要财务指标和经营目标完成情况,公司董事、高级管理人员分管工作范围及主要职责情况,董事及高级管理人员岗位工作业绩考评系统中涉及指标的完成情况,董事及高级管理人员的业务创新能力和创利能力等确定。

译文:

The annual remuneration of each of the executive Director and senior management of the Company fall between the range of RMB 200,000—RMB 5,000,000 while actual amount shall be determined based on the main financial indicators and operation target completion of the Company, the scope of work and main responsibilities of the Directors and senior management of the Company, the target completion of Directors and senior management as assessed by the duty and performance appraisal system, as well as business innovation capacity and profit generation ability of the Directors and senior management.

### 4. 遵循套语照搬原则

为照顾文体的一致性,相同套语、套段和套篇在样译可靠的情况下直接照搬。

 **案例**

H 集团将向本集团提供的产品和服务,不论以数量及种类计,均较本集团向 H 集团提供的多。按照以下的产品和服务类别分门别类:

工程技术服务,包括但不限于勘探技术服务、井下作业服务、油田建造服务、炼油厂建设服务及工程和设计服务;

生产服务,包括但不限于供水、发电和供电、供气和通信;

社会服务,包括但不限于保安服务、教育和医院;

生活服务,包括但不限于物业管理、培训中心和宾馆;

金融服务,包括但不限于贷款和存款服务。

译文:

More products and services are to be provided by H Group to the Group, both in terms of quantity and variety, than those to be provided by the Group to CNPC. Products and services to be provided by H Group to the Group have been classified together and categorized according to the following types of products and services:

Construction and technical services, including (but not limited to) exploration technology services, downhole operation services, oilfield construction services, oil refinery construction services and engineering and design services;

Production services, including (but not limited to) water supply, electricity generation and supply, gas supply and communications;

Supply of material services, including (but not limited to) the purchase of materials, quality control, storage of materials and delivery of materials;

Social services, including (but not limited to) security services, education and hospitals;

Ancillary services, including (but not limited to) property management, training centers and guesthouses;

Financial services, including (but not limited to) loans and deposits services.

## Section 4　Translating Strategies, Samples and Training

### ✓ Translating Strategies

#### 一、数词组成的常用短语

1. by hundreds（数以百计），by thousands（数以千计），by millions（数以百万计）。

2. hundreds of（数以百计，数百），thousands of（数以千计，数千），millions of（数以百万计），billions of（几十亿）。

3. ten to one（十之八九），nine cases out of ten（十之八九），nine tenths（几乎全部），fifty-fifty（对半的），a few tens of（十分之几），by one hundred percent（百分之百的）。

4. a decade of（十个），a dozen of（12个，一打），a score of（20个）。

#### 二、需要换算的数词

ten thousand（10千）一万，one hundred thousand（100千）十万，ten million（10百万）千万，one hundred million（100百万）亿，one billion 十亿，ten billion（10个十亿）百亿，one hundred billion（100个十亿）千亿，one trillion 万亿。

#### 三、概数的翻译

**1. 表示大约、不确定**

如 about，some，around，round，nearly，toward，somewhere about，estimated，approximately，in/of/on the border of，close to 等。

 **例句**

例 1. The price of this new machine is in the neighborhood of a thousand dollars.

这台新机器的价格大约是1,000元。

例 2. The output of this factory is about 17 times that of last year.

这家工厂的产量是去年的17倍。

**2. 表示高于、多于**

如 more than，odd，over，above，long，past，or more，upwards of，higher than，exceed，in excess of 等。

 **例句**

例 1. The staff of this company is said to be over one thousand.

据说这个公司有一千多名员工。

例 2. It took the manager more than 5 hours to finish the report.

经理花费了 5 个多小时才完成那份报告。

### 3. 表示少于、差一些、不到

如 less, less than, no more than, under, short of, off, to, within, as few as 等。

 例句

例 1. It took one month less than three years for them to develop the new material.

他们花了差一个月就到三年的时间才研制出了这种新材料。

例 2. They bought the electric kettle at 5 dollars off the list price.

他们以低于价目表 5 美元的价格买下了那个电热水壶。

## 四、倍数的译法

### 1. 倍数增加的译法

（1）"倍数+ as...as"表示"是原来的 n 倍"。

例 The grain output of this year is about 2 times as great as that of last year.

今年的粮食产量大约是去年的 2 倍。

（2）"倍数+比较级+ than"表示"比原来的多 n 倍"。

例 The revenue of this company is 15 times more than that of the little company.

这个大公司的收入比那个小公司多 15 倍。

（3）表示增加意义的动词+倍数。常见的动词有 increase, rise, exceed, grow, raise, expand, go up 等。

例 The total volume of state purchase in the first quarter rose by 4.5 percent, compared with the same period of last year.

和去年相同期比,第一季度的政府采购总额增长了 4.5 个百分点。

（4）表示增加意义的词+by a factor of+数词。表示"是原来的 n 倍"。

例 Today the speed of High-speed rail exceeds the ordinary speed by a factor of three.

现在火车的速度是平常速度的 3 倍。

（5）表示倍数意义的词+宾语/表语。这样的动词有 double, treble, quadruple。

例 The new airport will treble the capacity of the existing one.

新机场是现有机场容量的 3 倍。

### 2. 倍数减少的译法

（1）用表示"减少"的动词,如 decrease, reduce, fall, lower 等连接"by n 或 n%"表示净减量,还可以用系动词连接"n less（than）"表示净减量,n 表示数字。

**例句**

例 1. The cost decreased by 30%. 成本下降了 30%。

例 2. This new process used 20% less material. 这种新工艺少用了 20% 的材料。

（2）用表示"减少"的动词，如 decrease，reduce，fall，lower 等连接"by n times""n times""n times as +形容词/副词+as""by a factor of n"均可表示"减少了 n 分之 n−1 或减少到 n 分之一"，n 表示数字。

 **例句**

例 1. The enterprise management expenditure this year has decreased by 3 times as against that of 2020.

该企业今年的行政管理开支比 2020 年降低了 2/3。

例 2. The principal advantage of this technology is a four-fold reduction in volume.

这项技术的主要优点是体积缩小了 3/4。

**Translating Samples**

 **案例**

**例 1**

This company, founded in Oct. 1994 with the registered capital of RMB 30,000,000 Yuan, has passed qualification on construction decoration & building curtain wall Level I and qualification on special design of construction decoration, Grade A issued by Ministry of Construction, Safety Qualification Certificate Level I issued by Fujian Construction Bureau, as well as Fire-fighting Design & Construction Qualification Certificate Grade A issued by Fujian Public Security Bureau Fire Fighting Brigade.

**译文：**

该有限公司创立于 1994 年 10 月，注册资金 3,000 万元，现公司已具备建设部颁发的"建筑装饰、建筑幕墙施工一级资质"及"建筑装饰专项设计甲级资质"，福建省建设厅颁发的"一级安全资质证书"，福建省公安消防总队颁发的"甲级消防设计、施工资质证书"。

**例 2**

Currently, our company has a total of 300 employees, including 69 managerial staffs and 52 of which have professional titles, and 11 project managers. Since our establishment, the company performance is updating year after year under the joint efforts of our staffs, the design and construction performance that we have completed have been well accepted by the owner and people from all walks of life.

**译文：**

目前公司拥有员工总人数约 300 人，包括管理人员 69 人，具有专业职称管理人员 52 人，项目经理总数 11 人。公司自创办以来，在全体员工的不断努力下，公司业绩年年翻新，所完成的设计和施工业绩均得到业主乃至社会各界的普遍赞誉。

## 例 3

The board of directors （the "Board"）, the supervisory committee （the "Supervisory Committee"） and the directors （the "Directors"）, supervisors （the "Supervisors"） and senior management （the "Management"） of the Company hereby warrant that there are no false representations, misleading statements or material omissions contained in this report （the "Report"）, and jointly and severally accept full responsibility for the truthfulness, accuracy and completeness of its contents. This Report has been prepared in both Chinese and English. For any discrepancies, the Chinese version shall prevail.

**译文：**

本公司董事会、监事会及董事、监事、高级管理人员保证本报告所载资料不存在任何虚假记载、误导性陈述或者重大遗漏，并对其内容的真实性、准确性和完整性承担个别及连带责任。本报告分别以中、英文编制，在对中外文本的理解上发生歧义时，以中文文本为准。

## 例 4

Net profit attributable to owners of the Company in the consolidated Financial Statement 2021 prepared in accordance with Accounting Standards for Business Enterprises by the Company was RMB768,225,620.35, and net assets attributable to shareholders' equity of the Company were RMB12,000,210.15. The main differences with the net profit and net assets set out the financial statements prepared in accordance with International Financial Reporting Standards were as follow.

**译文：**

本公司按企业会计准则编制的 2021 年度合并财务报表归属于母公司所有者的净利润为人民币 768,225,620.35 元及归属于母公司所有者权益为人民币 12,000,210.15 元，其与按国际财务报告准则编制的财务报表列报的净利润和净资产的重要差异如下。

## 例 5

说明：公司在 2019 年以前年度，按照企业会计准则，将收到的与固定资产构建相关的国债专项资金及专项应付款计入资本公积中；而按照国际财务报告准则，则将收到的该等国债专项资金及专项应付款计入迟延收益，并按固定资产使用期限分期摊销。

**译文：**

Explanation：In years prior to 2019, according to the principles of the Accounting Standards for Business Enterprises, the Group will receive special fund for treasury bond received and special accounts payable related to construction of relevant fixed assets which are included in capital reserve. However, according to IFRS, the Group will account for special fund for treasury bond received and special accounts payable under deferred income and be amortized by installments over the useful lives of fixed assets.

**例6**

报告期内,公司离任董事、高管限售持股半年锁定期到期解禁,高管持股中的 825,870 股,股权性质由有限售条件高管持股变为无限售条件人民币普通股。公司新任董事所持有的 139,275 股,股权性质由无限售条件人民币普通股变为有限售条件高管持股。

译文:

During the reporting period, the half year lock-up period for the resigned Company was expired. Therefore, the nature of the 825,870 shares, used to be held by the Senior Management, was changed from restricted shares held by the senior management to the non-restricted RMB ordinary shares. The nature of the 139,275 shares held by the new Directors of the Company was changed from non-restricted RMB ordinary shares to restricted shares held by the senior management.

**例7**

采购、服务和其他支出的增加主要原因是:一,炼油厂加工量增加及原油价格上涨,外购原油支出相应增加;二,国内水、电等生产资料价格上涨及本集团生产规模扩大,油气生产支出相应增加。

译文:

The increase in purchases and services was primarily due to (1) an increase in the purchase expenses of crude oil from external suppliers, which resulted from an increase in crude oil prices and an increase in the purchases volume of crude oil by the Group's refineries, and (2) an increase in oil and gas production costs resulting from an increase in the rates for water and electricity and the prices of other production materials in the domestic market as well as an expansion of the production scale of the Group.

**例8**

2022 年 3 月 29 日,本公司控股股东持有公司 的 293,003,657 股限售股份已满承诺限售期,待控股股东确认有关解除限售的事项后,办理相关解除限售的手续。

译文:

The restriction period for the 293,003,657 restricted shares of the Company held by our Company, the controlling shareholder of the Company, expired on March 29 2022, the relevant procedures for the release from sales restriction will be processed upon confirmation from the controlling shareholder regarding such release from sales restriction.

### Translating Training

**A：Translate the following sentences about the annual report of listed companies into Chinese.**

1. The Register of Members of the Company will be closed from July 23 2021 to July 27 2021, both days inclusive, during which period no transfer of shares will be effected.

2. With the recognition by new customers from France and Germany to our Groups' fashionable design and workmanship, sales to these two markets improved during this year.

3. The Company was completely independent from the controlling shareholder, and had its independent and complete business operation controlling capacity.

4. According to the Restructuring Agreement entered into between the Company and the Group in 2021 upon the formation of the Company, the Group has undertaken to the Company the following.

5. None of Directors, Supervisors and the Senior Management is unable to guarantee the truthfulness, accuracy and completeness of the annual report.

6. The Company established a complete internal control system covering production management, financial management, connected transactions, external guarantee, use of proceeds, and material investment of the Company and its subsidiaries.

7. With the improving worldwide economy and a successful marketing strategy, the Group's overall turnover recorded satisfactory improvement over the course of the year. The improvement in turnover was mainly from the USA, Europe and the local market.

8. The performance of the Group's garment sales in the PRC was satisfactory in terns of the extension of its sales network and the increase in geographical coverage in major and second-to third-tier cities.

9. International administration departments were established to monitor the set-up, improvement and implementation of internal control system. Audit Committee reviewed and monitored the material connected transactions.

10. In terms of assets: There was only shareholding relationship between the Company and Chenming Holdings Company Limited. The assets of the company were completely separated from those of the controlling shareholder.

**B: Translate the following sentences about the annual report of listed companies into English.**

1. 2022 年 3 月 18 日召开了第五届监事会第十次会议。会议审议了公司 2021 年一季度报告全文和摘要。

2. 报告期内公司未发生持有公司股份 7%(含 7%)以上股东追加股份限售承诺的情况。

3. 现任董事、监事、高级管理人员 2021 年在公司领取的报酬情况请参见本节第一部分。

4. 按照深圳证券交易所上市规则的有关规定,报告期内,本集团无重大关联交易事项发生。

5. 募集资金使用情况:公司最近一次募集资金实际投入项目和承诺投入项目完全一致,没有变更。

6. 本公司董事会及董事保证本年度报告所载资料不存在任何虚假记载、误导性陈述或者重大遗漏,并对其内容的真实性、准确性和完整性承担个别及连带责任。

7. 我建议立即着手在东京和首尔建立两个亚洲地区的物流中心。三个月之内,这两个物流中心就可以投入使用,使我们在与客户直接打交道时处于更有利的地位。

8. 如果我们不马上采取行动,恐怕就不得不失去一部分市场份额。我们的主要竞争对手都已经在欧洲建立起了物流中心。再不及时反应的话,我们的一部分客户就会被他们吸引走。

9. 报告期内,根据香港联合交易所对《上市规则》有关条款的修改及中国证监会发布的《关于修改上市公司现金分红若干规定的决定》,公司根据其要求将公司章程做了相应修改。

10. 长虹集团的财务报表已经按照企业会计准则的规定编制,在所有重大方面公允反映了长虹集团 2021 年 12 月 31 日的公司及合并财务状况,以及 2021 年度的公司及合并经营成果。

## Section 5   Extensive Expression

### 一、企业财务会计报表封面（Financial Report Cover）

| | |
|---|---|
| 1. 报表所属期间之期末时间点 | period ended |
| 2. 所属月份 | reporting period |
| 3. 报出日期 | submit date |
| 4. 记账本位币币种 | local reporting currency |
| 5. 审核人 | verifier |
| 6. 填表人 | preparer |

### 二、资产负债表（Balance Sheet）

| | |
|---|---|
| 1. 资产 | assets |
| 2. 流动资产 | current assets |
| 3. 货币资金 | bank and cash |
| 4. 短期投资 | current investment |
| 5. 一年内到期委托贷款 | entrusted loan receivable due within one year |
| 6. 短期投资净额 | net bal of current investment |
| 7. 应收票据 | notes receivable |
| 8. 应收股利 | dividend receivable |
| 9. 应收利息 | interest receivable |
| 10. 应收账款 | account receivable |
| 11. 预付账款 | prepayment |
| 12. 应收补贴款 | subsidy receivable |
| 13. 存货 | inventory |
| 14. 已完工尚未结算款 | amount due from customer for contract work |
| 15. 待摊费用 | deferred expense |
| 16. 长期债权投资 | long-term debt investment |
| 17. 固定资产 | fixed assets |
| 18. 工程物资 | material holds for construction of fixed assets |
| 19. 固定资产清理 | fixed assets to be disposed of |
| 20. 固定资产合计 | total fixed assets |
| 21. 无形资产及其他资产 | other assets & intangible assets |

| 22. 无形资产 | intangible assets |
| 23. 长期待摊费用 | long-term deferred expense |
| 24. 融资租赁——未担保余值 | finance lease—unguaranteed residual values |
| 25. 融资租赁——应收融资租赁款 | finance lease—receivables |
| 26. 无形及其他长期资产合计 | total other assets & intangible assets |
| 27. 递延税项 | deferred tax |
| 28. 递延税款借项 | deferred tax assets |
| 29. 资产总计 | total assets |
| 30. 负债及所有者(或股东)权益 | liability & equity |
| 31. 流动负债 | current liability |
| 32. 短期借款 | short-term loans |
| 33. 递延收益 | deferred revenue |
| 34. 流动负债合计 | total current liability |
| 35. 长期借款 | long-term loans |
| 36. 长期负债合计 | total long-term liability |
| 37. 递延税款贷项 | deferred tax liability |
| 38. 负债合计 | total liability |
| 39. 少数股东权益 | minority interests |
| 40. 所有者权益(或股东权益) | owners' equity |
| 41. 实收资本(或股本) | paid in capital |
| 42. 实收资本(或股本)净额 | net bal of paid in capital |
| 43. 资本公积 | capital reserves |
| 44. 盈余公积 | surplus reserves |
| 45. 未确认投资损失 | unrealised investment losses |

## 三、利润及利润分配表（Income Statement and Profit Appropriation）

| 1. 主营业务收入 | revenue |
| 2. 减：主营业务成本 | less：cost of sales |
| 3. 主营业务税金及附加 | sales tax |
| 4. 主营业务利润(亏损以"－"填列) | gross profit（-means loss） |
| 5. 加：其他业务收入 | add：other operating income |
| 6. 减：其他业务支出 | less：other operating expense |
| 7. 营业费用 | selling & distribution expense |
| 8. 管理费用 | G&A expense |
| 9. 财务费用 | finance expense |
| 10. 营业利润(亏损以"－"填列) | profit from operation（-means loss） |
| 11. 加：投资收益(亏损以"－"填列) | add：investment income（-means loss） |
| 12. 补贴收入 | subsidy income |
| 13. 营业外收入 | non-operating income |

14. 减：营业外支出　　　　　　less：non-operating expense

15. 利润总额（亏损总额以"－"填列）　　profit before tax（-means loss）

16. 减：所得税　　　　　　　　less：income tax

17. 少数股东损益　　　　　　　minority interest

18. 加：未确认投资损失　　　　add：unrealized investment losses

19. 净利润（净亏损以"－"填列）　　net profit（-means loss）

20. 加：年初未分配利润　　　　add：retained profits

21. 其他转入　　　　　　　　　other transfer-in

22. 可供分配的利润　　　　　　profit available for distribution

23. 减：提取法定盈余公积　　　less：appropriation of statutory surplus reserves

24. 提取法定公益金　　　　　　appropriation of statutory welfare fund

25. 提取职工奖励及福利基金　　appropriation of staff incentive and welfare fund

26. 提取储备基金　　　　　　　appropriation of reserve fund

27. 提取企业发展基金　　　　　appropriation of enterprise expansion fund

28. 利润归还投资　　　　　　　capital redemption

29. 可供投资者分配的利润　　　profit available for owners distribution

30. 提取任意盈余公积　　　　　appropriation of discretionary surplus reserve

# Unit *15*

# Company Profile and Publicity Materials

Unit Objectives

In this unit you should

➤ familiarize yourself with the format of company profile and publicity materials.

➤ enable yourself to acquire the basic words and useful expressions of company profile and publicity materials.

➤ have a good command of the translating skills of in order and inversion.

## ❷ Section 1  Theme Lead-in

**Read the following passage to gain a better understanding of this unit.**

A company profile is one of the most important parts of any developing business. It is a brief summary about a company, its objectives and goals, its history to date, and milestones achieved along the way. It is one of the best tools to showcase your company's performance and acts as a marketing tool to grab new investors, employees, customers, or other parties interested in dealing with the company. Thus, a company profile can be an important form of advertisement.

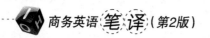

A company profile includes important basic information such as business phone number, e-mail address, fax number, physical address, company hours, and perhaps a map that shows the physical location of the company.

A company profile should include an introduction, brief company history, and relevant data on the company in terms of income, revenue, structure, infrastructure and resources, products, professional experience, and capacity. You should also include company goals and future plans, both in the short and long term, and anything in the line of a company mission statement, any company slogans, or guiding philosophies for the company.

A company profile also should include concise biographies for key members of the company. This includes the CEO and head specialists. Talk about their business experience, educational background and personality, and be sure to touch on any great achievements that staff members have accomplished during their tenure with the company.

A good profile must have no errors, and if it is designed as a brochure it is preferable to get it professionally made using quality paper, printing and structuring. As a page on the website, it should be attractive in appearance, immediately catching a reader's eye and interspersed with relevant pictures and sub-headings. The appropriate length of the profile is about 10-15 pages.

Once you've been in business for a couple of years, prepare the company profile and keep upgrading it at least once a year. Make sure to keep adding achievements and growth prospects when they happen. Keeping your company profile up to date is good business promotion for corporate branding.

## Section 2  Translation Warming-up

**A: Translate the following sentences about company profile and publicity materials into Chinese.**

1. Apple was founded in April 1976 by Steve Wozniak, then 26 years old, and Steve Jobs, 21.

2. In 2021, the company opened its firstretail outlet, a 6,000-square-foot store located in Virginia.

3. The company is a major retailer selling food, clothes and household furnishing. It also sells financial products.

4. Apple controlled more than 75 percent of the $2.5 billion digital audio player market in the United States.

5. Maersk（马士基公司）is one of the world's largest container shipping lines devoted to providing quality shipping and transportation services to its customers worldwide.

6. Haier has established 18 design institutes, 10 industrial complexes, 22 overseas production factories and 58,800 sales agents worldwide.

7. Established in Hong Kong in 1981, Red Apple Furniture Co., Ltd. moved its production base to Shenzhen in 1987. Red Apple owns an original value of fixed assets of H.K. $71.5 million, and total assets of H.K. $5.3 billion.

8. Our mission is to become the driving force in the Chinese information revolution, by promoting our innovative and original proprietary software solutions, and to become a truly international service provider.

9. We provide a broad portfolio of business and high-tech solutions to help our clients improve their business performance, and have many competitive advantages as evidenced by our history of excellent market performance.

10. White Swan Hotel keeps the constant international standard high level service from the very beginning till now, that makes hotel become the first choice for the customers no matter with business or leisure in Canton.

**B：Translate the following sentences about company profile and publicity materials into English.**

1. 本公司对所有产品实行三包。

2. TCL 集团股份有限公司创建于 1981 年,是一家综合性大型国有企业。

3. 近年来,康佳的生产经营格局取得了突破性的发展,在国内东北、西北、华南、华东、西南分别建立了五大生产基地。

4. 公司荣获"全国质量效益型先进企业""消费者满意企业"等称号。

5. 本公司重合同、守信誉。

6. 我们公司是欧洲最大的电子产品生产商。

7. 去年,我们收购了一家私营公司。

8. 2021 年,公司的营业额达到 20 亿元。

9. 2007 年苹果公司推出了 iPhone,2010 年推出了平板电脑 iPad。

10. 2020 年为止,公司在美国共开设 125 家商店,在加拿大、日本和英国也开设了商店。

# Section 3   Topic Features and Translation Principles

### 一、企业介绍的特点

一份企业简介,除概要性地介绍企业的情况外,对其产品也作了简略的宣传。

从文体上看,企业简介是说明书的一种,属于外贸应用文文体;从语篇类型上看,它属于"信息+鼓动类"语篇,有宣传和介绍的功能。因此其语言应充分考虑受众特点,以顾客为中心组织语言。

从内容上看,企业简介包括:

(1) 企业背景,包括如何成立,建立人,企业的历史、发展;

(2) 企业服务内容或者产品介绍;

(3) 企业员工和企业结构介绍;

(4) 企业的顾客群或者范围介绍;

(5) 企业近期内的重大发展介绍;

(6) 合作邀请。

从功能上看,企业简介主要有两种功能:提供企业信息和宣传公司。从第一种功能上看,企业简介应使用具有信息功能(informative)的语言,如"本公司成立于 2020 年,现有员工

2500人""本公司经营范围包括……"。而从第二个功能上看,企业简介也会采用一些具有呼唤功能(vocative)的语言,如"热诚欢迎海内外各界人士前来洽谈、投资、经济技术合作和友好往来""我们将以最上乘的质量、最低廉的价格、最优质的服务同广大客户密切合作,实现双赢、共创辉煌。热诚欢迎您的合作!"等。

企业介绍的语言应具有简洁性、逻辑性、紧凑性和客观性的特点,通常用语比较程式化,词汇上会出现大量的专业词汇,语法上则多用一般现在时态和被动语态。

## 二、企业介绍和宣传资料翻译的原则

### （一）英汉"企业介绍"的差异

英汉"企业介绍"在内容上和语言表达形式以及行文结构上都有很大不同。

**1. 内容上**

英语企业宣传资料注重突出公司形象及产品,充分表述事实,传递实质信息,用事实和数字说话;而汉语企业宣传资料则喜欢渲染一些信息,大量使用概念化及夸大的修饰语言,如"人杰地灵、历史悠久"等。习惯罗列权威机构的认证及各个级别的奖项。

**2. 语言表达形式以及行文结构上**

英语宣传材料一般语言平实、通俗易懂,注重客观介绍,具有口语特色。大量使用陈述句、祈使句、疑问句,以及名词、形容词、不定代词和介词短语等。企业简介常常分为几个小部分,并使用第一人称"We"以表示亲近消费者。而汉语则不同,公司简介中大量使用辞藻华丽的形容词和修饰语,通常会使用一些标语口号式的文字,多为短语形式,如:"质量第一、信誉第一、服务至上、平等互利""严管理、高品质、讲信誉、重服务"等,具有简短醒目的特点。

### （二）翻译原则

简洁、达意、交代清楚企业的基本内涵是翻译企业资料的基准。公司介绍的翻译要力求准确,做到完整全面。应使用平实的语调,简洁的措辞,译出企业的核心内容,如企业性质、股东情况等,一些渲染性的宣传词可以删去。语言尽量简单,有亲和力,接近口语。要遵循以下原则:

**1. 忠实原文。通常采用的方法为直译法,将句子按字面意思直接翻译过来**

 **例句**

例 1. Founded in 1837, Procter & Gamble is one of the largest consumer products companies in the world.

宝洁公司创始于 1837 年,是世界上最大的日用消费品公司之一。

例 2. A Fortune 100 company with global presence and impact, it had sales of US $ 35.3 billion in 2021.

它是世界财富百强企业之一,拥有全球性的业务和影响力。2021 年销售额为 353 亿美元。

**2. 通顺易懂。符合语言规范、语言习惯及时代特点,避免死译、硬译**

 例句

例 1. Founded in 1979, Harbin Zhengda Group is a large corporation focusing on construction and development of real estate.

译文 A: 成立于 1979 年的哈尔滨正大集团是以建筑及房地产开发为主的企业。

译文 B: 哈尔滨正大集团成立于 1979 年,是以建筑及房地产开发为主的企业。

分析:第一种译法参照了英文的语法,将定语翻译在名词之前,但是不符合汉语表达的习惯,相比较而言,第二种译法更符合汉语语言规范。

例 2. 产品多次荣获国家经委新产品"金龙奖"、中国新技术"金奖",山东省优质产品奖、省市科学技术进步奖。

译文 A: Our products have been awarded "Gold Dragon Award" of New Product issued by National Economy Committee, National New Technique "Gold Award", Shangdong Province Superior Quality Product Award and Provincial(Municipal) Technology Advance Award.

译文 B: The company has been awarded with many titles for its quality products and excellent service by local, provincial and national institutions.

分析:译文 A 如实翻译出了原文所列的各种奖项和颁奖机构。但是这些名称对于英文读者而言没有任何意义,他们无法理解这些奖项名称和颁奖机构的含义及其权威性,所以无需全部翻译。译文 B 简洁、直白地列出了奖项的级别,达到应有的效果。

**3. 注重保持原文的风格,用词准确,必要时采用意译法**

 例句

例 1. Haier was ranked 95th after such household names as Coca-Cola, McDonald's and Nokia, which were the top three.

海尔排名第 95 位。排行榜上,可口可乐荣登榜首,麦当劳排名第二,诺基亚名列第三。

分析:这句话的翻译就是将句子结构进行了转换,使意思的表达更为清楚,同时也起到了强调的作用。

例 2. 本公司拥有雄厚的技术力量,本科毕业以上的技术、管理人员占员工总数的 60% 以上。

The company boasts tremendous technological strength with a well-qualified management and staff.

分析:在中文环境中,"本科毕业以上的技术、管理人员占员工总数的 60% 以上",也可作为"雄厚的技术力量"的证据,但是在英语环境下会显得牵强。如果直译成"Boasting tremendous technological strength, the company owns a technical and managerial staff with bachelor degrees or above who account for 60% of the total number of its employees." 会不利于译文功能的实现,因此不能硬译,可做必要的删减,进行概括性的论述。

**4. 语言相对正式,用词多以褒义词或中性词为先,不能夸大**

中文宣传材料常有大量的形容词,起到烘托渲染作用。如果把这些形容词如实翻译,译

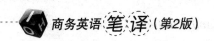

文会很夸张,因此翻译时,不应受这些词语的干扰,对信息要进行整理,只翻译那些对译文读者有用的信息。

 例句

今天的城市已经成为了东北地区繁华地带中一片富有生机和希望的投资热土。

译文 A：Today, the city has become an investment spot full of investment opportunities. It is one of the promising prosperous areas in the Northeast part of the country.

译文 B：The city has become an investment spot for investment in the Northeast part of the country.

分析：译文 A 文体累赘,意思重复,外国人不易理解。事实上,译文 B 已经足以表达原文所有的信息。因为英文的宣传材料文体平实、用词具体,重在提供信息,因此在翻译的时候,不要受中文渲染词语的干扰,只需翻译那些对译文读者有用的信息。

## 三、常见企业介绍失误表现

### 1. 译文中的文化缺省,造成失误

公司简介中往往涉及一些汉文化中所特有的机构名称、政治术语、历史事件、典故、奖项名称等。这些内容所涉及的文化背景知识极具中国特色。而对英文读者来说,却是必须明示不可的。如果对这些内容不加解释地直接译为英文,就会形成译文中的文化缺省,使英语读者无法正确理解其含义。例如:"邓小平南行讲话""大锅饭""三个代表""实行三包"等,翻译时必须作简要说明,以便使译文明白易懂。

### 2. 忽视中英文化、价值观念差异而导致失误

汉语公司简介的夸张、溢美之词容易使人产生反感,导致语用失误。比如,"在总经理的英明领导下,我公司开拓创新、锐意进取、不畏困难、不惧艰辛,正努力开创本行业新局面。""先进的生产设备,独特的开发力量和完美的售后服务使我们的产品在国内外市场深受欢迎。""我们的任务就是以最佳品质、最优服务、最低价格为您带来最高价值。"

这种典型的中文语言在语篇结构、表达方式、思维习惯上与英文截然不同,在国外客户眼中并无实在意义。他们关注的是具体的而不是空泛的"最佳品质、最优服务、最低价格"。英语中类似材料通常直奔主题,用具体数据说明问题。这种文章如果逐字直译,势必让英文读者不知所云。因此,翻译此类材料之前,应对原文进行删减、重组或改写等处理,注重传达原文的信息和语用意图。

### 3. 片面字面意义的翻译,忽视暗含意义

这类语用失误产生的原因在于不懂得在特定的情景中,英语有相应的习惯表达方式,因而在翻译中不恰当地采用某种表达方式,或误用英语的其他表达方式,结果不能准确地表达原文的信息和用意,甚至引起误解。

例如:"我公司专门生产腰包"被译为 Our company is specialized in producing body bags. "body bag" 在英语中意为"遗体袋",而不是我们所认为的与身体(body) 有关的包,这样翻

译完全是贻笑大方。"腰包"其实就是简单的"waist packs"或"wallets/purses"。

再如:我国出口美国的减肥片,开始时无人问津,后发现英语译名为"obesity-reducing tablets",在美国人看来,此药片是专门给特大胖子(obese people)服用的,不符合消费心理,后来,改译名为"slimming pills",便打开了销路。

针对上述企业介绍的失误现象,译文应以目标语(target language)为准,针对目标受众翻译出地道准确的英文。

 **Section 4   Translating Strategies, Samples and Training**

### ✔ Translating Strategies

### 一、顺译

顺译(translation in order)法,又称为"顺序法"或"原序译法"。英汉语句中的主要成分主语、谓语、宾语或表语的词序基本上是一致的。有些英文复合句所叙述的动作按照发生的时间先后安排,或按逻辑关系安排,与汉语的表达方式也比较一致,就可按原文顺序翻译。

如果句子较长,可以按照所听到的原句的顺序,把整个句子分割成若干个意义单位或信息单位逐一译出。有的时候也需要使用增补、删减等手段进行句子衔接,形成完整的句子。顺译法能够减轻记忆负担,便于及时处理信息。

### 📝 例句

例 1. Our company is dedicated to delivering high quality products and services.
我们公司致力于提供高质量的产品和服务。

例 2. Today, 6 Johnson & Johnson affiliations are operating in China, /employing more than 3,000 people/and producing a wide range of consumer, pharmaceutical and medical products/in our mission to promote the healthcare of Chinese people.
今天,强生公司在中国已经拥有 6 家子公司和机构,员工 3,000 多名,生产的产品涉及消费品,药品和医疗器械等领域,并且始终致力于促进中国人民健康事业的发展。

**分析**:该句子中使用了两个现在分词(employing,producing)做伴随状语的结构,可以直译过来。

例 3. Business is a combination/of all these activities/: production, distribution and sale/, through which profit or economic surplus will be created.
商务是指生产、配送、销售等一切活动的组合,通过这些活动,创造利润和经济盈余。

**分析**:英语中的定语从句绝大部分都是后置的。根据限制意义的强弱不同,分为限制性和非限制性定语从句两种。汉语中作定语的成分则都是前置,也不涉及限制意义的强弱。翻译的关键在于译文是否符合汉语语序。在定语从句英译汉的时候,如果符合汉语表达习惯,可以依据英语原文顺序进行直译。在该句子中,定语从句的先行词是 production, distribution and sale,关系代词是 which,前面使用了介词 through,可直接将介词结构翻译成

"通过这些活动"，然后加上后面的句子，正好符合汉语的表达方式。

例4. It is indeed a pleasure/to stand before the Assembly/and extend to you, Sir,/in the name of my country,/my most sincere congratulations/on your election/as president of the present session of the General Assembly. /

的确非常愉快，能够在大会上，向阁下先生转达，以我国家的名义转达，我最真诚的祝贺,（祝贺）您当选本届联合国大会的主席。

## 二、逆译

逆译（inverse translation）又称"倒置译法"。主要指句子的前后倒置。有些英文句子的表达次序与汉语习惯不同，如，英语时间状语可前可后。表达结果、条件、说明等的状语从句也很灵活，既可以先述也可以后述。而汉语表达往往是按时间或逻辑的顺序进行的，一般重要的内容放在句子的最后。因此，为了与汉语的习惯相一致，当语序不同时，需要采用逆译法。

**1. 简单句中的顺序调整**

 **例句**

例1. Coca-Cola has operated outside the US since 1897.
可口可乐公司从1897年开始开拓国外市场。（状语）

例2. It is our task to gain 30% market share in China by the end of this year.
我们的任务是于今年年底在中国获得30%的市场份额。（状语）

**分析**：上述两个例子可见，汉语中通常习惯是把时间状语放在句子的前面来使用。

例3. Sunshine Co. Ltd is the franchised distributor of a number of famous brands and products.
阳光有限公司是众多知名品牌的特许经销商和总代理。（定语）

**分析**：带有of的结构通常翻译成定语"……的……"，表示所属关系。

例4. The automaker was founded by Henry Ford in 1903, backed by 12 local businessmen.
1903年，亨利·福特在当地12位商人的支持下建立了福特公司。（状语）

**分析**：该句子中是过去分词backed引起的短语作状语。

例5. 在美丽的金秋时节，我很高兴，能在古老又充满现代活力的古都南京，迎来参加"2022中国东部论坛"的各位嘉宾。

In this beautiful golden fall, I am very happy to welcome the distinguished guests to China East Forum 2022/in the ancient capital Nanjing,/an age-old and mysterious city full of dynamism of the modern era.

**分析**：汉语句式习惯把地点（在古老又充满现代活力的古都南京）和定语（参加"2022中国东部论坛的"）放在前面，但是翻译英文时，一定要按照英文习惯，翻译在后面。

**2. 复合句中因时间、条件、假设、目的等关系，而导致翻译顺序不同**

 **例句**

例1. Apple Inc. is an American multinational corporation that designs and markets consumer electronics, computer software, and personal computers.

苹果公司是一家设计销售电子消费品、计算机软件和电脑的美国跨国公司。(定语)

例 2. Traditional is a word <u>that characterizes our company because we have a long and proud history</u>.

因为公司历史悠久、成绩斐然,所以"传统"是适合用来形容本公司的词汇。(原因状语从句)

例 3. Our company has taken full advantage of many synergies generated within the group <u>while retaining our identity and remaining faithful to our distinctive difference</u>.(时间状语从句)

公司在努力保持自己的特色的同时,也充分利用集团内部的合力与优势。

例 4. In 1985 a power struggle developed between Jobs and CEO John Sculley, <u>who had been hired two years earlier</u>.(定语从句)

1985 年,乔布斯和两年前入主苹果的 CEO 约翰·斯卡利之间产生严重的分歧。

例 5. The cost is a major consideration <u>if you want to buy office appliances</u>.(条件状语从句)

如果你想选购办公设备,成本是主要考虑的问题。

## Translating Samples

## 一、公司背景(包括如何成立,建立人,公司的历史、内容和发展)

 **案例**

### 例 1

福特汽车公司是美国的跨国汽车企业,总部在底特律。1903 年,亨利·福特在当地 12 位商人的支持下建立了福特公司。除了福特和林肯品牌之外,公司还有马自达、阿斯顿·马丁和路虎品牌。福特公司是美国第二大汽车生产商。2010 年,福特的年汽车销售量全球排名第五。世界五百强名单中,凭借 2009 年 1183 亿的财政收入,在美国公司中福特公司排名第八。2008 年,福特公司生产汽车 553.2 万辆,到 2019 年年底全世界范围内共有员工 19 万人。

**译文:**

Ford Motor Company is an American multinational automaker based in Detroit. The automaker was founded by Henry Ford in 1903, backed by 12 local businessmen. In addition to the Ford and Lincoln brands, Ford also has Mazda, Aston Martin and Land Rover. Ford is the second largest automaker in the U.S. and the fifth largest in the world based on annual vehicle sales in 2010. Ford is the eighth-ranked overall American-based company in the 2010 Fortune 500 list, based on global revenues in 2009 of $118.3 billion. In 2008, Ford produced 5.532 million automobiles and employed about 190,000 employees at around worldwide by the end of 2019.

### 例 2

Marks and Spencer plc is a British retailer headquartered in London, with over 700 stores in the United Kingdom and over 300 stores across more than 40 countries. It specializes in the selling of clothing and food products. M&S was founded in 1884 by Michael Marks and Thomas Spencer in

Leeds. It made its reputation in the early 20th century on a policy of only selling British-made goods. It entered into long term relationships with British manufacturers, and sold clothes and food under the "St Michael" brand. M&S opened stores in continental Europe in 1975 and in Ireland four years later. In 1988 the company opened two stores in Hong Kong. Marks & Spencer launched an online shopping service in 1999. In February 2007, it announced the opening of the world's largest M&S shop outside the UK at Dubai Festival City. M&S is currently ranked ahead in The Times "Top 100 Graduate Employers 2020-2021".

**译文：**

玛莎百货是英国著名零售商，总部位于伦敦，在英国本土有700多家分店，在全球40多个国家开设了300多家分店，主要销售服装和食品。1884年，米歇尔·马克斯和汤姆·斯宾塞两人在利兹成立了玛莎百货。20世纪早期，玛莎百货以只销售国产产品而著名，与英国制造商有长期的合作关系，销售"圣米歇尔"品牌的服装与食物。1975年，玛莎百货在欧洲大陆开设分店，四年后登陆爱尔兰。1988年，在香港开设两家分店。1999年，开通互联网购物。2007年2月，玛莎百货宣布在迪拜开设英国境外最大的分店。在《泰晤士报》2020年至2021年度100名最佳雇主中，玛莎百货名列前茅。

## 二、公司服务内容或者产品介绍

 **案例**

**例1**

比克公司以生产一次性产品而闻名。公司主要生产一次性刮胡刀、圆珠笔和打火机。比克书写用品遍布160个国家，每天销售量超过2,000万。打火机的日销售量将近400万。

**译文：**

Bic is well-known for its disposable products. The company focuses on producing disposable razors, ballpoint pens and lighters. Today sales of Bic writing instruments total more than 20 million a day in 160 countries and daily sales of disposable lighters now numbers almost 4 millions.

**例2**

We are one of the UK's leading retailers, with over 21 million people visiting our stores each week. We offer stylish, high quality, great value clothing and home products, as well as outstanding quality foods, responsibly sourced from around 2,000 suppliers globally. We employ over 78,000 people in the UK and abroad, and have over 700 UK stores, plus an expanding international business.

We are the number one provider of womenswear and lingerie in the UK, and are rapidly growing our market share in menswear, kidswear and home, due in part to our growing online business. Overall, our clothing and homeware sales account for 49% of our business. The other 51% of our business is in food.

**译文：**

我们是英国最优秀的零售商之一，每周客流量超过2,100万人。我们经营时尚、优质、超值的服装和家用产品,还出售优质食品。所有产品来源于全球 2,000 多家供应商。我们在全球和英国国内共有员工 7.8 万人,国内店面达 700 多家,境外业务不断扩大。

在女装和女性内衣经营方面,我们在国内位居首位。因为网上购物的不断增长,目前男装、儿童服装和家用产品的市场份额也不断扩大。总体上说,服装与家用产品占了总销量的 49%,另外的 51% 主要是食品。

## 三、公司员工和公司结构介绍

 **案例**

### 例 1

公司分为三个部门：生产部、市场营销部和人力资源部。生产部下分两个部门：开发部和质检部。人力资源部下分人事部和培训部两个部门。

**译文：**

The company is divided into three departments: the Production Department, the Sales & Marketing Department and the Human Resources Department. The Production Department is subdivided into two sections: the Development Section and the Quality Assurance Section. Under the Human Resources Department, there are two sections: the Personnel Section and the Training Section.

### 例 2

With headquarters in Seattle, Boeing employs more than 165,000 people across the United States and in 70 countries. More than 123,000 employees hold college degrees. Boeing is organized into two business units: Boeing Commercial Airplanes and Boeing Defense, Space & Security.

**译文：**

波音公司的总部位于西雅图,在美国境内及全球 70 个国家共有员工达 16.5 万余名。员工中超过 12.3 万人拥有大学学历。波音公司下设两个业务部门：波音民用飞机集团和波音防务、空间与安全集团。

## 四、企业的顾客群和业务介绍

 **案例**

### 例 1

我们的能力包括：电脑辅助工程与制造、CNC 技术、高效率的加工中心及镀金等。我们具有足够的研究与开发能力,拥有一支富有经验的工程技术人员队伍。目前我们正在制造用于防卫设施和通信电子部件的仪表工作装置。

**译文：**

Our facilities include computer aided engineering and manufacturing, CNC technology, efficient processing centers, etc., including gold plating. We have adequate facility for research and development and a team of experienced engineers and technicians. Presently we are manufacturing

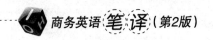

clockwork mechanisms for defense applications and communication electronic components.

### 例 2

GE is truly a global company in the top ten in the world in market valuation. It has operations all over the world and is particularly complex in that it is not a one product company. It has 13 major businesses ranging from aircraft engines and turbine generators to plastics and appliances.

译文：

GE 的确是一家全球性公司。在市场评估中，是世界前 10 大公司之一。在全世界范围内进行运作。因为不是单一产品公司，所以运作比较复杂。公司经营 13 种业务，从飞机发动机、涡轮发电机、塑料一直到各种器械。

## 五、企业近期的重大发展

 **案例**

### 例 1

去年起，公司对 3G 网络的研发投入了重金。目前，在中国广东省、上海、北京，以及美国、英国、德国等世界各地的分公司内，有 2,000 余名工程师在从事 3G 网络研发工作。

译文：

The company has been investing heavily in the R&D of 3G systems since last year. Currently there are over 2,000 engineers engaged in the R&D of 3G systems in our branch offices in Guangdong, Shanghai and Beijing of China and USA, UK and Germany.

### 例 2

The company has been a global leader in innovation in telecommunications. In China, it has invested US $ 600 million in R&D, building 17 R&D centers and labs in Beijing, Tianjin, Shanghai, Nanjing, Chengdu and Hangzhou so far. The number of R&D staff is about 3,000 now.

Its China R&D Institute has now become one of the world-class R&D bases at its own brand. It has also evolved into the largest R&D institute global companies have ever set up in China.

译文：

这家公司一直是全球电子通信领域创新的带头人。它在中国的研发投资达 6 亿美元，到目前为止，在北京、天津、上海、南京、成都和杭州等 6 个城市建立了 17 个研发中心和实验室，研发人员约 3,000 人。

它的中国研究院已经成为世界级的自有品牌研发基地之一，也是跨国公司在中国建立的最大的研发机构。

## 六、合作邀请

 **案例**

### 例 1

中煤总公司（CNCIEC）的宗旨是信誉第一、质量第一、服务第一。它热诚欢迎海内外各界人士前来洽谈、投资、经济技术合作和友好往来！

**译文：**

Abiding by the enterprise principle of "high prestige through quality products and service", CNCIEC awaits with great enthusiasm people from all walks of life both at home and abroad coming for talks over business, investment, technical and economic cooperation.

### 例 2

If you are a qualified supplier with good products, we look forward to working with you in delivering high quality products to the customers. If you are an importer who wants to buy good products at a reasonable price, our company, with its extensive range of products, can be your most reliable business partner.

**译文：**

如果您是一家产品质量可靠的供应商，我们愿意与您合作，协助您打开本地区市场。如果您是一家希望以合理价格购买优质产品的进口商，我们公司将凭借齐全的产品种类成为您最可靠的商业伙伴。

### Translating Training

**A：Translate the following words or phrases about company profile and publicity materials into Chinese.**

1. company profile
2. company history
3. corporate culture
4. corporate strategy
5. company policy
6. business administration
7. development plan
8. management objective
9. management principle
10. management mechanism
11. annual turnover
12. high-end market
13. market share
14. general asset
15. production line
16. R&D base
17. product range
18. product information
19. event news
20. brochure

**B：Translate the following words or phrases about company profile and publicity materials into English.**

1. 创建于
2. 位于，坐落于
3. 更新设备
4. 与国际接轨
5. 打进国际市场
6. 开发产品
7. 树立公司良好形象
8. 跻身于，被列入
9. 设计公司标识
10. 从事于
11. 盈利
12. 研究开发
13. 打造公司形象
14. 日常运作
15. 耐用消费品
16. 产品定位

17. 公司口号　　　　　　　　18. 商标
19. 技术革新　　　　　　　　20. 全球总部

**C：Translate the following Sentences about company profile and publicity materials into Chinese.**

1. The GUMOTEX, Joint Stock Company, is a manufacturing and trade organization, which has been around domestic and international markets for more than 50 years.

2. We put people who want to lend in touch with credit-worthy people who want to borrow.

3. The annual financial gross turnover of the company hovers at around the two billion CZK mark, where roughly one half of the annual production goes for export.

4. Metrostav's main weapons in competition for new projects will include a reasonable pricing policy and a can-do approach to customers' requirements.

5. The business volume puts the company into the top fifty of Czech exporters.

6. It further manufactures inflatable kayaks, canoes and rafts for general and special uses, inflatable mattresses, lounge chairs, pillows and special products for industry and retail.

7. Medilink Ltd. is a membership-based professional association, which provides arrange of specialist consultancy services, developed specifically to meet the needs of the Healthcare Technologies Sector (medical system and biomedical).

8. XXX's experience of managing regional, national and European grants ensures that its members secure both quality and cost-effected services.

9. It manufactures polyurethane-based foams under the brand name of MOLITAN and products made from it, mainly bed mattresses based on MOLITAN or latexfoam, shaped pieces for furniture upholstery, sound and thermal insulations and other products.

10. Swiss International Air Lines Ltd. is a Swiss company, because it is established under the laws of Switzerland, has its legal domicile in Switzerland and its Board of Directors consists mainly of Swiss nationals.

**D：Translate the following sentences about company profile and publicity materials into English.**

1. 公司自创建以来，始终以"六赢"理念为准则，即确保"大众、代理、员工、公司、供方、社会"参与合作的六方共同受益、共同发展，使公司能够坚实、稳定地发展。

2. 北京加维通信电子技术有限公司是美国通用宽带卫星公司于 1993 年 10 月在中国内地投资设立的子公司，是外商独资企业，现有员工 500 人。

3. 亮马河大厦位于北京中央商务休闲区，拥有商务酒店、酒店式服务公寓、办公楼和大型会议餐饮设施，形成完整的国际化商务中心。

4. 公司专为特体、特殊需求的顾客量体加工定制皮衣，并开展"上门量衣、上门送货、电话预约订购"等各项服务。

5. 馄饨侯于 1948 年起开始在王府井地区经营，由于"料精、味美、方便实惠、服务周全"，深得食客的喜爱，远近闻名。

6. 我公司自 20 世纪 70 年代末开始陆续在海外建立了一批独资、合资企业和代表机构，在原有海外销售渠道的基础上,为进一步强化这些海外企业的职能,并为公司向国际化经营发展创造条件,公司已着手在亚洲、欧洲、美洲地区组建三个独立的跨国集团公司,实行自主经营、独立核算、自负盈亏。

7. 美国通用宽带卫星公司总部设在美国佐治亚州亚特兰大市,为跨国经营的综合性集团公司,在美国、欧洲、中东、东南亚、香港均设有子公司、工厂、代表处、发货仓库和维修中心,已形成高效而快速的技术开发、设计、生产、销售和服务网络体系。

8. 本公司拥有写字楼全部产权,是中国反病毒领域办公条件和开发环境最好的公司;上缴国家利税进入 2019 年、2020 年度中关村科技园区"前 100 名缴税大户"和"其他行业总收入前 50 名"大名单,也是杀毒软件行业唯一一家进入以上排名的公司。

9. 为弘扬民族文化遗产,挖掘清真菜珍品,挽救濒于失传的北京西派菜系,"老西来顺"饭庄在保持原有风味的基础上,发扬清真菜肴选料广泛、制作精良的特点,为宾客提供四季菜肴、精致烤涮、甜食面点。

10. 北京民营新世纪养殖场位于中国生态农业第一村民营生态农场内,优良的生态环境,标准化的生产模式,快捷的配送渠道,保证了所有上市鸡蛋的安全、新鲜!

## Section 5   Extensive Expression

### 一、公司种类(Types of company)

| | |
|---|---|
| 1. company/corporation | 公司 |
| 2. multinational corporation | 跨国公司 |
| 3. group corporation | 集团公司 |
| 4. limited company | 有限公司 |
| 5. parent company | 母公司 |
| 6. subsidiary company | 子公司 |
| 7. share holding company | 股份公司 |
| 8. listed company | 上市公司 |

### 二、管理(Management)

| | |
|---|---|
| 1. corporate culture | 企业文化 |
| 2. corporate identity | 公司形象 |
| 3. corporate image | 企业形象 |
| 4. corporate strategy | 公司策略 |
| 5. develop high-tech products | 开发高新产品 |
| 6. team-building | 团队建设 |
| 7. promote team spirit | 提出团队精神 |
| 8. introduce advanced science and technology | 引进先进科学技术 |
| 9. organizational performance | 公司绩效 |
| 10. management skills | 管理技能 |

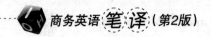
## 三、产品介绍（Product introduction）

| | |
|---|---|
| 1. selected materials | 用料上乘 |
| 2. superior materials | 优质原料 |
| 3. perfect in workmanship | 做工精细 |
| 4. exquisite craftsmanship | 技艺精湛 |
| 5. skillful manufacture | 制作精巧 |
| 6. sophisticated technology | 工艺精良 |
| 7. latest technology | 最新工艺 |
| 8. finely processed | 加工精细 |
| 9. modern design | 造型新颖 |
| 10. professional design | 设计合理 |
| 11. rational construction | 结构合理 |
| 12. various styles | 款式齐全 |
| 13. superior quality | 质量上乘 |
| 14. stable quality | 质量稳定 |
| 15. reliable quality | 质量可靠 |
| 16. wide varieties | 品种繁多 |
| 17. complete in specifications | 规格齐全 |
| 18. quality and quantity assured | 保质保量 |
| 19. dependable performance | 性能可靠 |
| 20. easy and simple to handle | 操作简便 |
| 21. easy to use | 使用方便 |
| 22. durable in use | 经久耐用 |

# Unit *16*

# Tourist Publicity Materials

Unit Objectives

In this unit you should

➢ familiarize yourself with the information and format of tourist materials.

➢ enable yourself to acquire the basic words and useful expressions of tourist publicity materials.

➢ have a good command of the translating skills of the words application and the words ellipsis.

## ❷ Section 1   Theme Lead-in

**Read the following passage to gain a better understanding of this unit.**

Thomas Cook took the first tourists to Paris in 1855. On the return journey, gathering for the buses/coaches some people got arrested for waiting in the park. In Paris people were not allowed to have gatherings. His first excursion was Leicester to Loughborough in 1841. Prior to 1834, the Bank of England observed about thirty-three saints' days and religious festivals as holidays, but in 1834, this was reduced to just four: 1 May, 1 November, Good Friday, and Christmas Day. In

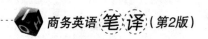

1871, the first legislation relates to bank holidays.

Wealthy people have always traveled to distant parts of the world, to see great buildings, works of art, learn new languages, experience new cultures and taste different cuisines. Long ago, at the time of the Roman Republic, places such as Baiae were popular coastal resorts for the rich. The word *tourist* was used by 1772 and *tourism* by 1811. In 1936, the League of Nations defined *foreign tourist* as "someone traveling abroad for at least twenty-four hours". Its successor, the United Nations, amended this definition in 1945, by including a maximum stay of six months.

### Leisure travel

Leisure travel was associated with the Industrial Revolution in the United Kingdom—the first European country to promote leisure time to the increasing industrial population. Initially, this applied to the owners of the machinery of production, the economic oligarchy, the factory owners and the traders. These comprised the new middle class. Cox & Kings was the first official travel company to be formed in 1758.

The British origin of this new industry is reflected in many place names. In Nice, France, one of the first and best-established holiday resorts on the French Riviera, the long esplanade along the seafront is known to this day as the *Promenade des Anglais*; in many other historic resorts in continental Europe, old, well-established palace hotels have names like the *Hotel Bristol*, *the Hotel Carlton* or the *Hotel Majestic*—reflecting the dominance of English customers.

Many leisure-oriented tourists travel to the tropics, both in the summer and winter. Places of such nature often visited are: Bali in Indonesia, Colombia, Brazil, Cuba, the Dominican Republic, Malaysia, Mexico the various Polynesian tropical islands, Queensland in Australia, Thailand, Saint-Tropez and Cannes in France, Florida, Hawaii and Puerto Rico in the United States, Barbados, Sint Maarten, Saint Kitts and Nevis, The Bahamas, Anguilla, Antigua, Aruba, Turks and Caicos Islands and Bermuda.

### Winter tourism

Although it is acknowledged that the Swiss were not the inventors of skiing it is well documented that St. Moritz, Graubünden, became the cradle of the developing winter tourism: Since that year of 1865 in St. Moritz, many daring hotel managers choose to risk opening their hotels in winter but it was only in the seventies of the 20th century when winter tourism took over the lead from summer tourism in many of the Swiss ski resorts. Even in winter, portions of up to one third of all guests (depending on the location) consist of non-skiers.

### Mass tourism

Mass tourism could only have developed with the improvements in technology, allowing the transport of large numbers of people in a short space of time to places of leisure interest, so that greater numbers of people could begin to enjoy the benefits of leisure time.

## Section 2　Translation Warming-up

**A：Please match the Chinese translation in column B with the English expressions in column A.**

| A | B |
|---|---|
| 1. 御花园 | A. the Hall of Prayer for Good Harvest |
| 2. 故宫博物院 | B. Longevity Hill |
| 3. 观音阁 | C. Heaven Pool |
| 4. 天池 | D. Dufu Cottage |
| 5. 杜甫草堂 | E. Huaqing Hot Spring |
| 6. 华清池 | F. the Culture Palace for Nationalities |
| 7. 甘露寺 | G. the Imperial Garden |
| 8. 民族文化宫 | H. Sweet Dew Temple |
| 9. 万寿山 | I. Goddess of Mercy Pavilion |
| 10. 祈年殿 | J. the Palace Museum |

**B：Translate the following phrases and sentences about tourist materials into English.**

1. 大观园按古典小说《红楼梦》中所描写的中国传统园林建筑风格建造。

2. 这些兵马俑再现了秦始皇率领的军队在南北多条战线征战的壮丽图景。

3. 关外的孟姜女庙用来纪念孟姜女,一位传说中的女中豪杰。

4. 故宫博物院,也称紫禁城,位于北京市中心。里面的明清帝王的皇宫是世界上规模最大、最完整的古代木结构建筑群。

5. 苏州是江苏省著名的超过 2500 年历史的文化名城,拥有 200 多座古典园林。其中,小型私家花园尤其名扬全国,反映了宋、元、明、清时期的建筑风格。

6. 一座古老风车的风叶像张开的翅膀,迎风转动。与绿草、野花构成了独特的景致,更为这童话般的世界增添了神奇的色彩。

7. 浙江素有"鱼米之乡、丝茶之乡、文物之乡、旅游胜地"之称,自然风光和人文景观交相辉映。

8. 这些广场都铺着迷人的鹅卵石,富有魅力;商铺林立、餐馆密集、人来人往、独具特色。

9. "七夕节"已成为中国情人节,它承载着古典而浪漫的中国爱情文化。

10. 度假村四面青山环抱、依山傍水、万松挺翠、奇花异草、空气清新、清净优雅、景色宜人。

## Section 3　Topic Features and Translation Principles

### 一、旅游宣传资料

在旅游活动开始前,人们通过阅读旅游宣传资料,不仅可以欣赏到风景名胜与文物古迹,还可以深入了解异国的风土人情和文化传统,从而进行有意义的文化艺术交流。因此,旅游宣传资料翻译在旅游中起着至关重要的作用,可以吸引更多的外国友人来中国旅游,弘

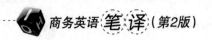

扬我国的历史文化。

旅游宣传资料的特点：

**1. 体裁多样性**

旅游宣传资料可以用描写、记叙和说明的形式来展现旅游产品，以达到不同的效果，吸引游客的关注。

**2. 功能多样性**

首先，具有信息功能，游客通过阅读旅游宣传资料可以获取旅游产品的大量相关信息，以达到对旅游产品的初步了解；其次，具有美感功能，旅游宣传资料可以图片和短片的形式展出，配以优美的语言，更生动地展示出旅游产品的特色，更有效地达到宣传的目的。

**3. 浓郁的文化气息**

旅游宣传资料中可以包含古迹的诗词曲赋、佳句楹联、文人墨客、传说典故以及散文游记，从而富有浓厚的文学性。

**4. 祈使功能**

文字介绍以优美的表达方式来传达其诱人的信息，达到令游客心驰神往，欲一睹为快的功能，从而弘扬文化，促进旅游业的发展。

### 二、旅游宣传资料的翻译原则

旅游宣传资料的翻译是指以国外普通旅游者为对象，介绍中国旅游事业和旅游资源的各种资料的翻译，是跨国界、跨文化的旅游宣传形式，是传播文化的载体。因此，旅游宣传资料的翻译尤为重要。要求译者在翻译时应忠实原文又不拘泥于原文，灵活运用翻译技巧，进行文字的转换和文化的传播，使用符合译语的文化和观念的语言表达和结构模式，有效地传达旅游目的国的信息。译者在翻译旅游宣传资料时，应遵循以下翻译原则：

（1）以中文旅游资料为本，要传达原文的信息，要表现出原文的文化历史色彩，如典故、寓言、神话以及俗语的翻译。

 **例句**

例1. 早采三天是个宝，迟采三天路边草。（龙井茶）

Picked three days earlier, it's a priceless asset; picked three days late, it's a worthless grass, which is a kind of tea called Longjing in China.

**分析**：译文用非限制性定语从句对文中的 grass 进行解释，使读者更易理解文中所讲述的是关于龙井茶采茶的习语。

例2. 美国人说"滚石不聚苔"，但在中国却是滚石不聚墨。

In America, "rolling stones gather no moss." in China, they gather no inscriptions.

**分析**：译文采用美国的俗语"滚石不聚苔"解释中国俗语，使读者易于联想理解。

例3. 大肚能容容天下难容之事；开口便笑笑天下可笑之人。（赞颂弥勒佛）

His belly is big enough to contain all intolerable things in the world; his mouth is ever ready to laugh at all snobbish persons under heaven. (the eulogy of Buddha)

**分析**：译文后增加对原文解释,词句是对佛教中弥勒佛的赞美,使读者对原文有更好的理解。

例 4. 中国有句俗话"赶得早不如赶得巧",赶上地坛庙会那就是巧。

A Chinese saying goes, "Timing is everything" and this applies to Ditan Temple Fair ( a temple fair held in the Park of Earth Temple).

**分析**：译文中增加了括号中的解释性语言,把中国的庙会文化韵味表现出来,让读者更清楚明白原文的表达。

例 5. 秦始皇统一六国后,一方面拆毁诸国间的长城,另一方面为防御北边匈奴,又修筑了横亘万余里的长城,成为我国最早的万里长城。

After unifying all other six states, Emperor Qinshihuang, the first emperor of the Qin Dynasty, while pulling down the walls between the former states, had new walls built in the north to defend the Hun. The walls stretched more than five thousand kilometers, forming the oldest Great Wall.

**分析**：译文中对秦始皇进行解释,使读者更易理解句中所讲述秦始皇为秦朝的历史人物。

(2) 以旅游资料的译文为重点,既忠实于原文又不拘于原文,从译文读者的角度出发,根据文化语言的差异性,对信息进行适当调整,使读者易懂。

 **例句**

例 1. 天下西湖三十六,就中最好是杭州。

Of the thirty-six West Lakes east or west, the West Lake in Hangzhou is the best.

**分析**：译文中采用状语的表达来传达原文的意思,指杭州的西湖才是最好的,使译文简洁易懂,符合英语的表达习惯。

例 2. 西安的六十四米高的大雁塔是玄奘西游印度回国后的居留之地。

The 64-meter-high Dayan Pagoda in Xi'an is the place where Xuan Zang, a great monk in the Tang Dynasty, once lived after returning from India.

**分析**：译文中增加了对玄奘的解释,让读者对原文中所讲述的唐朝僧人玄奘有更好的理解,从读者的角度增加了部分解释信息。

例 3. 湖南省位于长江中下游南部,东经 108 度至 114 度,北纬 24 度至 30 度。因地处洞庭湖之南,所以叫做湖南。

Hunan Province lies just south of the middle reaches of the Yangtze River between 108° and 114° E longitude and 24° and 30° N latitude. As it is also situated south of Lake Dongting, the Province has the name Hunan, which means "south of the lake".

**分析**：译文增加了非限定性定语从句,对湖南的得名进行了解释,让读者更好地理解湖南是以地理位置而得名的。

例 4. 海南岛上全年常绿,全年都鲜花盛开,是个只有夏季没有冬季的地方,年平均气温在 24℃ 左右。

Greenery and flowers can be seen throughout the year in Hainan, where the annual average temperature is 24 degrees centigrade.

**分析**：译文中省去原文中"是个只有夏季没有冬季的地方"，使译文更简洁，更符合英文的表达习惯。

例 5. 每当舍身岩畔云雾弥漫，云层中会幻化出一道七色光环，光环中能映出自己的身影，犹如面对明镜。

Whenever the Sacrifice Rock is enveloped in cloud, a circle of seven colors will appear. On the mountain top, one feels as if caught in the circle, like being in front of a mirror.

**分析**：译文中增加了语境的描写"on the mountain top"使译文清晰，使读者易懂。

## Section 4   Translating Strategies, Samples and Training

### Translating Strategies

#### 一、增词法

增词（words amplication），亦称补充，是指在译文中增加某些原文中虽无其字但有其意的词，以便更忠实通顺地表达原文的思想内容。翻译时倘若过于拘泥于原文的表达形式，往往会使译文晦涩难懂，甚至会背离原文。增词可分为语义性增词、语法性增词和修辞性增词。

语义性增词指为使译文语义明确，根据意义上的需要在译文中增加原文中没有的词。

语法性增词指由于汉英词法、句法不同，汉译英时，往往要补充代词、介词、连词、冠词和动词以表达完整的语法性。

修辞性增词出于行文上的考虑，所增加的词多为不改变原意的语气词、强调性副词或其他修辞上需要的词汇，以使意义明确。

 例句

例 1. A red sun rose slowly from the calm sea.

一轮红日从风平浪静的海面冉冉升起。（增加量词）

例 2. A stream is winding its way through the valley into the river.

一湾溪水蜿蜒流过山谷，汇合到江里去了。（增加量词、动词）

例 3. 寺山门一对石狮子，雕凿精细。

In front of the gate of Temple stand a pair of exquisitely carved stone lions.（增加状语）

例 4. 琼岛东北部有"琼岛春荫"碑，为 1751 年所建，附近风光秀丽，过去是燕京八景之一。

In the northeast of Qiongdao Island, there is a stone tablet, erected in 1751, with "Qiong Dao Chun Yin" engraved on it. It is said the inscription was written by Emperor Qianlong. This area, noted for its beautiful scenery, was counted as one of the eight outstanding views of Beijing.（增加解释）

例 5. 故宫的修建耗时 14 年，整个过程于 1420 年结束。

The construction of the Forbidden City took 14 years and was completed in 1420, 72 years before Christopher Columbus discovered the New World.(增加解释)

## 二、减词法

减词(words ellipsis),亦称省略,指不译出原文中的某些词的意思,但不是删去原文的意思,而是省去那些在译文中不言而喻的字词,或省去那些译出来不合语言表达习惯的词语。在旅游宣传资料翻译中,中文的旅游文本更符合汉语美学的特点,使用一些修辞手法让读者产生一种美感,更激起旅游者的观光游览欲望。

但中西方的文化存在差异性,汉语的修辞手法和渲染的词句,西方人肯定无法理解,在翻译的过程中就可以删掉不译,减少在翻译过程中文化差异带来的误解或是歧义。另外,英语句式构架严整,用词简洁自然,语言上忌重复累赘,这恰恰与汉语表达相反,所以在翻译过程中可以避免重复表达,使文章更简洁易懂。

 例句

例 1. 林边有一个洞,叫白龙洞。

Near the forest is the White Dragon Cave.

例 2. 寺外建有"药师琉璃光如来宝塔",简称"药师塔"。

By the side of the temple there stands the Yaoshita Pagoda(the Druggist Pagoda).

例 3. 鲤鱼门以海鲜美食驰名,最适宜三五知己晚饭共餐。

This fishing village is popular for its seafood and ideal for a night out with friends.

例 4. Travel to Belvoir Castle for a visit and drive through the area associated with D. H. Lawrance and Robin Hood.

驾车去巴勒瓦城堡。

例 5. Over the past ten years the Fitzroy district has changed itself from a dodgy place that you'd be scared to walk around in at night, to the arts and avant-garde district of the city.

费滋罗区曾经是人们晚上不敢出去逛的危险地方,但在过去 10 年里,这里变成了这座城市里充满艺术性的前卫地区。

Translating Samples

## 一、旅游指南

案例

例 1

### 雍和宫介绍

雍和宫位于北京市东城区内城的东北角即雍和宫大街路东,是北京市内最大的藏传佛教寺院。清康熙三十二年(1693 年),成为皇四子胤禛的府邸。该寺院主要由三座精致的牌坊和五进宏伟的大殿组成。被中国政府列为重要的历史性保护建筑。雍正驾崩后,乾隆将雍和宫改建为藏传喇嘛寺。

译文：

Yonghegong(The Lama Temple) is a largest lamasery located in the northeastern part of the old city of Beijing. It was a palatial residence built in 1693 by Qing Emperor Kangxi for his fourth son, Prince Yongzheng who later succeeded to the throne. This magnificent temple consists of three memorial archway and five main buildings. The temple is listed by the Chinese Government as one of the important historical monuments under special preservation. After the death of his father, Emperor Qianlong converted the palace into a lamasery.

例2

## Mt. Lusan

Mt.Lushan, situated in the north of Jiangxi Province, is one of China's famous scenic spots. Surrounded by rivers and lakes and with its special features of geological structure, Mt.Lushan is a unique mountain with queer peaks and beautiful ridges, lingering clouds and mists, rolling waterfalls and running springs, and dense forests, giving it romantic charm with rivers and hills adding radiance and beauty to each other.

译文：

庐山位于江西省北部，是中国著名旅游景点之一。四面环水，富有独特的地质结构。庐山以奇怪的山峰，优美的山脊，缠绵的云雾，气势澎湃的瀑布，川流不息的泉水以及茂密的森林而闻名，赋予庐山浪漫迷人的色彩，优美的河流以及山峰给彼此增添了光芒和美丽。

## 二、旅游行程

 案例

北京一日游简介

主要游览项目

1. 故宫

2. 漫游天安门广场

3. 颐和园

旅程安排

9:00 出发

9:30 故宫

12:00 天安门广场

13:00 颐和园

15:00 回旅馆

译文：

Highlights of One-day Tour of Beijing

Special Features：

1. Visiting Forbidden City

2. Strolling at Tian'anmen Square

3. Visiting Summer Palace

Itinerary：

9：00 Taking the touring bus at the hotel gate

9：30 Arrival at Forbidden City

12：00 Arrival at Tian'anmen Square

13：00 Arrival at Summer Palace

15：00 Back to the hotel

## 三、旅游通知

 案例

Dear Guest：

The hotel does not subscribe to credit cards. As a registered guest, you may settle your account by cash, traveler's checks or personal checks. For your convenience, counter check are available. Thanks.

General Manager

译文：

尊敬的游客：

　　本店不受理信用卡, 住店客人可以用现金、旅行支票或者私人支票结账。为了给您提供方便, 本店备有银行取款单。

总经理

### Translating Training

**A：Translate the following tourist publicity material into Chinese.**

1. Foods such as authentic Beijing roast duck and instant-boiled mutton have proved popular with tourists as well.

2. In winter, Shangri-la is a sleeping beauty in the snow-covered world, which can be admired afar rather than closely.

3. The characteristic of Guilin's scenery is its oddly-shaped solitary hills, rising out of flat ground, in various shapes.

4. A wide range of hotels, motel and apartment accommodation is available in most cities, major resorts and many rural areas.

5. If you like kitsch, you won't want to miss the bizarre melange of cultural artifacts at the National Museum of American History.

6. As the Big Ben is ringing the hour, a long queue of visitors from all over the world moves slowly forward into the Houses of Parliament.

7. The process mentioned above can be divided into three：night fog, hanging ice branch morning, and falling icy flowers at the noon.

8. The extraordinary vale of this park can be best condensed in a sentence: one step promptly takes you into the history of China, one day adequately enables you to tour the whole of China.

9. It is said that the Tuojiang River and the Ancient Street are embodiments of Fenghuang's glamour, a harmony between natural landscape and local customs.

10. You'll experience the scenery in a playful way that takes advantage of alternative ways of getting around, whether it is hiking, mountain biking, walking or climbing on the ropes course.

11. Tourists can ride a bamboo raft to enjoy the picturesque landscape along the Nine-bend Stream, as reflected in the ancient lines that landscape on the Wuyi Mountains is as marvelous as a fairyland.

12. This holiday resort provides an excellent environment for holiday seekers with hills, lakes, pines, trees and flowers all around which captivate you by its beautiful scenery, tranquility, and the fresh air.

13. Endowed with special geological landforms and a mild climate, Qingcheng Mountain enjoys exuberant vegetation and forests through which the paths wind and the ancient temples disperse in ranges of mountains.

14. Qingdao, like a cluster of brilliant pearls, is located on the southwestern coast of Shangdong Peninsula boarding the Yellow Sea. With a mild climate, Qingdao is famous for its scenic beauty and is renowned as the seaside summer resort in China.

15. Shanghai, a shopping center for best buys, is the largest city in China. Tourists will be satisfied with what the city supplies, form various snacks and cakes to handicrafts and textiles. Neighboring Suzhou and Hangzhou, only a couple of hours away from Shanghai by train, are two garden cities, each considered by Chinese to be "paradise on earth".

**B: Translate the following tourist publicity material into English.**

1. 黄龙风景，自海拔近 3600 米处，沿山谷而下，地上覆盖着一层淡黄色碳酸钙沉积，形成大大小小的众多水池，状如梯田。

2. 九寨沟的奇美风光，就在于它有着天然的 108 个翠海，从风光的结构上讲，它是以水为主体的，这就有别于其他山水的特色了。

3. 中国的手工艺品、丝绸、瓷器、地毯、棉纺织品在世界上享有盛名，而且比在世界其他地方购买价格更合理，挑选余地更大。

4. 故宫又称紫禁城，究其由来，是由天文学说和民间传说相互交融而形成的。古人认为紫微垣（即北极星）是天帝之座，故皇帝的居所又称紫禁城。

5. 北京是中国的政治、文化中心。在这里您可以游览万里长城中的一段——八达岭；明清两代皇室居住的地方——故宫；清朝御花园——颐和园和北海。

6. 把杭州比喻成人间天堂，很大程度是因为有了西湖。千百年来，西湖风景有着经久不衰的魅力，它的丰姿情影，令人一见钟情。就连唐朝诗人白居易离开杭州时还念念不忘西湖，"未能抛得杭州去，一半勾留是此湖。"

7. 丽江古城，位于云南丽江，是一个古老的小镇，主要居住着纳西族人。该镇建于 1127 年，古镇道路铺上了在丽江生产的彩色鹅卵石，镇上有明清时期建造的许多石头桥和牌坊。

大部分住宅都是由泥土和木头制成的。纳西民族传统的东巴文化一直保存在丽江。

8. 迪拜的帆船酒店,又名"阿拉伯塔""阿拉伯之星",是世界上第一家 7 星级酒店。位于中东地区阿拉伯联合酋长国迪拜酋长国的迪拜市。酒店由英国设计师 W. S. Atkins 设计,外观如同一张鼓满了风的帆,一共有 56 层、321 米高,是全球最高的酒店之一。酒店套房分别设在 27 个楼层,有自己的客户服务和管家服务。

9. 黄石公园内奇观比比皆是,充满了各种各样令人惊奇的地理奇观,间歇泉、温泉、喷气孔四处可见,更有高峡深谷、飞瀑流泉,令人叹为观止。然而,最引人注目的还是这儿受保护的大批野生动物群——野牛、麋鹿、驼鹿、熊、狮、鹰、野天鹅以及其他成群出没的动物。作为全球第一个国家公园,黄石公园占地 200 多万英亩,约合 8.1 万公顷。每年到访的游客成千上万。

10. 上海希尔顿酒店位于城市商业中心,距两大高档商业街——南京路商圈及淮海路商圈仅咫尺之遥;并且毗邻静安寺、静安公园及地铁交通。酒店拥有各式客房 714 间套,酒店设有行政房,配备有位于 38 层、占地 510 平方米的行政酒廊。客房拥有明亮的落地窗户、宽敞的办公区域及高速宽带。酒店拥有占地 32,000 平方英尺的现代化全功能 SPA 馆、健身中心、网球场及壁球馆、美发中心。

## Section 5　Extensive Expression

### 一、旅游交通类(Travel Transport)

| | |
|---|---|
| 1. airport | 机场 |
| 2. terminal building | 候机楼 |
| 3. waiting lounge | 候机室 |
| 4. international line | 国际航线 |
| 5. boarding card | 登机牌 |
| 6. captain | 机长 |
| 7. steward | 乘务员 |
| 8. stewardess | 空中小姐 |
| 9. air route | 航线 |
| 10. one way ticket | 单程车票 |
| 11. round trip ticket | 往返车票 |

### 二、旅游住宿类(Travel Accommodation)

| | |
|---|---|
| 1. inn | 旅馆,饭店 |
| 2. lodge | 小旅馆 |
| 3. tavern | 酒店 |
| 4. hostel | 招待所 |
| 5. hotel | 饭店,酒店 |
| 6. motel( =motor hotel) | 汽车旅店 |

| | |
|---|---|
| 7. budget hotel | 廉价旅馆 |
| 8. economy hotel(one-star hotel) | 一星级饭店 |
| 9. some comfort hotel(two-star hotel) | 二星级饭店 |
| 10. average comfort hotel(three-star hotel) | 三星级饭店 |
| 11. high comfort hotel(four-star hotel) | 四星级饭店 |
| 12. luxury hotel(five-star hotel) | 五星级饭店 |
| 13. single room | 单人房 |
| 14. double room | 大床房 |
| 15. twin room | 标准房 |
| 16. tripe room | 三人房 |
| 17. en-suite | 套房 |
| 18. family suite | 家庭套房 |
| 19. economy room(ER) | 经济间 |
| 20. standard room(SR) | 标准间 |
| 21. superior room(UR) | 高级套房 |
| 22. standard suit(SS) | 套间 |
| 23. deluxe room(DR) | 豪华间 |
| 24. presidential suit(PS) | 总统套房 |
| 25. studio room | 工作室型客房 |
| 26. multi-functional room | 多功能客房 |
| 27. combined type rooms | 组合客房 |

## 三、其他类(Others)

| | |
|---|---|
| 1. guidebook | 旅游指南 |
| 2. guild practice | 导游实践 |
| 3. international tourism | 国际导游 |
| 4. itinerary | 旅行计划,节目 |
| 5. tour guide | 导游 |
| 6. local guide | 地陪,地方导游 |
| 7. minimum tour price | 最低旅游价格 |
| 8. multilingual guide | 会多种语言的导游 |
| 9. national guide | 全陪,全程导游 |
| 10. off-peak season | 淡季 |
| 11. peak season | 旺季 |
| 12. programme | 节目 |
| 13. sightseeing | 游览 |
| 14. state-list famous historical and culture cities | 国家级历史文化名城 |
| 15. tour arrangement | 旅游安排 |
| 16. tour catalog | 旅游目录 |

| 17. tour escort/conductor/director | 旅游团陪同 |
| 18. tour operation | 旅游业务 |
| 19. tour talker | 自动导游磁带机 |
| 20. tourism | 旅游业，旅游 |
| 21. tourism activities | 旅游活动 |
| 22. tourism circles | 旅游界 |
| 23. tourist | 游客 |
| 24. tourist authority/office | 旅游局 |
| 25. tourist destination | 旅游目的地 |
| 26. tourist destination area | 旅游目的地地区 |
| 27. tourist spots | 旅游点 |
| 28. travel business | 旅游业务 |
| 29. travel expert | 旅游专家 |
| 30. travel press | 旅游报纸 |

## 四、中国著名景点翻译（Chian Famous Scenery）

| 1. Beihai Park | 北海公园 |
| 2. the Palace Museum | 故宫博物院 |
| 3. the Museum of Revolutionary History | 革命历史博物馆 |
| 4. Tian'anmen Square | 天安门广场 |
| 5. Chairman Mao Zedong Memorial Hall | 毛主席纪念堂 |
| 6. the Hall of Preserving Harmony | 保和殿 |
| 7. the Hall of Central Harmony | 中和殿 |
| 8. the Great Wall | 长城 |
| 9. the Meridian Gate | 午门 |
| 10. the Forbidden City | 紫禁城 |
| 11. Imperial Garden | 御花园 |
| 12. Summer Palace | 颐和园 |
| 13. Temple of Heaven | 天坛 |
| 14. Zhoukoudian Ancient Site | 周口店遗址 |
| 15. the Hall of Supreme Harmony | 太和殿 |
| 16. the Hall of Prayer for Good Harvest | 祈年殿 |
| 17. the Children's Palace | 少年宫 |
| 18. the Beacon Tower | 烽火台 |
| 19. the Great Hall of the People | 人民大会堂 |
| 20. Fairy Cave | 仙人洞 |
| 21. Huangguoshu Falls | 黄果树瀑布 |
| 22. the Imperial Mountain Summer Resort | 避暑山庄 |
| 23. Longmen Stone Cave | 龙门石窟 |

| | |
|---|---|
| 24. Suzhou Gardens | 苏州园林 |
| 25. Lushan Mountain | 庐山 |
| 26. Heaven Pool | 天池 |
| 27. Penglai Water City | 蓬莱水城 |
| 28. Big Wild Goose Pagoda | 大雁塔 |
| 29. Potala Palace | 布达拉宫 |
| 30. Grand Canal | 大运河 |
| 31. Dianchi Lake | 滇池 |
| 32. Du Fu Cottage | 杜甫草堂 |
| 33. Dujiang Dam | 都江堰 |
| 34. Gulangyu Islet | 鼓浪屿 |
| 35. Goddess of Mercy Pavilion | 观音阁 |
| 36. Lijiang River | 漓江 |
| 37. Hanshan Temple | 寒山寺 |
| 38. Yellow Crane Tower | 黄鹤楼 |
| 39. Huangshan Mountain | 黄山 |
| 40. the First Pass Under Heaven | 天下第一关 |
| 41. Guilin Scenery with Hills and Waters | 桂林山水 |
| 42. Qin Terra-Cotta Warriors and Horses Figurines | 秦始皇兵马俑 |

# 参 考 文 献

1. 孙万彪. 高级翻译教程(第二版)[M]. 上海：上海外语教育出版社,2000.

2. 约翰·A. 凯里. 商务书信速查速写[M]. 北京：电子工业出版社,2006.

3. 许建平. 英汉互译实践与技巧[M]. 北京：清华大学出版社,2007.

4. 谭卫国. 外贸英语的语言特点与翻译[M]. 上海：上海交通大学出版社,2008.

5. 彭萍. 实用商务文体翻译(英汉双向)[M]. 北京：中国编译出版社,2008.

6. 玛丽·默里·博斯罗克. 欧洲商务礼仪手册[M]. 北京：东方出版社,2009.

7. 彭萍. 实用旅游英语翻译[M]. 北京：对外经济贸易大学出版社,2010.

8. 李明. 商务英语翻译(汉译英)[M]. 北京：高等教育出版社,2010.

9. 冯祥春. 国际经贸英语文章精选[M]. 北京：对外经济贸易大学出版社,2010.

10. 丁小丽. 商务英语翻译 [M]. 北京：清华大学出版社,北京交通大学出版社,2011.

11. 傅敬民. 实用商务英语翻译教程[M]. 上海：华东理工大学出版社,2011.

12. 李海峰. 经贸英语翻译教程[M]. 西安：陕西师范大学出版社,2013.

13. 翁凤翔. 论商务英语翻译的4Es标准[J]. 上海翻译,2013(1).

14. 岳峰,刘茵. 商务英语笔译[M]. 厦门：厦门大学出版社,2014.

15. 王秋菊,邹和成. 商务英语翻译[M]. 重庆：重庆大学出版社,2015.

16. 赵春燕. 商务英语翻译[M]. 广州：广东高等教育出版社,2015.

17. 彭萍. 实用商务翻译[M]. 北京：中国宇航出版社,2015.

18. 张丽华. 国际组织概论[M]. 北京：科学出版社,2015.

19. 段云礼,江治刚. 经贸英语翻译[M]. 北京：对外经济贸易大学出版社,2016.

20. 唐慧丽,王志宏. 商务英语翻译[M]. 上海：复旦大学出版社,2016.

21. 廖芸. 商务英语翻译教程[M]. 北京：对外经济贸易大学出版社,2016.

22. 董晓波. 商务英语翻译[M]. 北京：对外经济贸易大学出版社,2017.

23. 余慕鸿,章汝雯. 商务英语谈判[M]. 北京：外语教学与研究出版社,2020.

24. 陈德彰. 英汉翻译入门[M]. 2版. 北京：外语教学与研究出版社,2020.

# 教师服务

感谢您选用清华大学出版社的教材！为了更好地服务教学，我们为授课教师提供本书的教学辅助资源，以及本学科重点教材信息。请您扫码获取。

## ≫ 教辅获取

本书教辅资源，授课教师扫码获取

## ≫ 样书赠送

**公共基础课类**重点教材，教师扫码获取样书

 清华大学出版社

E-mail: tupfuwu@163.com
电话: 010-83470332 / 83470142
地址: 北京市海淀区双清路学研大厦 B 座 509

网址: http://www.tup.com.cn/
传真: 8610-83470107
邮编: 100084